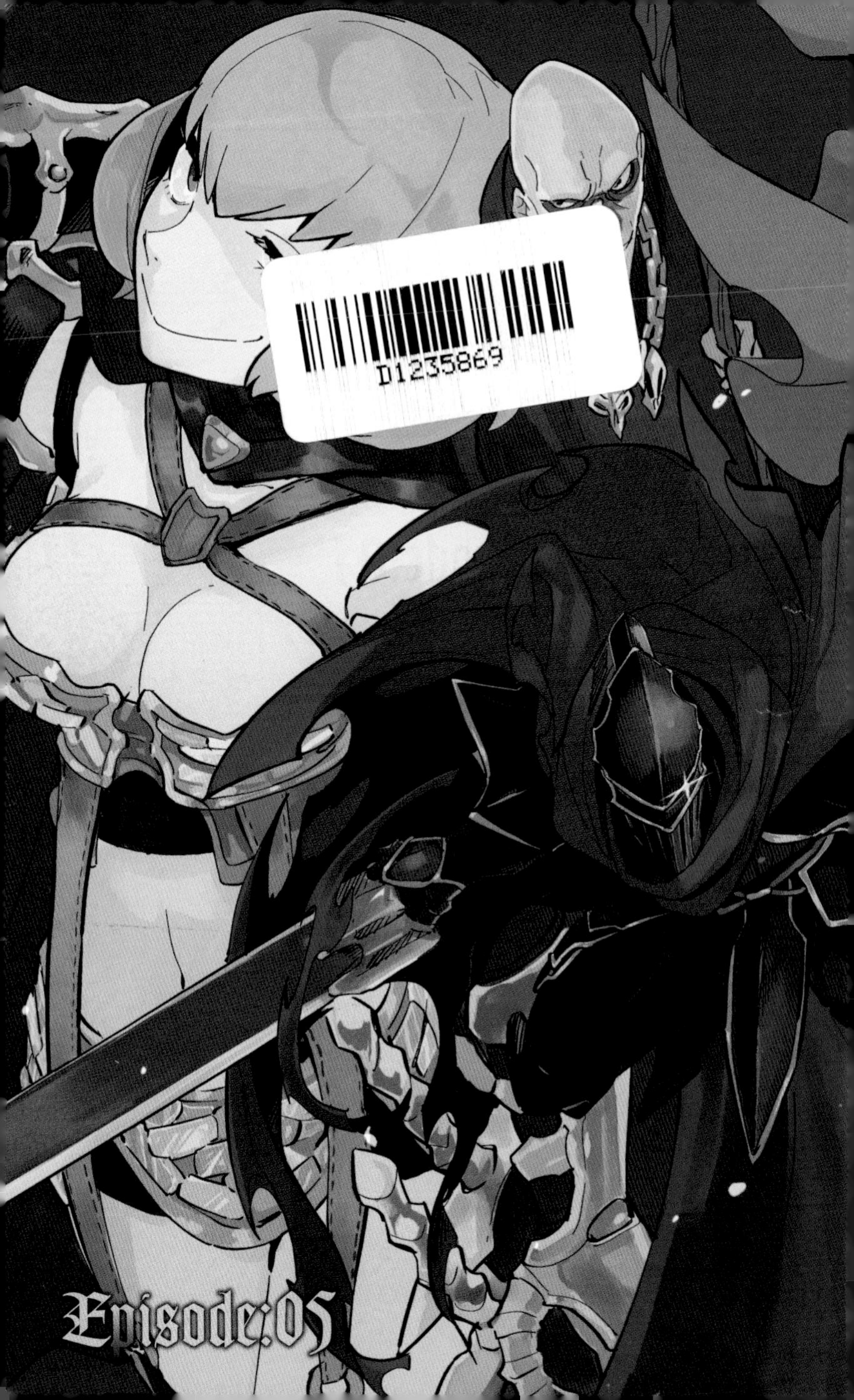
Episode:05

OVERLORD

2

Original Story:
Kugane Maruyama

Art:
Hugin Miyama

OVERLORD

2

Original Story:
Kugane Maruyama

Character Design:
so-bin

Art:
Hugin Miyama

Scenario:
Satoshi Oshio

Interpretive notes of the OVERLORD

Outline of Volume: 1

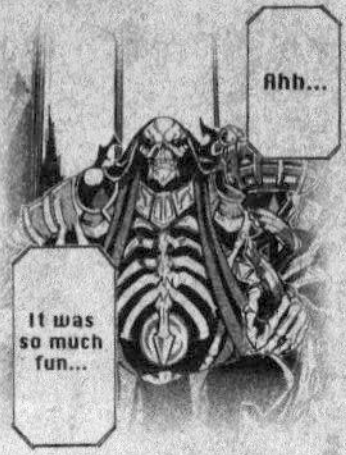
Ahh...
It was so much fun...

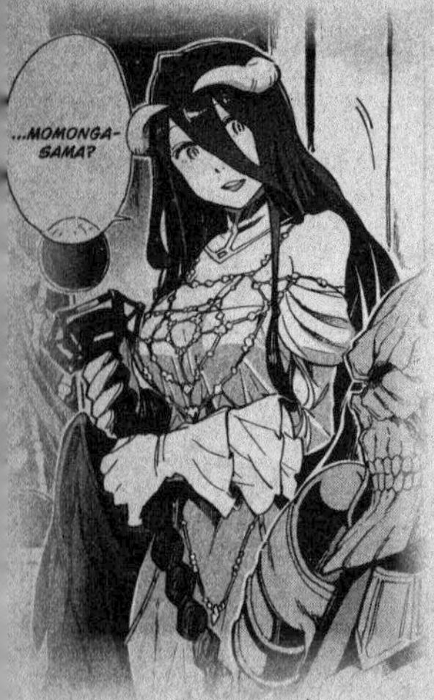
...MOMONGA-SAMA?

The protagonist, Momonga, is a player of the massively popular DMMO-RPG *Yggdrasil*. He is guild master of Ainz Ooal Gown, one of the greatest guilds in the game. But time has passed, and *Yggdrasil* faces the closing of its servers. Abandoned by his old guildmates, Momonga sits alone in their headquarters, the Great Tomb of Nazarick, waiting for the shutdown.

However, once the shutdown time passes, something odd happens. The world of the game hasn't disappeared. As Momonga wonders if the shutdown was postponed, Albedo, who was supposed to be an NPC, smiles at him and asks what's wrong. The other NPCs are also very animated and have conversations with him as though they can think for themselves.

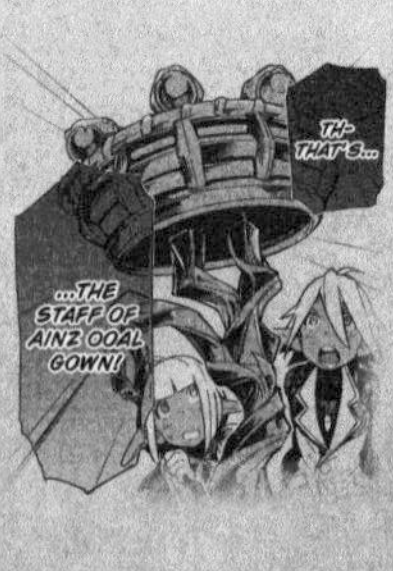
TH-THAT'S...
...THE STAFF OF AINZ OOAL GOWN!

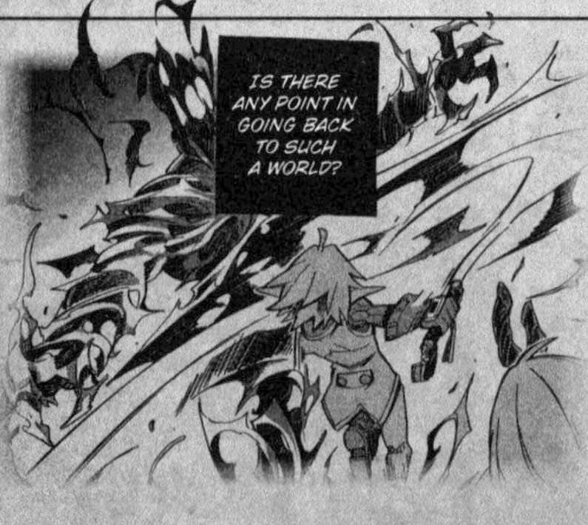
IS THERE ANY POINT IN GOING BACK TO SUCH A WORLD?

Seeing all the NPCs moving around as if they're alive, Momonga figures that something strange must be going on. He orders the NPC Sebas to investigate the Tomb's surroundings. It turns out that Momonga was not sucked into the game world but was transported to another world entirely.

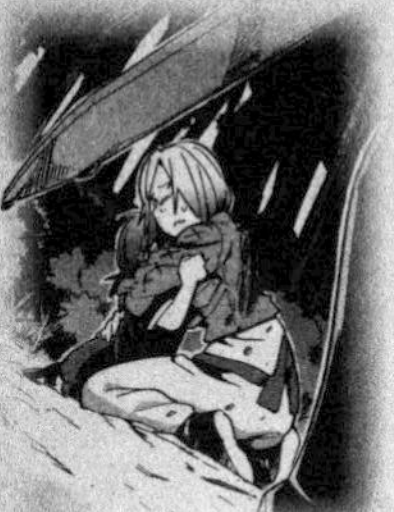

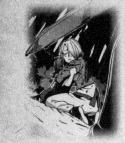

Feeling at a loss due to all the sudden changes, he nonetheless takes stock of his situation and feels it's not worth returning to his own world. Then, hoping that perhaps some of his old guildmates were also transported here, he decides to make a name for himself throughout this new world so that they can find him.

With this goal in mind, Momonga is investigating things in the area when he discovers a village being overrun by mysterious soldiers. He intends to ignore it, but after remembering wise words his guildmate Touch Me once said to him, he heads out to save the day. Partway through, he meets the captain of the Re-Estize Kingdom's Royal Select, Gazef, who is also fighting on the side of the villagers. Momonga admires his strong will.

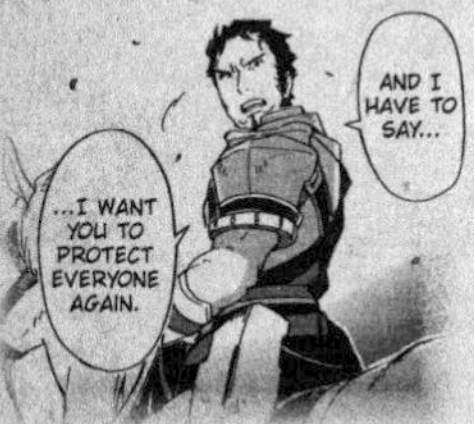
AND I HAVE TO SAY...
...I WANT YOU TO PROTECT EVERYONE AGAIN.

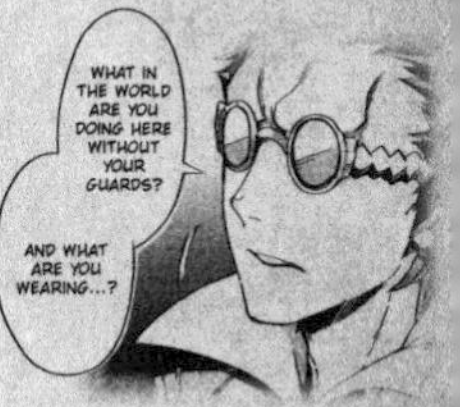
WHAT IN THE WORLD ARE YOU DOING HERE WITHOUT YOUR GUARDS?
AND WHAT ARE YOU WEARING...?

When Gazef is almost defeated by the captain of the Slane Theocracy's Sunlit Scripture, Nigun, Momonga jumps in to save him. He defeats Nigun without a struggle and earns the respect and gratitude of the villagers.

After the battle, Momonga decides to take his guild's name, Ainz Ooal Gown, as his own. He begins planning how to improve his reputation in order to reunite with his former guildmates.

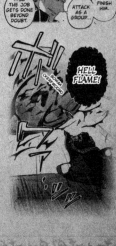

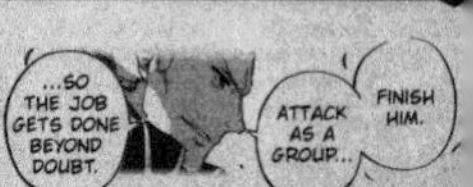
FINISH HIM.
ATTACK AS A GROUP...
...SO THE JOB GETS DONE BEYOND DOUBT.

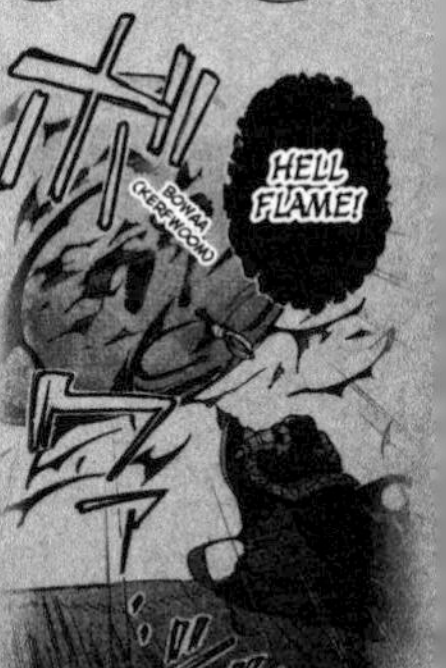
HELL FLAME!
BOWAA (KERFWOOM)

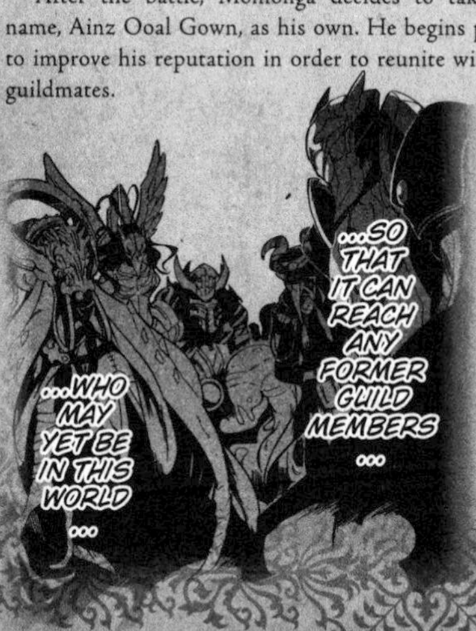
...SO THAT IT CAN REACH ANY FORMER GUILD MEMBERS...
...WHO MAY YET BE IN THIS WORLD...

Interpretive notes of the OVERLORD

Character Profile

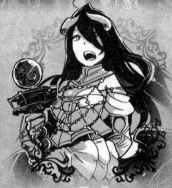

Ainz Ooal Gown (Momonga)

The protagonist and ruler of the guild Ainz Ooal Gown. In order to spread that name, he takes it on for himself and abandons his own name. Clad in raven-black armor, he plans to gather information as an adventurer under the name "Momon."

Ainz Ooal Gown

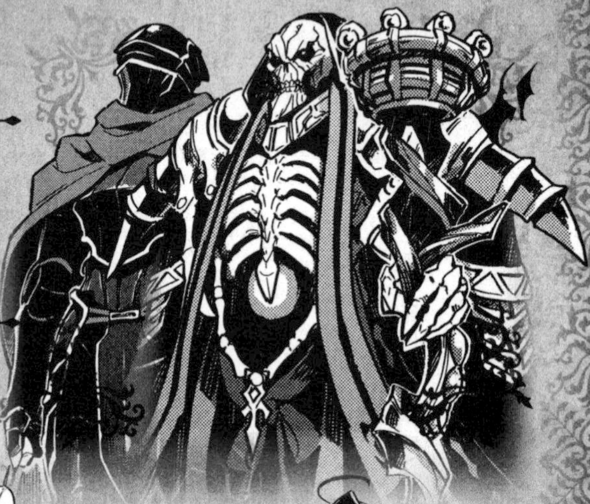

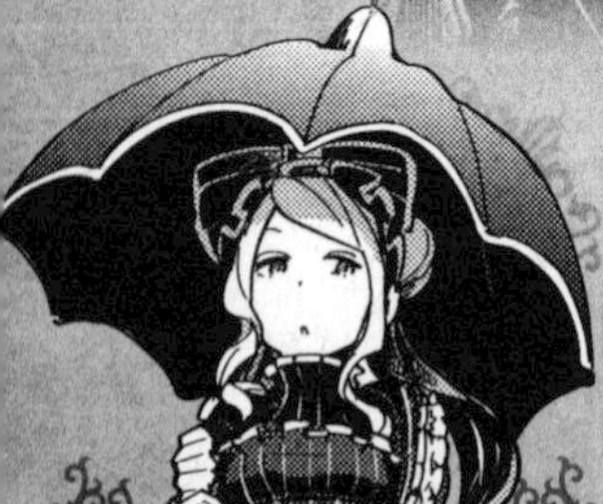

Shalltear Bloodfallen

A True Vampire who is superhuman at both melee and magical combat. Since her creator was into games with pretty little girls, the way she talks and acts borders on contrived. Her breasts look big, but they're fake.

Shalltear Bloodfallen

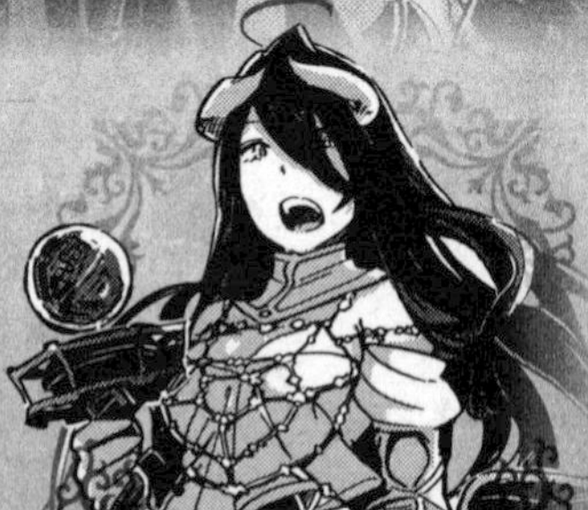

Albedo

A succubus who runs administrative operations. Her stats are focused on defense. She's crazy about Ainz because he edited her backstory code and made it so that she was in love with him.

Albedo

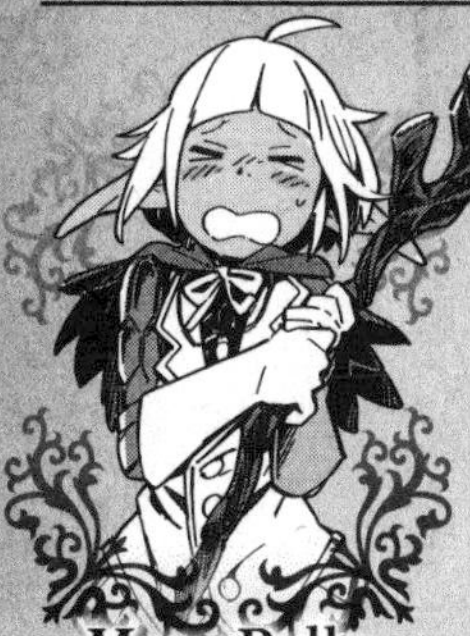

Mare Bello Fiore

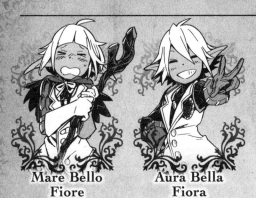

Aura's twin brother with the skills of a druid. He's so timid, he's practically shaking half the time, and he can't seem to compete with his sister. He's dressed like a girl because his created wanted him to be.

Mare Bello Fiore

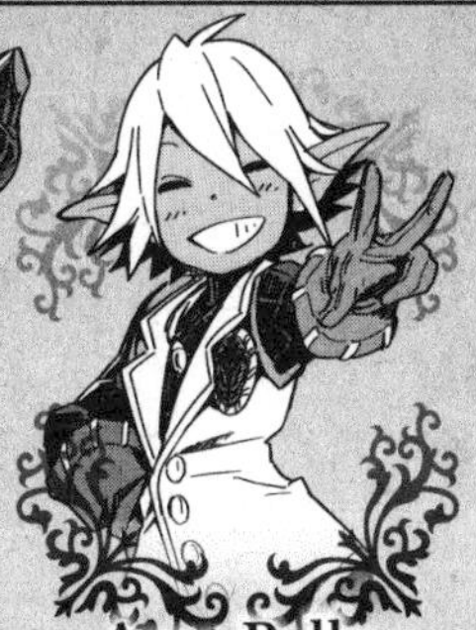

Aura Bella Fiora

A beast tamer-ranger dark elf girl. She looks young, but she's seventy-six. Even so, she's as innocent and spunky as she appears. She's dressed like a boy because her creator wanted her to be.

Aura Bella Fiora

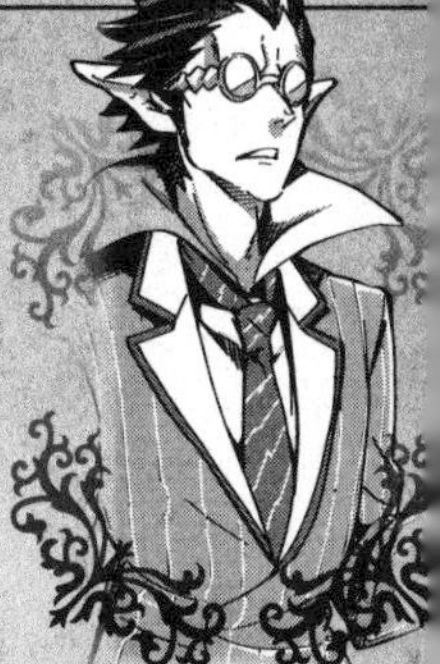

Demiurge

A demon in charge of strategic planning, and the brains of Nazarick with the nickname, "Creator of the Inferno." Behind his mild-mannered demeanor lurks his true cold-blooded nature. He's a grotesque with multiple forms.

Demiurge

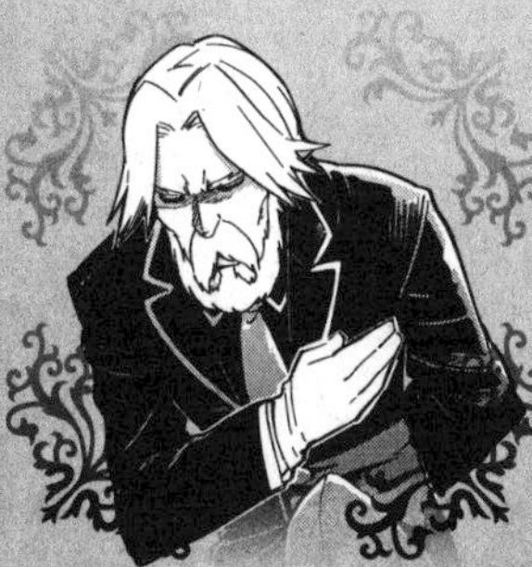

Sebas Tian

The stern old butler who manages Nazarick's affairs. Like the floor guardians, he is often roped into helping carry out Ainz's plans.

Sebas Tian

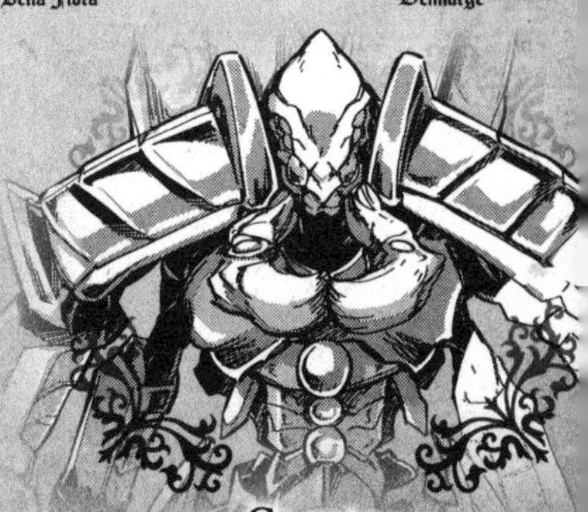

Cocytus

An earnest warrior with the body of a giant insect. He owns twenty-one types of weapons and uses them deftly with his four arms. Enemies are intimidated by his spiked tail.

Cocytus

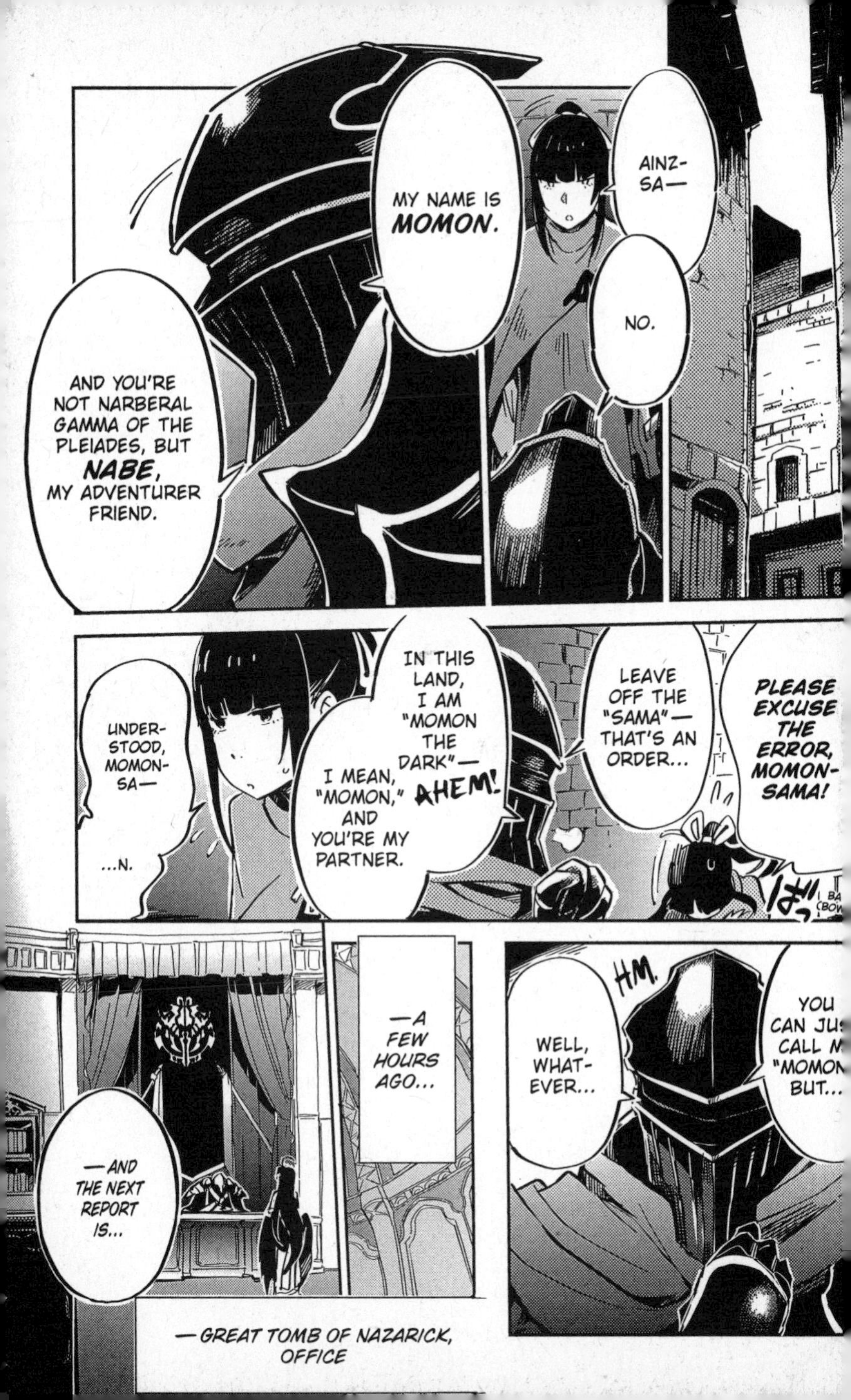
AINZ-SA—
NO.
MY NAME IS MOMON.
AND YOU'RE NOT NARBERAL GAMMA OF THE PLEIADES, BUT NABE, MY ADVENTURER FRIEND.
PLEASE EXCUSE THE ERROR, MOMON-SAMA!
LEAVE OFF THE "SAMA"— THAT'S AN ORDER...
IN THIS LAND, I AM "MOMON THE DARK"—
AHEM!
I MEAN, "MOMON," AND YOU'RE MY PARTNER.
UNDER-STOOD, MOMON-SA—
...N.
YOU CAN JUS CALL M "MOMON BUT...
HM.
WELL, WHAT-EVER...
—A FEW HOURS AGO...
—AND THE NEXT REPORT IS...
—GREAT TOMB OF NAZARICK, OFFICE

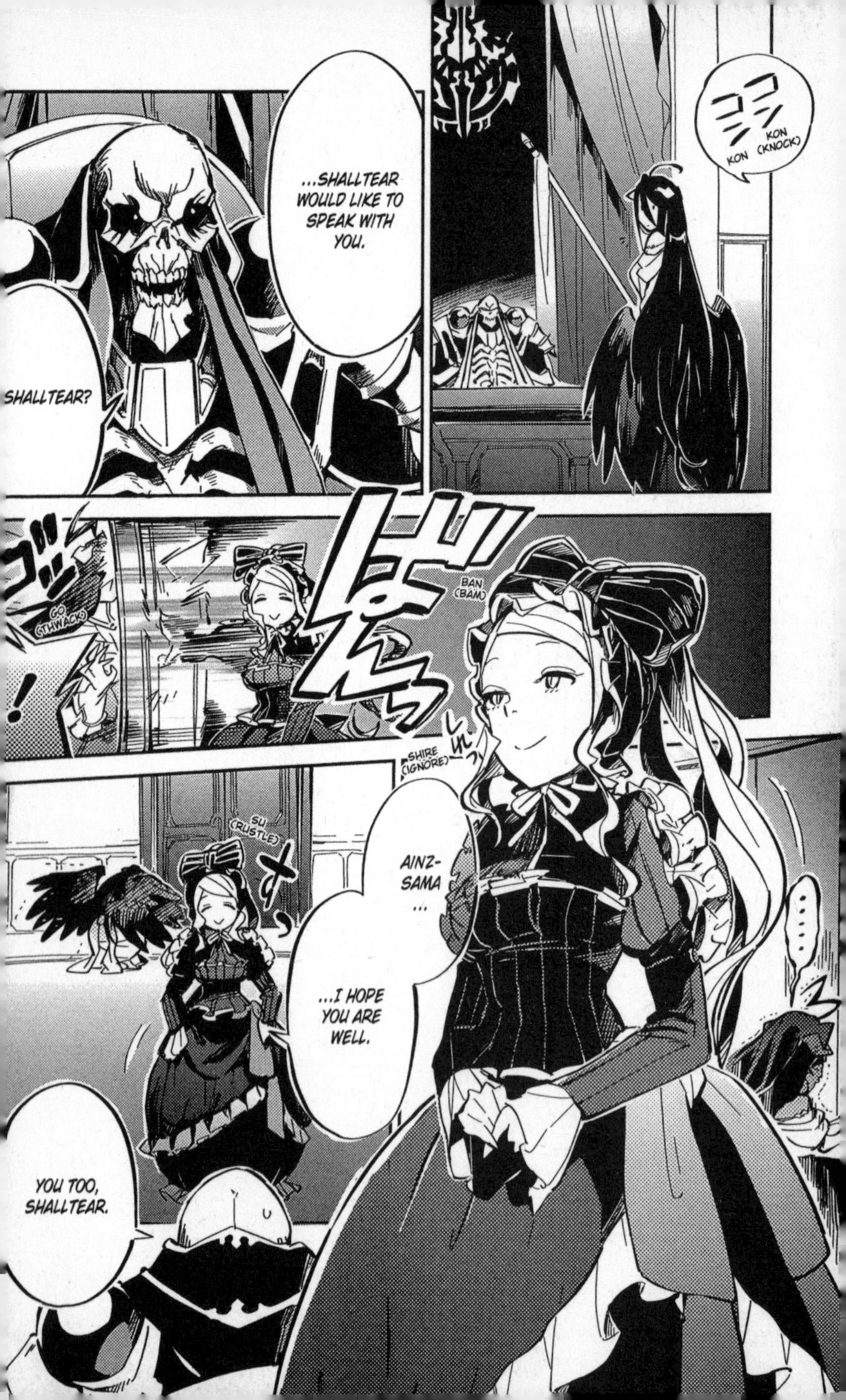
コンコン
KON KON (KNOCK)
...SHALLTEAR WOULD LIKE TO SPEAK WITH YOU.
SHALLTEAR?
BAN (BAM)
GO (THWACK)
!
SHIRE (IGNORE)
SU (RUSTLE)
AINZ-SAMA ...
...I HOPE YOU ARE WELL.
....
YOU TOO, SHALLTEAR.

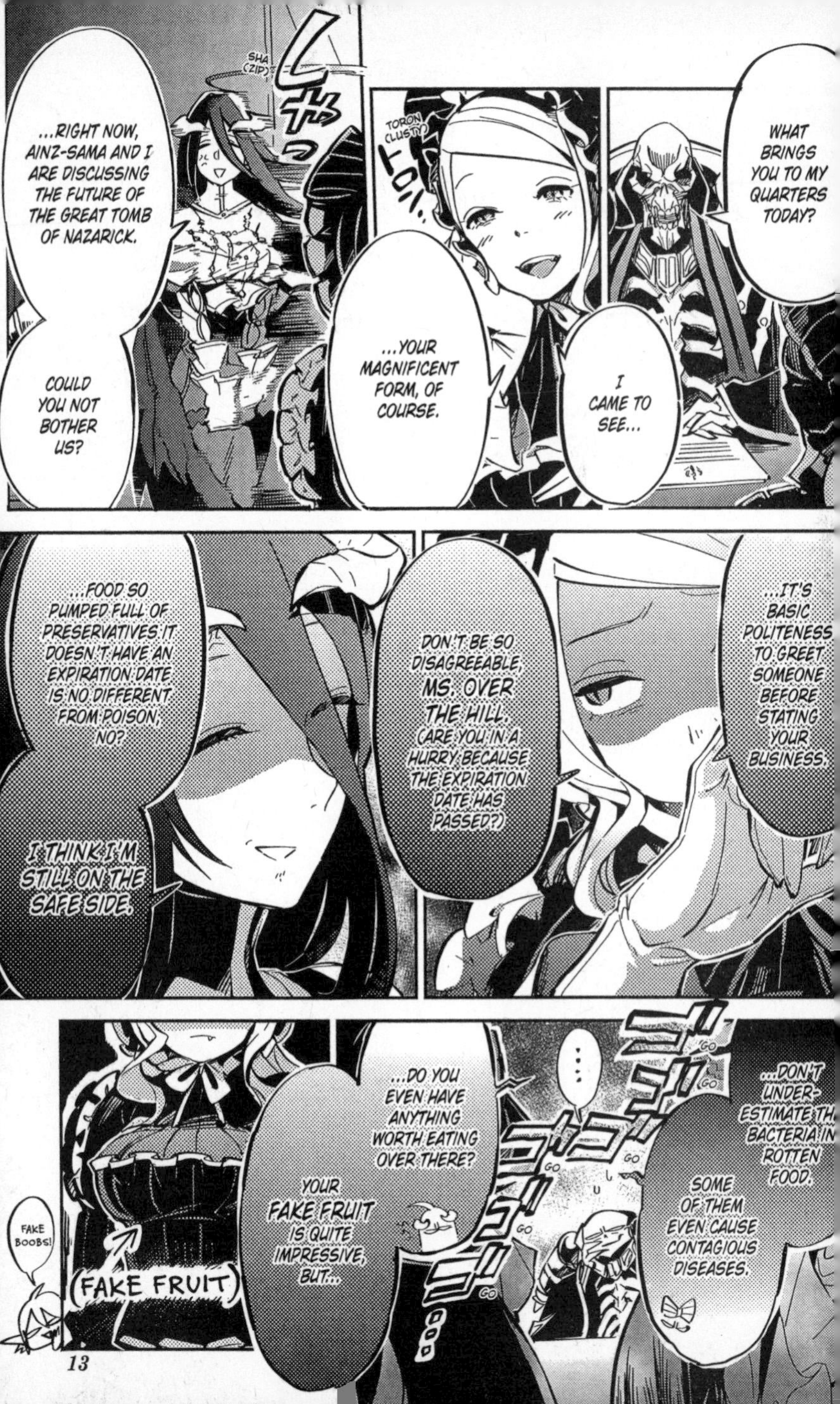

WHAT BRINGS YOU TO MY QUARTERS TODAY?
TORON (LUSTY)
I CAME TO SEE...
...YOUR MAGNIFICENT FORM, OF COURSE.
SHA (ZIP)
...RIGHT NOW, AINZ-SAMA AND I ARE DISCUSSING THE FUTURE OF THE GREAT TOMB OF NAZARICK.
COULD YOU NOT BOTHER US?
...IT'S BASIC POLITENESS TO GREET SOMEONE BEFORE STATING YOUR BUSINESS.
DON'T BE SO DISAGREEABLE, MS. OVER THE HILL. (ARE YOU IN A HURRY BECAUSE THE EXPIRATION DATE HAS PASSED?)
...FOOD SO PUMPED FULL OF PRESERVATIVES IT DOESN'T HAVE AN EXPIRATION DATE IS NO DIFFERENT FROM POISON, NO?
I THINK I'M STILL ON THE SAFE SIDE.
...DON'T UNDER-ESTIMATE TH BACTERIA IN ROTTEN FOOD.
SOME OF THEM EVEN CAUSE CONTAGIOUS DISEASES.
GO GO GO GO GO GO
...
...DO YOU EVEN HAVE ANYTHING WORTH EATING OVER THERE?
YOUR FAKE FRUIT IS QUITE IMPRESSIVE, BUT...
(FAKE FRUIT)
FAKE BOOBS!

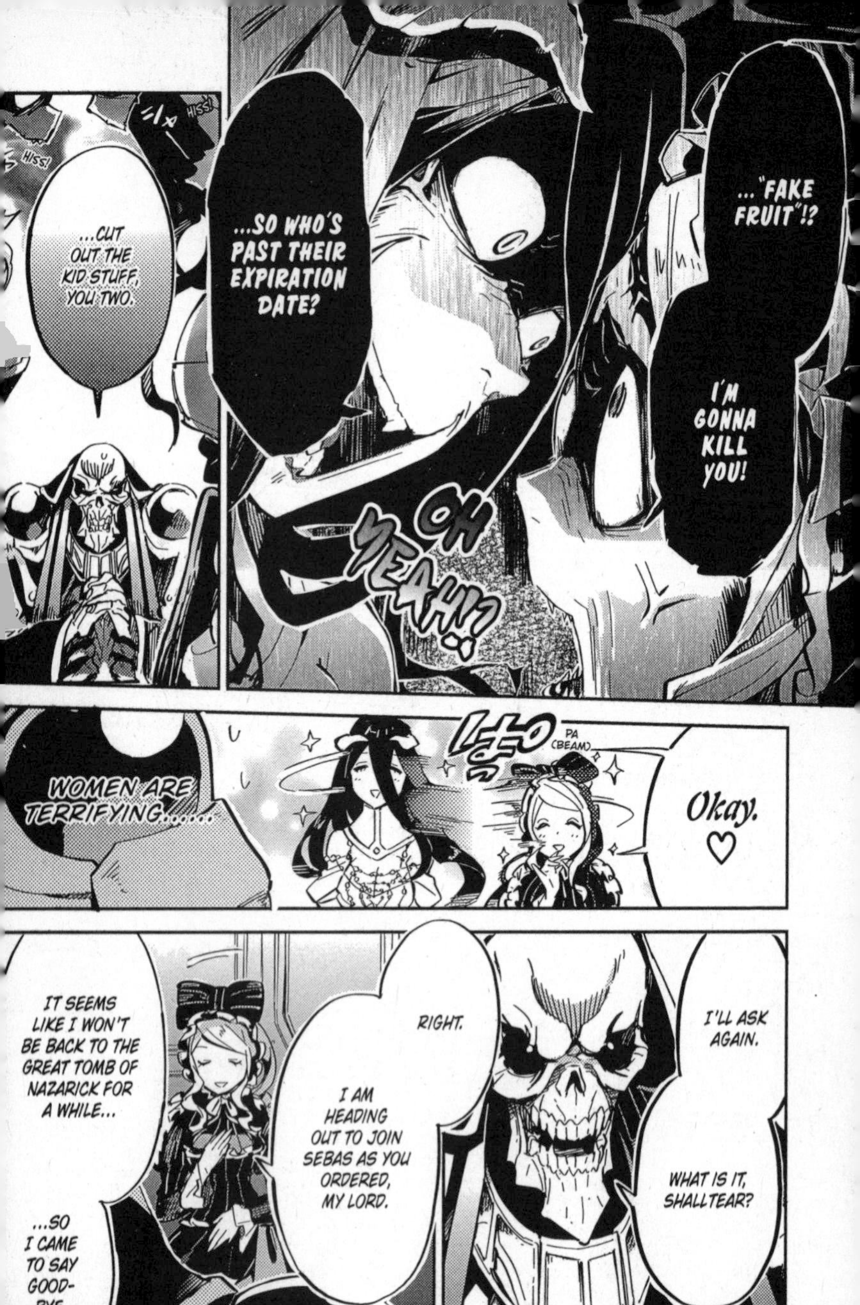
..."FAKE FRUIT"!?
I'M GONNA KILL YOU!
...SO WHO'S PAST THEIR EXPIRATION DATE?
OH YEAH!?
HISS!
HISS!
...CUT OUT THE KID STUFF, YOU TWO.
Okay. ♥
PA (BEAM)
WOMEN ARE TERRIFYING......
I'LL ASK AGAIN.
WHAT IS IT, SHALLTEAR?
RIGHT.
I AM HEADING OUT TO JOIN SEBAS AS YOU ORDERED, MY LORD.
IT SEEMS LIKE I WON'T BE BACK TO THE GREAT TOMB OF NAZARICK FOR A WHILE...
...SO I CAME TO SAY GOOD-BYE.

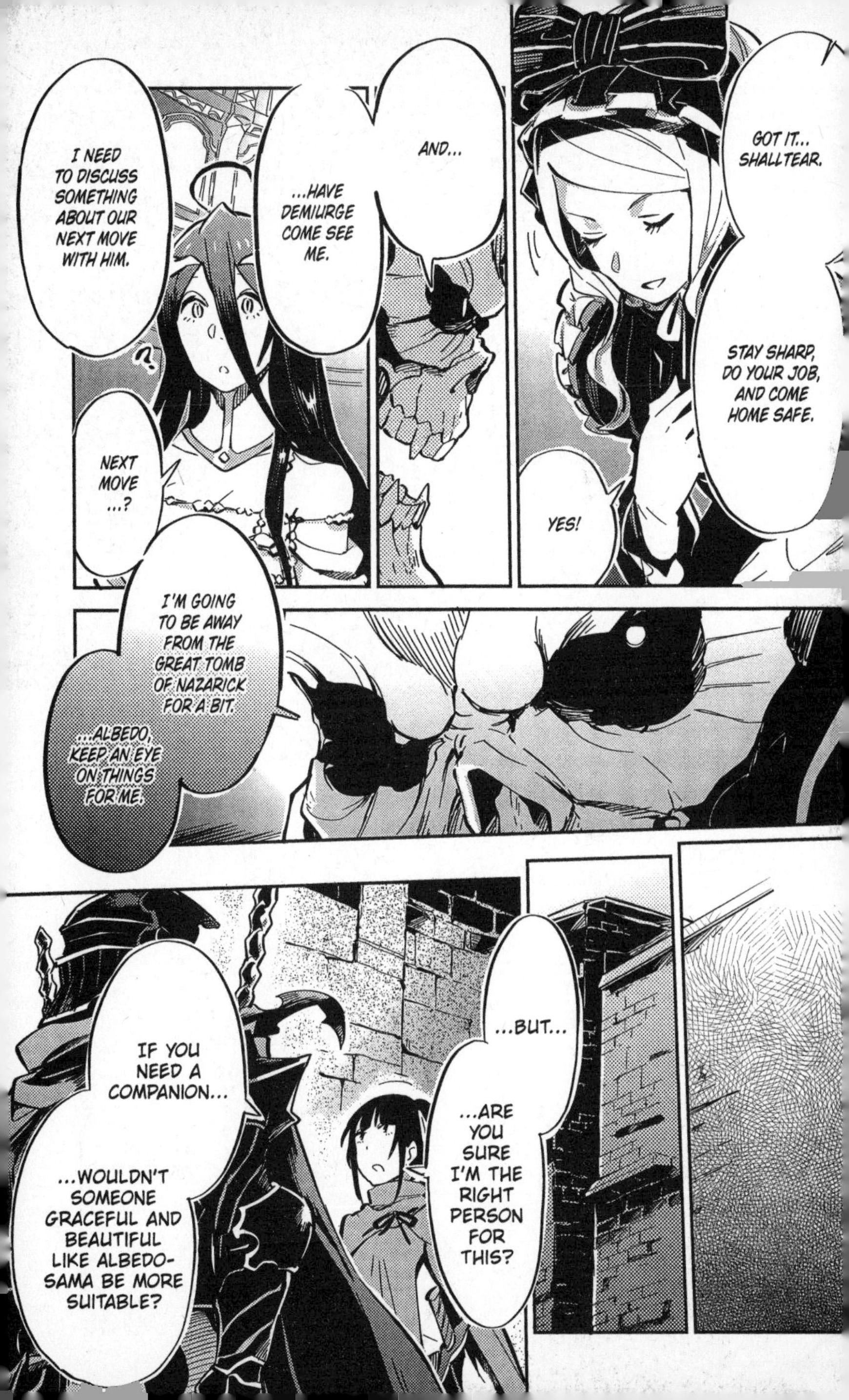
GOT IT... SHALLTEAR.
STAY SHARP, DO YOUR JOB, AND COME HOME SAFE.
YES!
AND...
...HAVE DEMIURGE COME SEE ME.
I NEED TO DISCUSS SOMETHING ABOUT OUR NEXT MOVE WITH HIM.
NEXT MOVE ...?
I'M GOING TO BE AWAY FROM THE GREAT TOMB OF NAZARICK FOR A BIT.
...ALBEDO, KEEP AN EYE ON THINGS FOR ME.
...BUT...
...ARE YOU SURE I'M THE RIGHT PERSON FOR THIS?
IF YOU NEED A COMPANION...
...WOULDN'T SOMEONE GRACEFUL AND BEAUTIFUL LIKE ALBEDO-SAMA BE MORE SUITABLE?

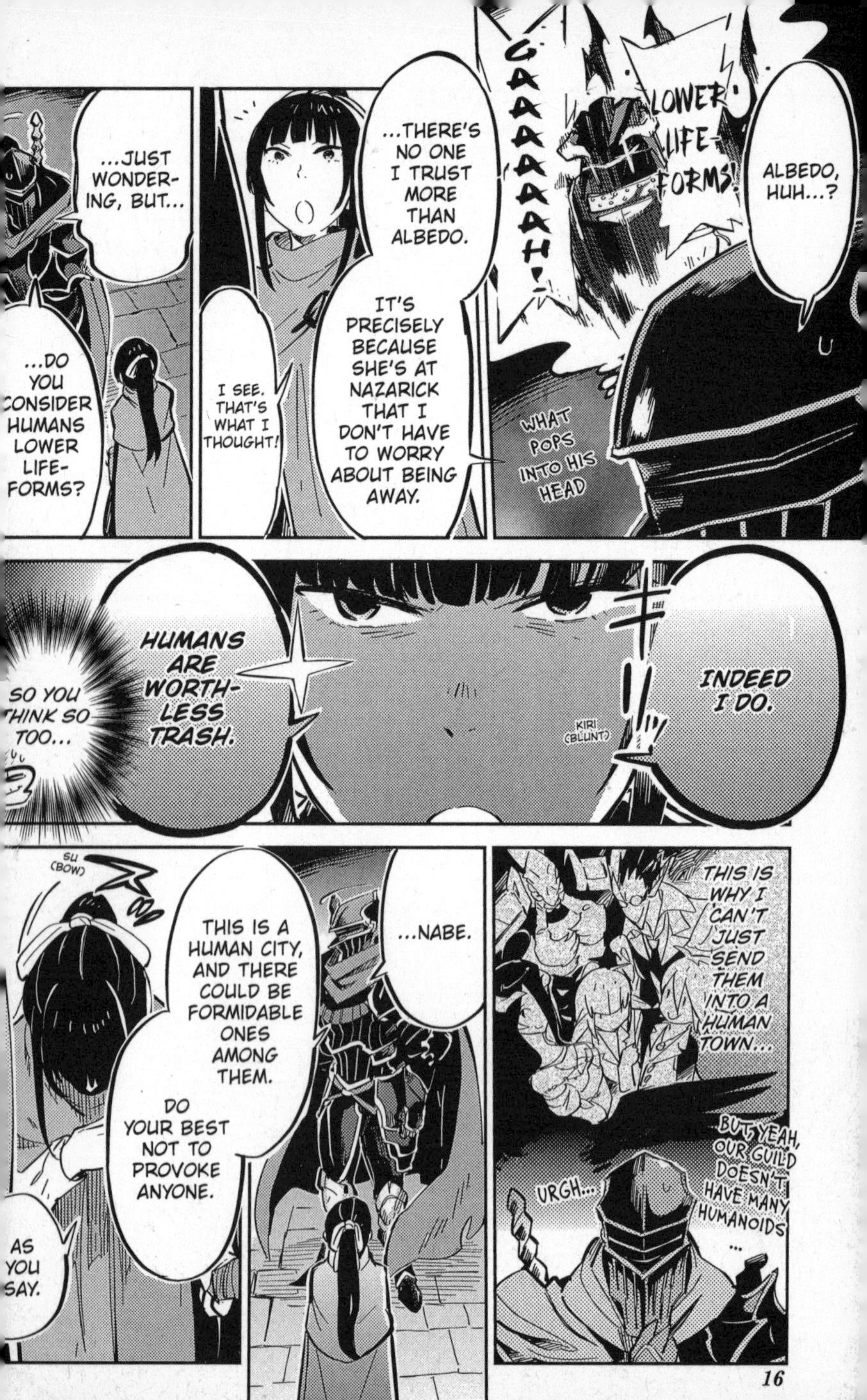
ALBEDO, HUH...?
LOWER LIFE-FORMS!
GAAAAAAAAH!
WHAT POPS INTO HIS HEAD
...THERE'S NO ONE I TRUST MORE THAN ALBEDO.
IT'S PRECISELY BECAUSE SHE'S AT NAZARICK THAT I DON'T HAVE TO WORRY ABOUT BEING AWAY.
I SEE. THAT'S WHAT I THOUGHT!
...JUST WONDERING, BUT...
...DO YOU CONSIDER HUMANS LOWER LIFE-FORMS?
INDEED I DO.
KIRI (BLUNT)
HUMANS ARE WORTH-LESS TRASH.
SO YOU THINK SO TOO...
THIS IS WHY I CAN'T JUST SEND THEM INTO A HUMAN TOWN...
BUT, YEAH, OUR GUILD DOESN'T HAVE MANY HUMANOIDS...
URGH...
...NABE.
THIS IS A HUMAN CITY, AND THERE COULD BE FORMIDABLE ONES AMONG THEM.
DO YOUR BEST NOT TO PROVOKE ANYONE.
SU (BOW)
AS YOU SAY.

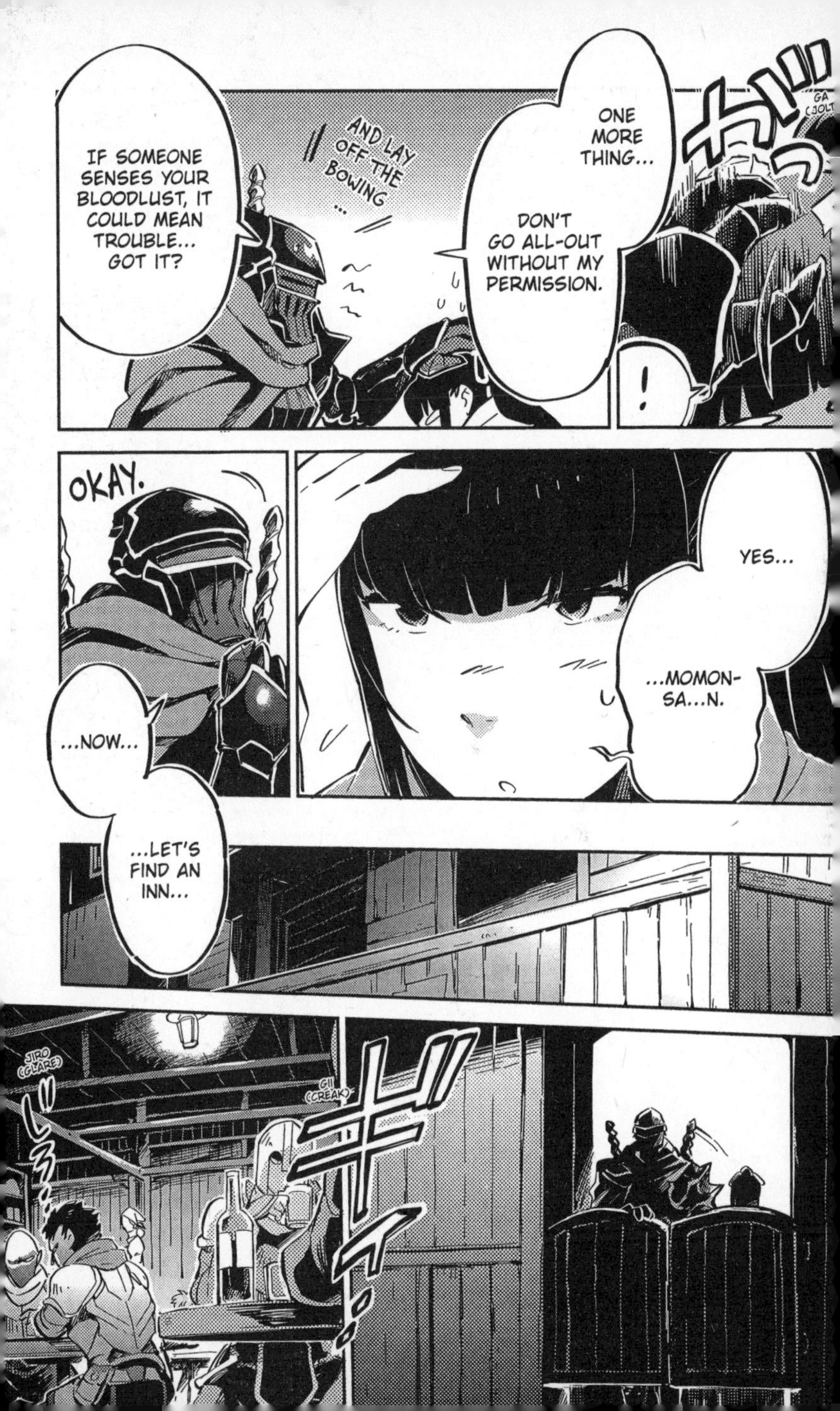
GA (JOLT
!
ONE MORE THING...
DON'T GO ALL-OUT WITHOUT MY PERMISSION.
AND LAY OFF THE BOWING...
IF SOMEONE SENSES YOUR BLOODLUST, IT COULD MEAN TROUBLE... GOT IT?
YES...
...MOMON-SA...N.
OKAY.
...NOW...
...LET'S FIND AN INN...
GII (CREAK)
JIRO (GLARE)

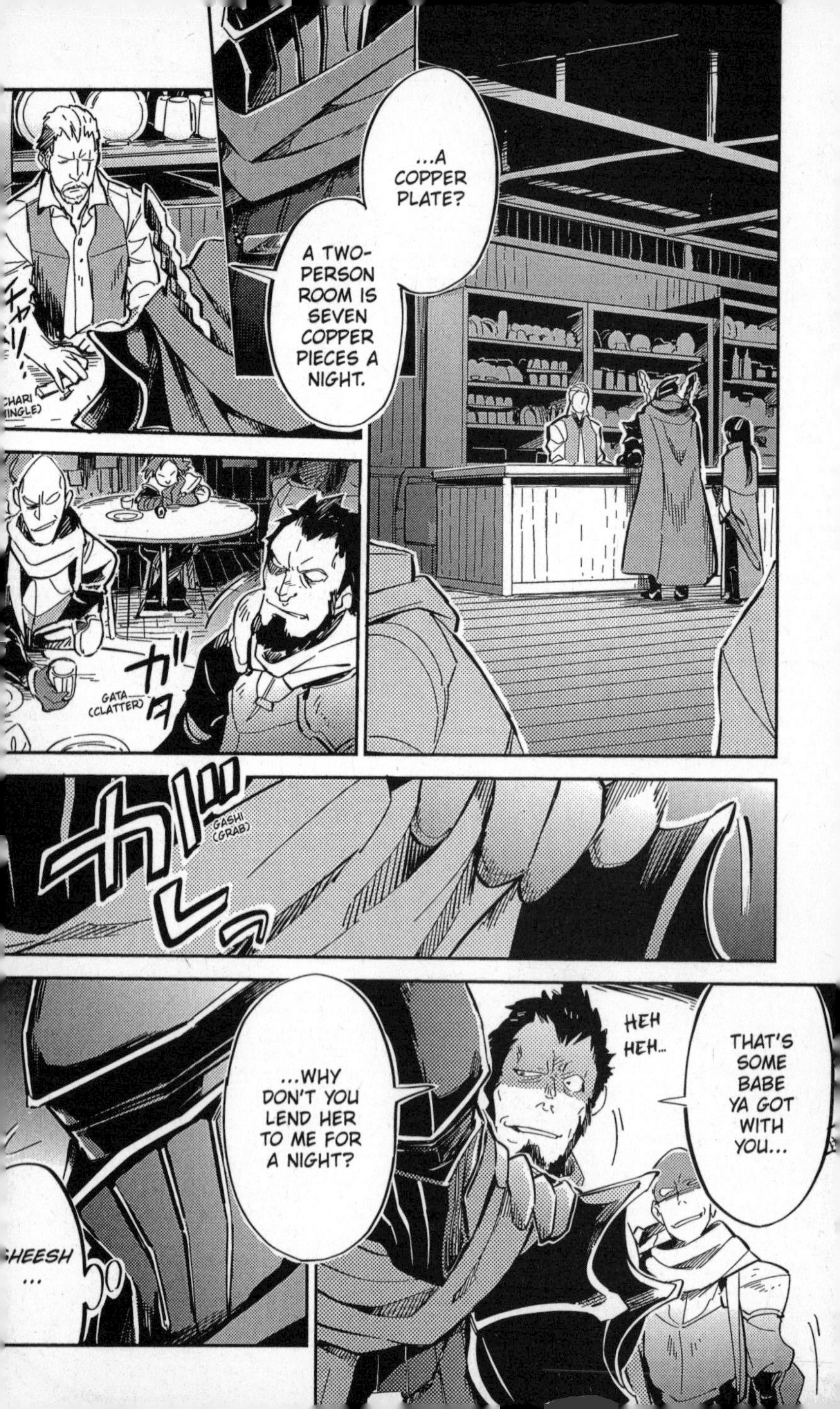

...A COPPER PLATE?
A TWO-PERSON ROOM IS SEVEN COPPER PIECES A NIGHT.
CHARI (JINGLE)
GATA (CLATTER)
GASHI (GRAB)
THAT'S SOME BABE YA GOT WITH YOU...
HEH HEH...
...WHY DON'T YOU LEND HER TO ME FOR A NIGHT?
SHEESH ...

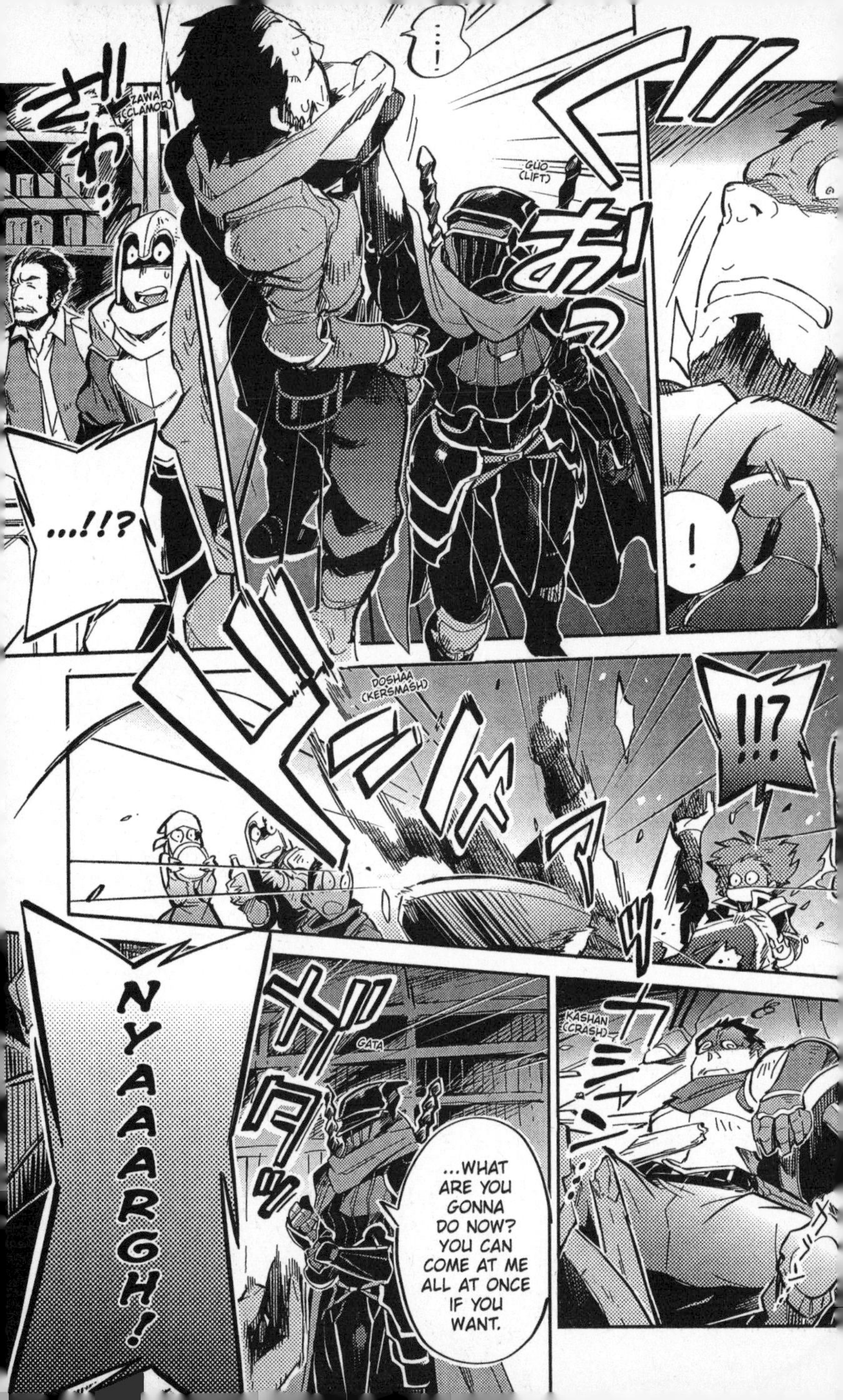
!
GUO (LIFT)
...!
ZAWA (CLAMOR)
...!!?
!!?
DOSHAA (KERSMASH)
KASHAN (CRASH)
GATA
...WHAT ARE YOU GONNA DO NOW? YOU CAN COME AT ME ALL AT ONCE IF YOU WANT.
NYAAARGH!

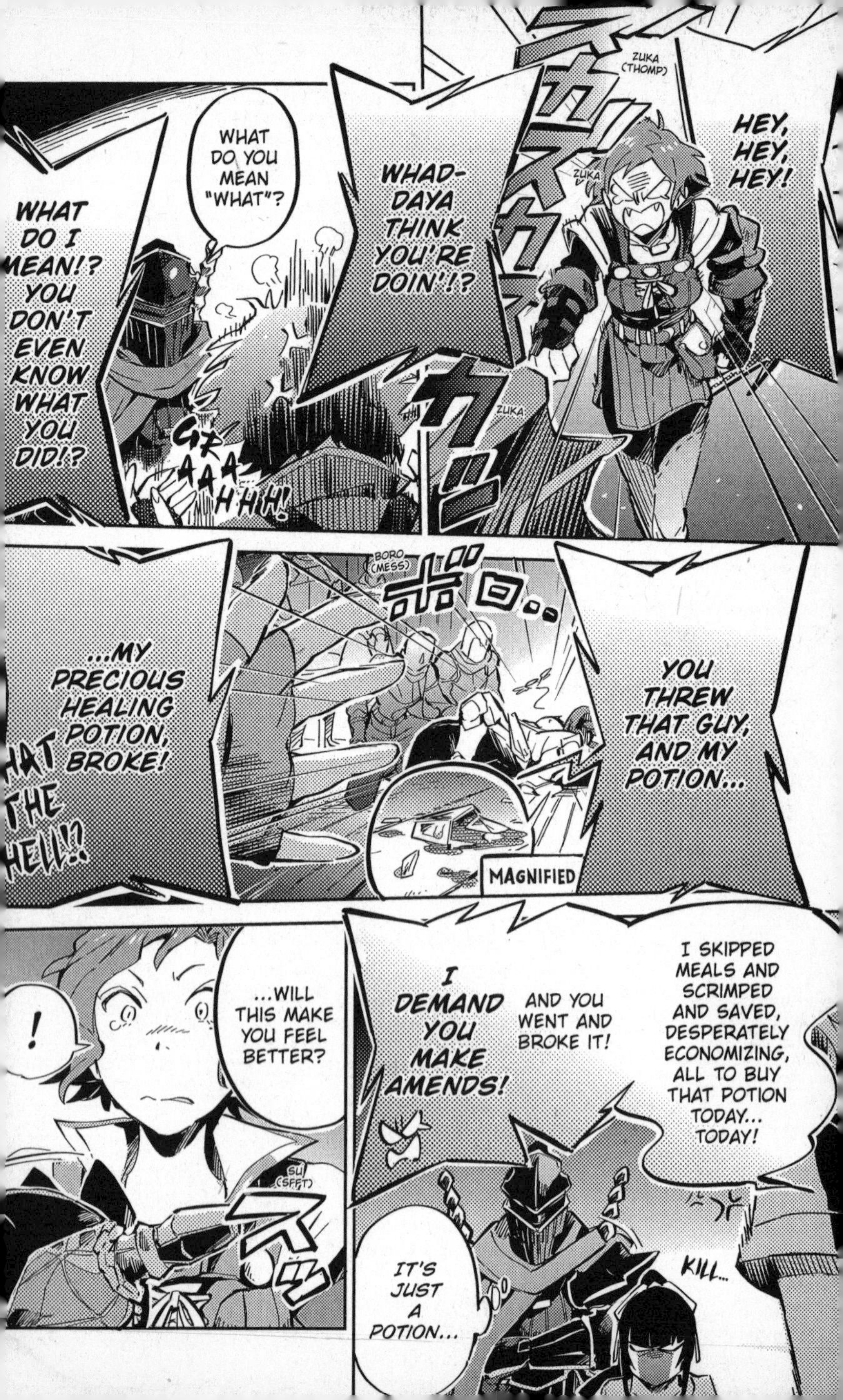
ZUKA (THOMP)
HEY, HEY, HEY!
ZUKA
WHAD-DAYA THINK YOU'RE DOIN'!?
ZUKA
WHAT DO YOU MEAN "WHAT"?
WHAT DO I MEAN!? YOU DON'T EVEN KNOW WHAT YOU DID!?
GRAAAHHH!
BORO (MESS)
YOU THREW THAT GUY, AND MY POTION...
MAGNIFIED
...MY PRECIOUS HEALING POTION, BROKE!
HAT THE HELL!?
I SKIPPED MEALS AND SCRIMPED AND SAVED, DESPERATELY ECONOMIZING, ALL TO BUY THAT POTION TODAY... TODAY!
AND YOU WENT AND BROKE IT!
I DEMAND YOU MAKE AMENDS!
KILL...
IT'S JUST A POTION...
...WILL THIS MAKE YOU FEEL BETTER?
!
SU (SFFT)

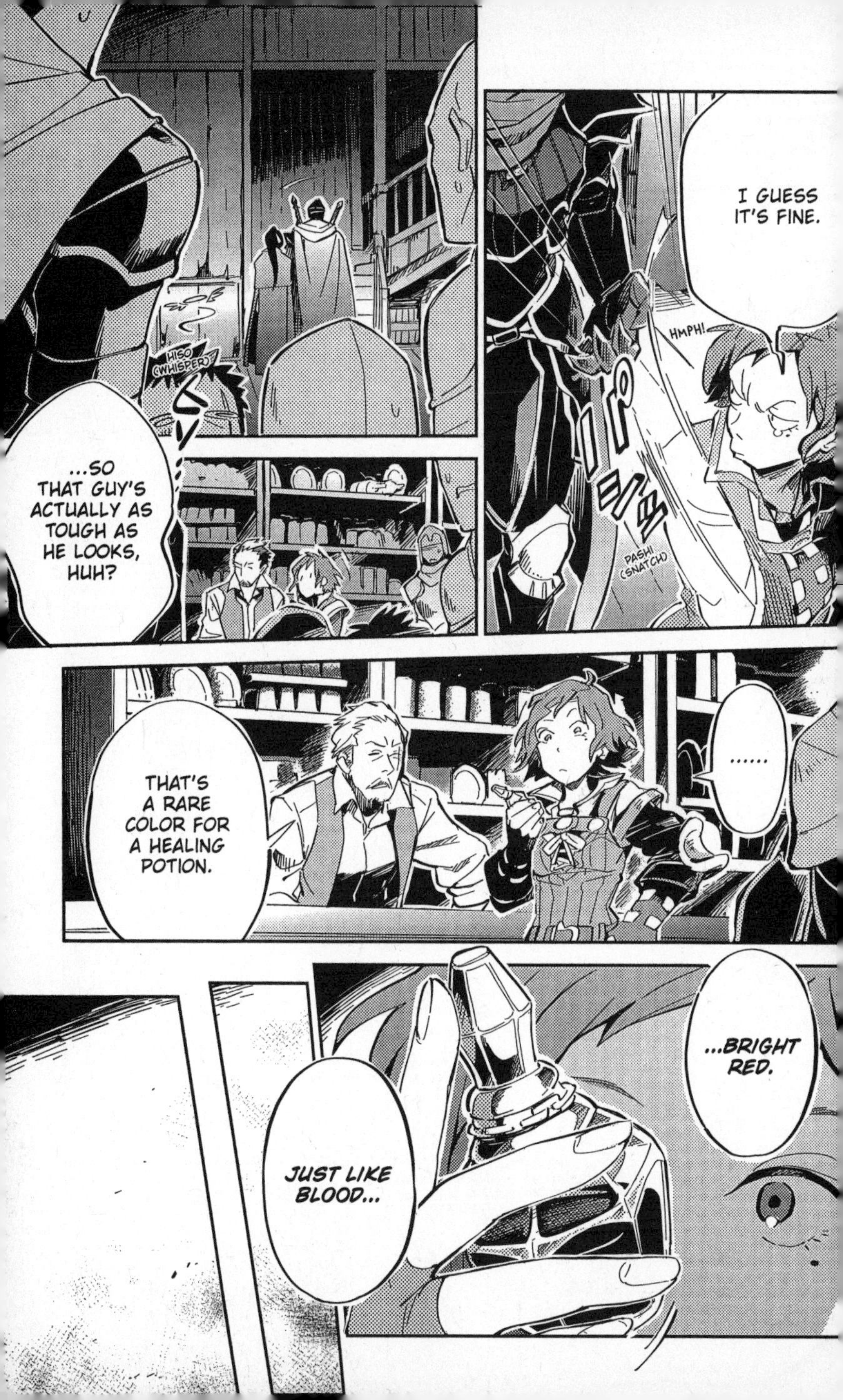
I GUESS IT'S FINE.
HMPH!
PASHI (SNATCH)
HISO (WHISPER)
...SO THAT GUY'S ACTUALLY AS TOUGH AS HE LOOKS, HUH?
......
THAT'S A RARE COLOR FOR A HEALING POTION.
...BRIGHT RED.
JUST LIKE BLOOD...

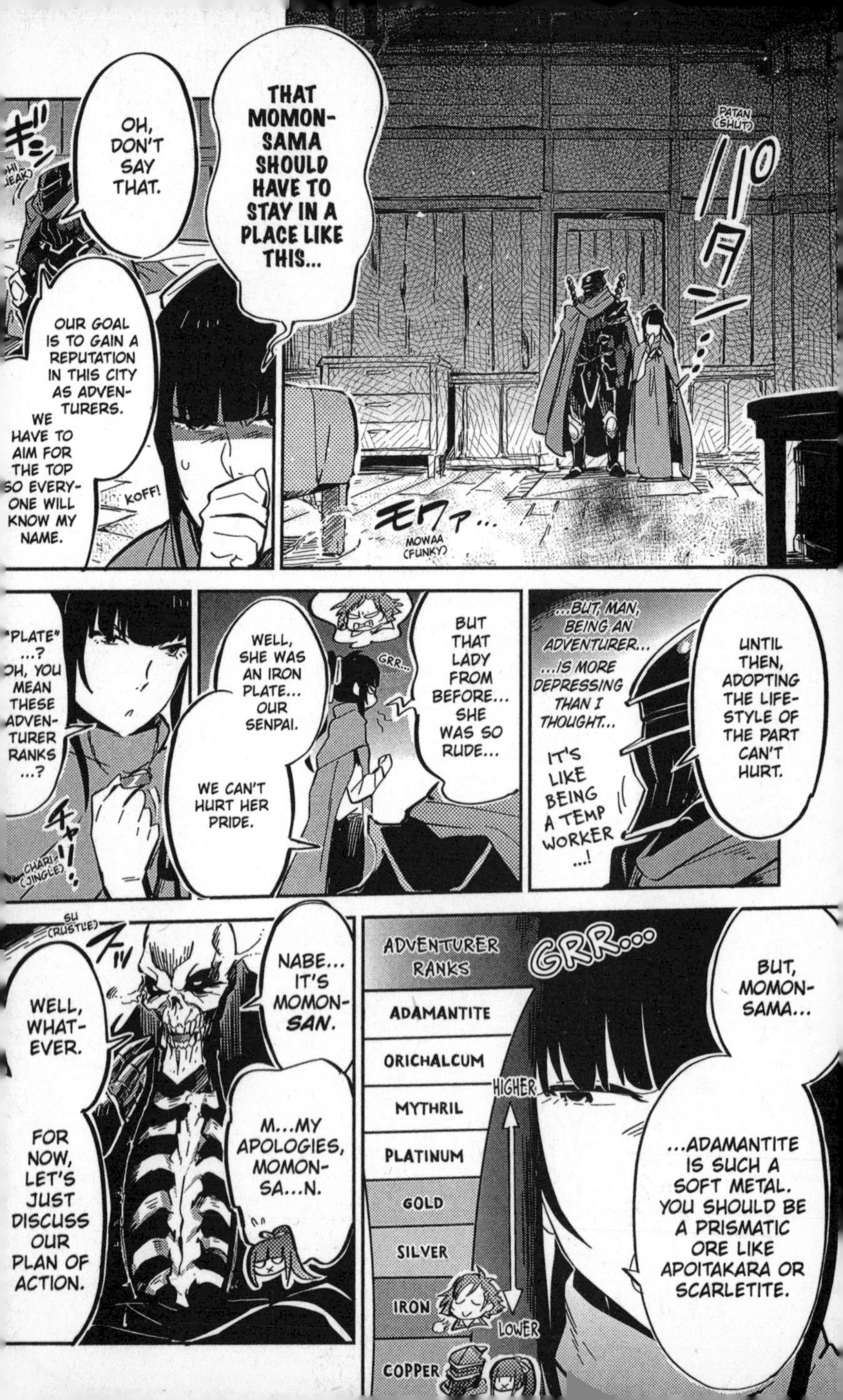
PATAN (SHUT)
THAT MOMON-SAMA SHOULD HAVE TO STAY IN A PLACE LIKE THIS...
MOWAA (FUNKY)
OH, DON'T SAY THAT.
OUR GOAL IS TO GAIN A REPUTATION IN THIS CITY AS ADVENTURERS.
WE HAVE TO AIM FOR THE TOP SO EVERYONE WILL KNOW MY NAME.
KOFF!
UNTIL THEN, ADOPTING THE LIFESTYLE OF THE PART CAN'T HURT.
...BUT, MAN, BEING AN ADVENTURER... ...IS MORE DEPRESSING THAN I THOUGHT...
IT'S LIKE BEING A TEMP WORKER...!
BUT THAT LADY FROM BEFORE... SHE WAS SO RUDE...
GRR...
WELL, SHE WAS AN IRON PLATE... OUR SENPAI.
WE CAN'T HURT HER PRIDE.
"PLATE"...? OH, YOU MEAN THESE ADVENTURER RANKS...?
CHARI (JINGLE)
GRR...
BUT, MOMON-SAMA...
...ADAMANTITE IS SUCH A SOFT METAL. YOU SHOULD BE A PRISMATIC ORE LIKE APOITAKARA OR SCARLETITE.
ADVENTURER RANKS
ADAMANTITE
ORICHALCUM
MYTHRIL
PLATINUM
GOLD
SILVER
IRON
COPPER
HIGHER
LOWER
NABE... IT'S MOMON-SAN.
SU (RUSTLE)
WELL, WHATEVER.
M...MY APOLOGIES, MOMON-SA...N.
FOR NOW, LET'S JUST DISCUSS OUR PLAN OF ACTION.

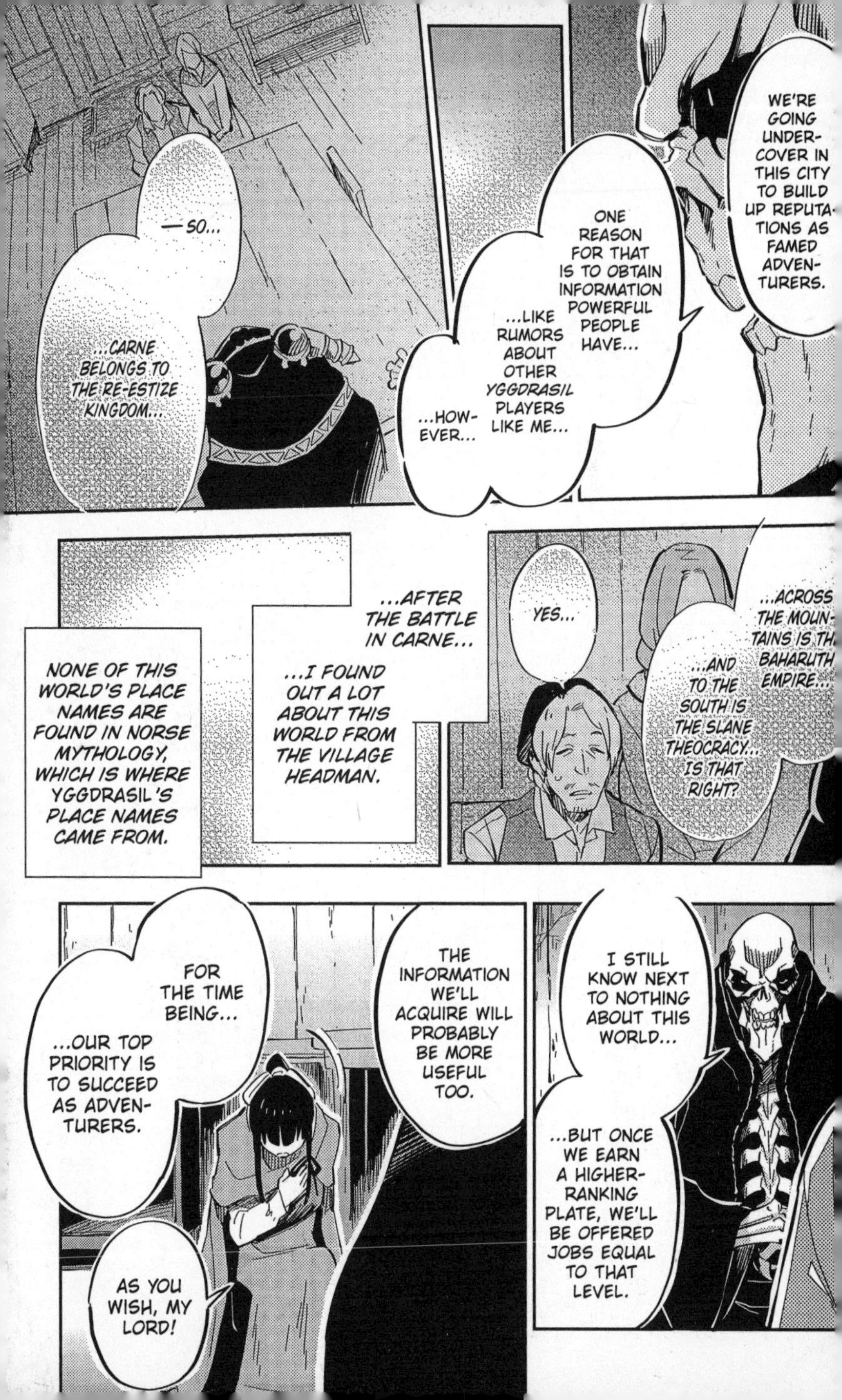
WE'RE GOING UNDERCOVER IN THIS CITY TO BUILD UP REPUTATIONS AS FAMED ADVENTURERS.
ONE REASON FOR THAT IS TO OBTAIN INFORMATION POWERFUL PEOPLE HAVE...
...LIKE RUMORS ABOUT OTHER YGGDRASIL PLAYERS LIKE ME...
...HOWEVER...
—SO...
...CARNE BELONGS TO THE RE-ESTIZE KINGDOM...
...ACROSS THE MOUNTAINS IS TH BAHARUTH EMPIRE...
...AND TO THE SOUTH IS THE SLANE THEOCRACY... IS THAT RIGHT?
YES...
...AFTER THE BATTLE IN CARNE...
...I FOUND OUT A LOT ABOUT THIS WORLD FROM THE VILLAGE HEADMAN.
NONE OF THIS WORLD'S PLACE NAMES ARE FOUND IN NORSE MYTHOLOGY, WHICH IS WHERE YGGDRASIL'S PLACE NAMES CAME FROM.
I STILL KNOW NEXT TO NOTHING ABOUT THIS WORLD...
...BUT ONCE WE EARN A HIGHER-RANKING PLATE, WE'LL BE OFFERED JOBS EQUAL TO THAT LEVEL.
THE INFORMATION WE'LL ACQUIRE WILL PROBABLY BE MORE USEFUL TOO.
FOR THE TIME BEING...
...OUR TOP PRIORITY IS TO SUCCEED AS ADVENTURERS.
AS YOU WISH, MY LORD!

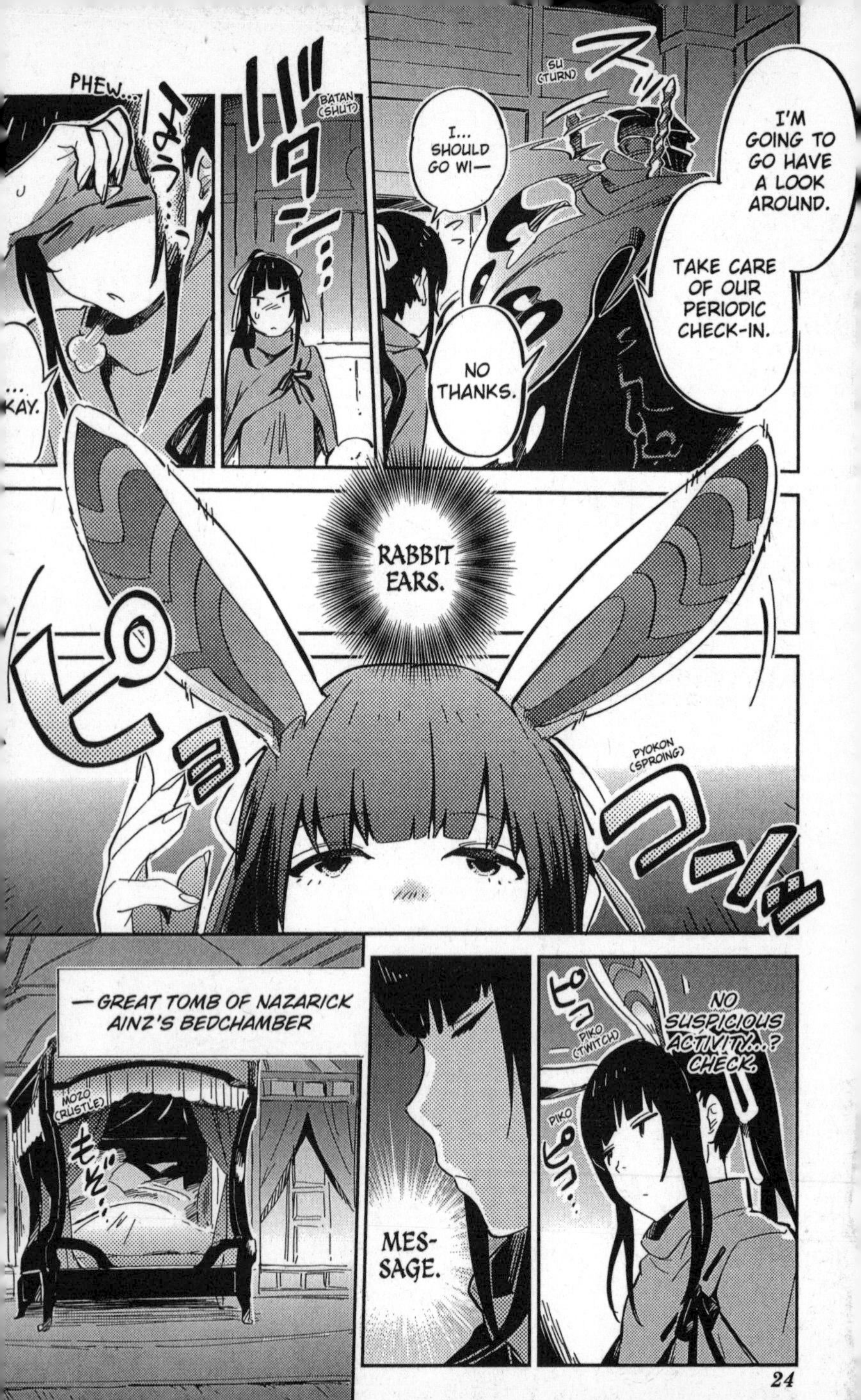
SU (TURN)
I'M GOING TO GO HAVE A LOOK AROUND.
TAKE CARE OF OUR PERIODIC CHECK-IN.
I... SHOULD GO WI—
NO THANKS.
BATAN (SHUT)
PHEW...
...KAY.
RABBIT EARS.
PYOKON (SPROING)
PIKO (TWITCH)
NO SUSPICIOUS ACTIVITY...? CHECK.
PIKO
MES-SAGE.
—GREAT TOMB OF NAZARICK AINZ'S BEDCHAMBER
MOZO (RUSTLE)

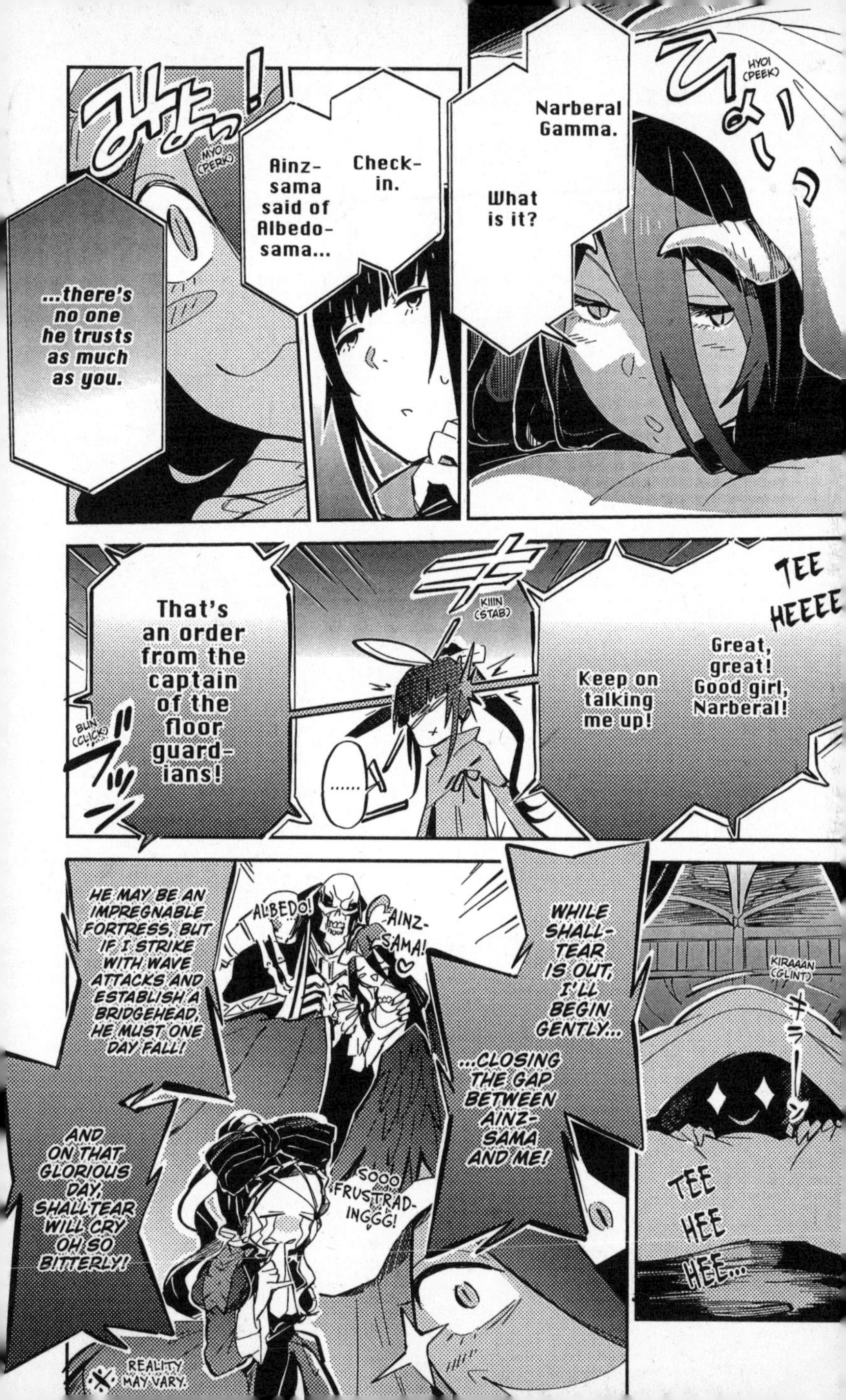
HYOI (PEEK)
Narberal Gamma.
What is it?
Check-in.
Ainz-sama said of Albedo-sama...
MYO (PERK)
...there's no one he trusts as much as you.
TEE HEEEE
Great, great! Good girl, Narberal!
Keep on talking me up!
KIIN (STAB)
......
That's an order from the captain of the floor guardians!
BUN (CLICK)
KIRAAAN (GLINT)
TEE HEE HEE...
WHILE SHALLTEAR IS OUT, I'LL BEGIN GENTLY...
...CLOSING THE GAP BETWEEN AINZ-SAMA AND ME!
HE MAY BE AN IMPREGNABLE FORTRESS, BUT IF I STRIKE WITH WAVE ATTACKS AND ESTABLISH A BRIDGEHEAD, HE MUST ONE DAY FALL!
AINZ-SAMA!
ALBEDO!
SOOO FRUSTRADINGGG!
AND ON THAT GLORIOUS DAY, SHALLTEAR WILL CRY OH SO BITTERLY!
※ REALITY MAY VARY.

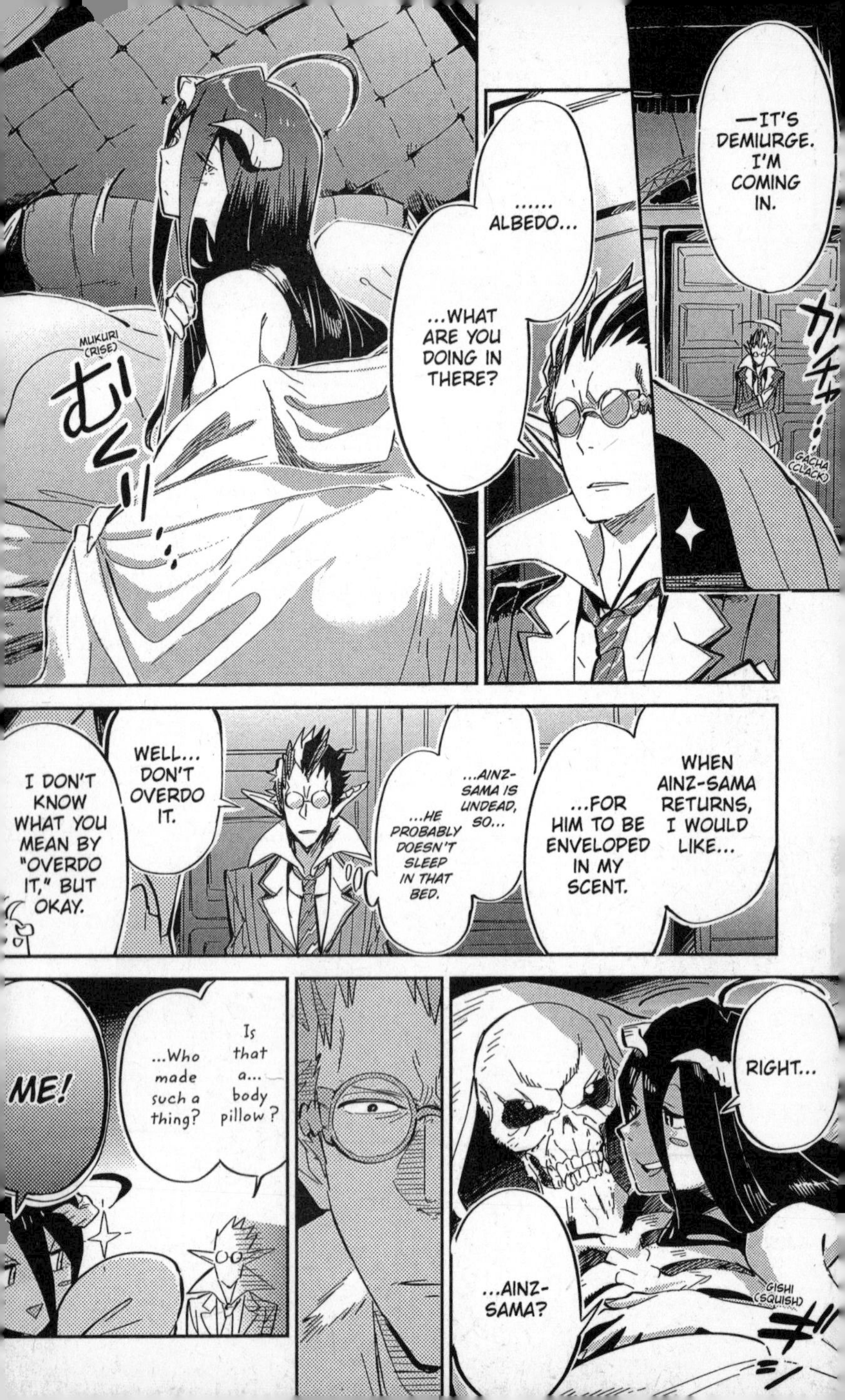
—IT'S DEMIURGE. I'M COMING IN.
カチャ…
GACHA (CLACK)
......ALBEDO...
...WHAT ARE YOU DOING IN THERE?
むくり
MUKURI (RISE)
WHEN AINZ-SAMA RETURNS, I WOULD LIKE...
...FOR HIM TO BE ENVELOPED IN MY SCENT.
...AINZ-SAMA IS UNDEAD, SO...
...HE PROBABLY DOESN'T SLEEP IN THAT BED.
WELL... DON'T OVERDO IT.
I DON'T KNOW WHAT YOU MEAN BY "OVERDO IT," BUT OKAY.
RIGHT...
...AINZ-SAMA?
GISHI (SQUISH)
Is that a... body pillow?
...Who made such a thing?
ME!

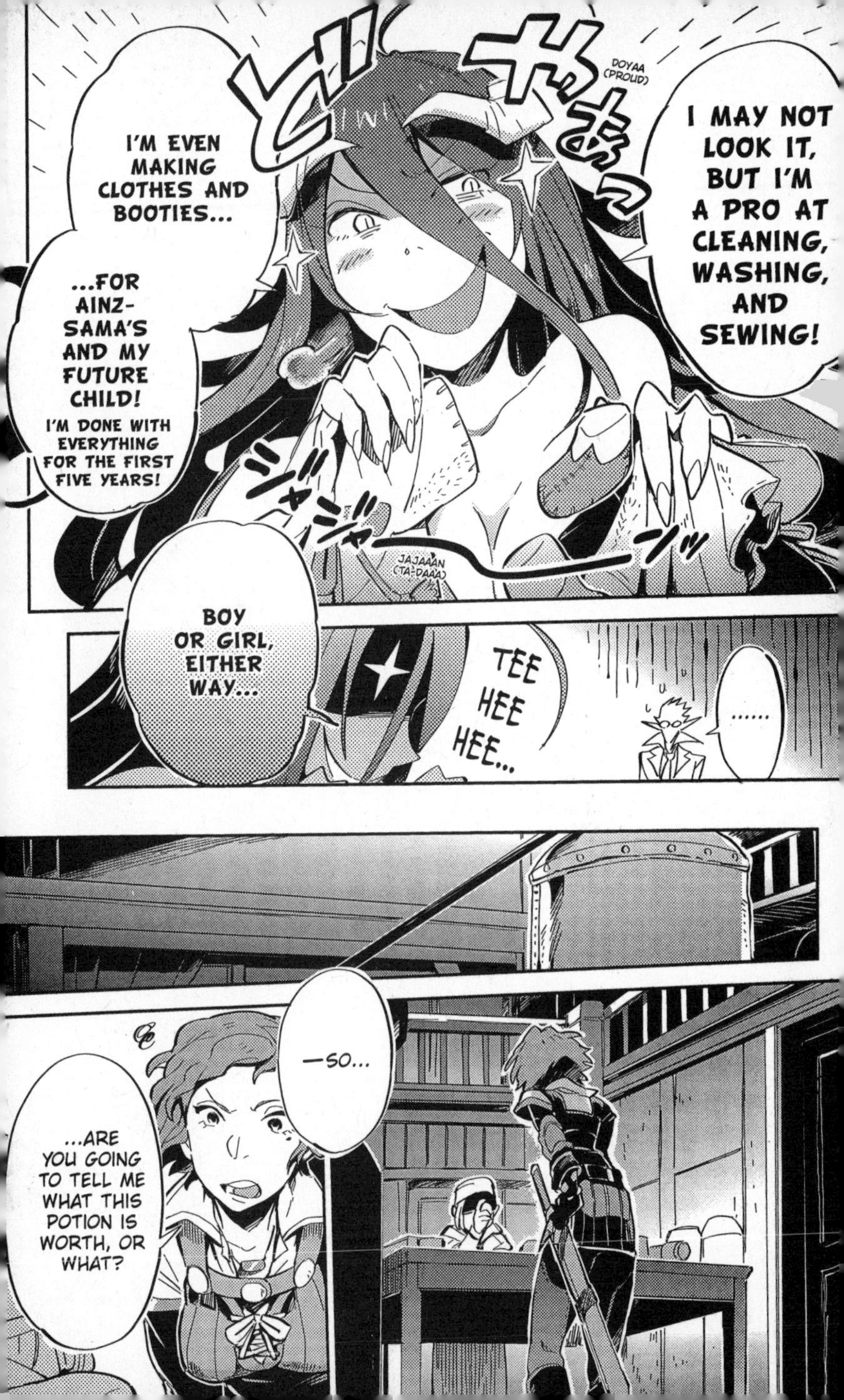
DOYAA (PROUD)
I MAY NOT LOOK IT, BUT I'M A PRO AT CLEANING, WASHING, AND SEWING!
I'M EVEN MAKING CLOTHES AND BOOTIES...
...FOR AINZ-SAMA'S AND MY FUTURE CHILD!
I'M DONE WITH EVERYTHING FOR THE FIRST FIVE YEARS!
JAJAAAN (TA-DAAA)
......
TEE HEE HEE...
BOY OR GIRL, EITHER WAY...
—SO...
...ARE YOU GOING TO TELL ME WHAT THIS POTION IS WORTH, OR WHAT?

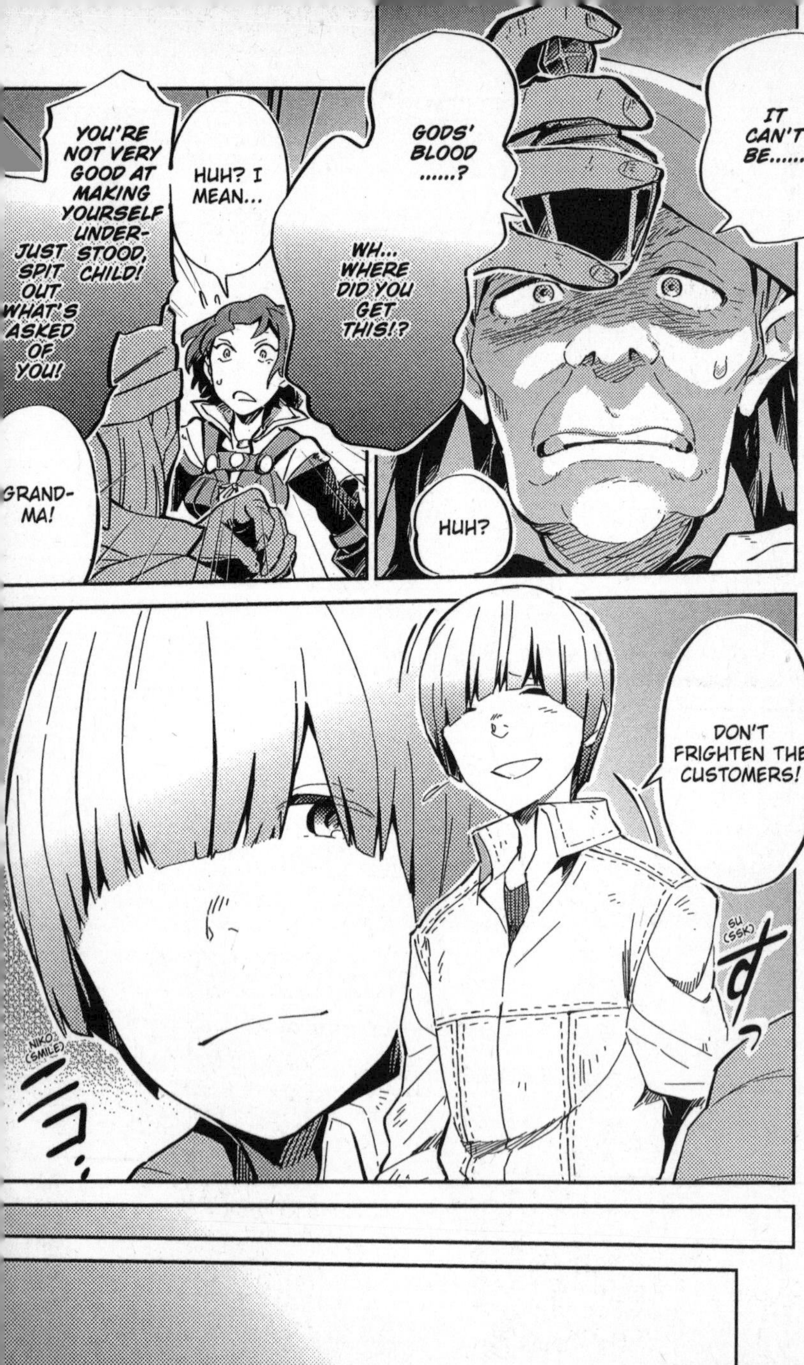
IT CAN'T BE......
GODS' BLOOD ......?
WH... WHERE DID YOU GET THIS!?
HUH?
HUH? I MEAN...
YOU'RE NOT VERY GOOD AT MAKING YOURSELF UNDER-STOOD, CHILD!
JUST SPIT OUT WHAT'S ASKED OF YOU!
GRAND-MA!
DON'T FRIGHTEN THE CUSTOMERS!
SU (SSK)
NIKO (SMILE)

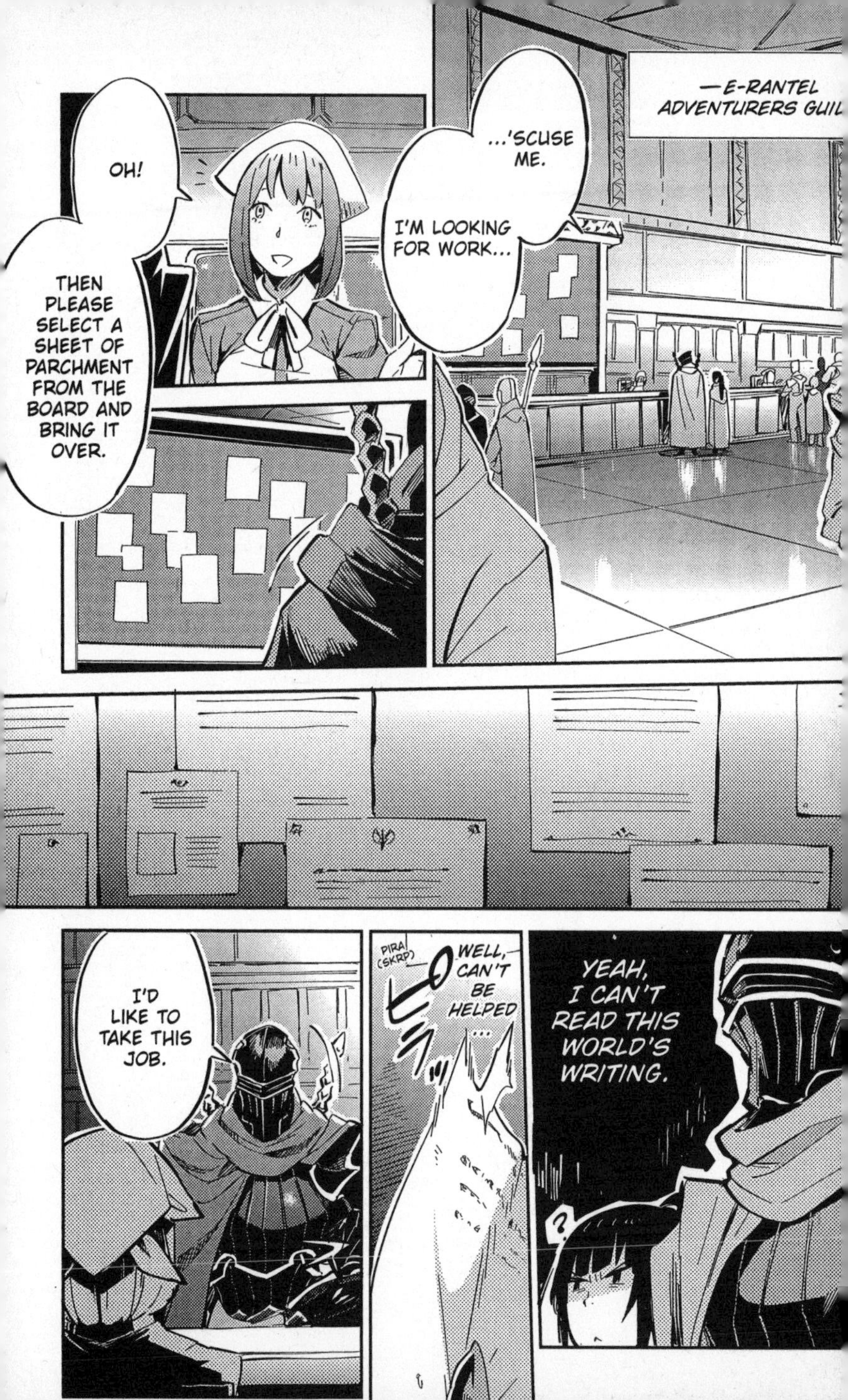
—E-RANTEL ADVENTURERS GUIL
...'SCUSE ME.
I'M LOOKING FOR WORK...
OH!
THEN PLEASE SELECT A SHEET OF PARCHMENT FROM THE BOARD AND BRING IT OVER.
YEAH, I CAN'T READ THIS WORLD'S WRITING.
PIRA (SKRP)
WELL, CAN'T BE HELPED...
I'D LIKE TO TAKE THIS JOB.

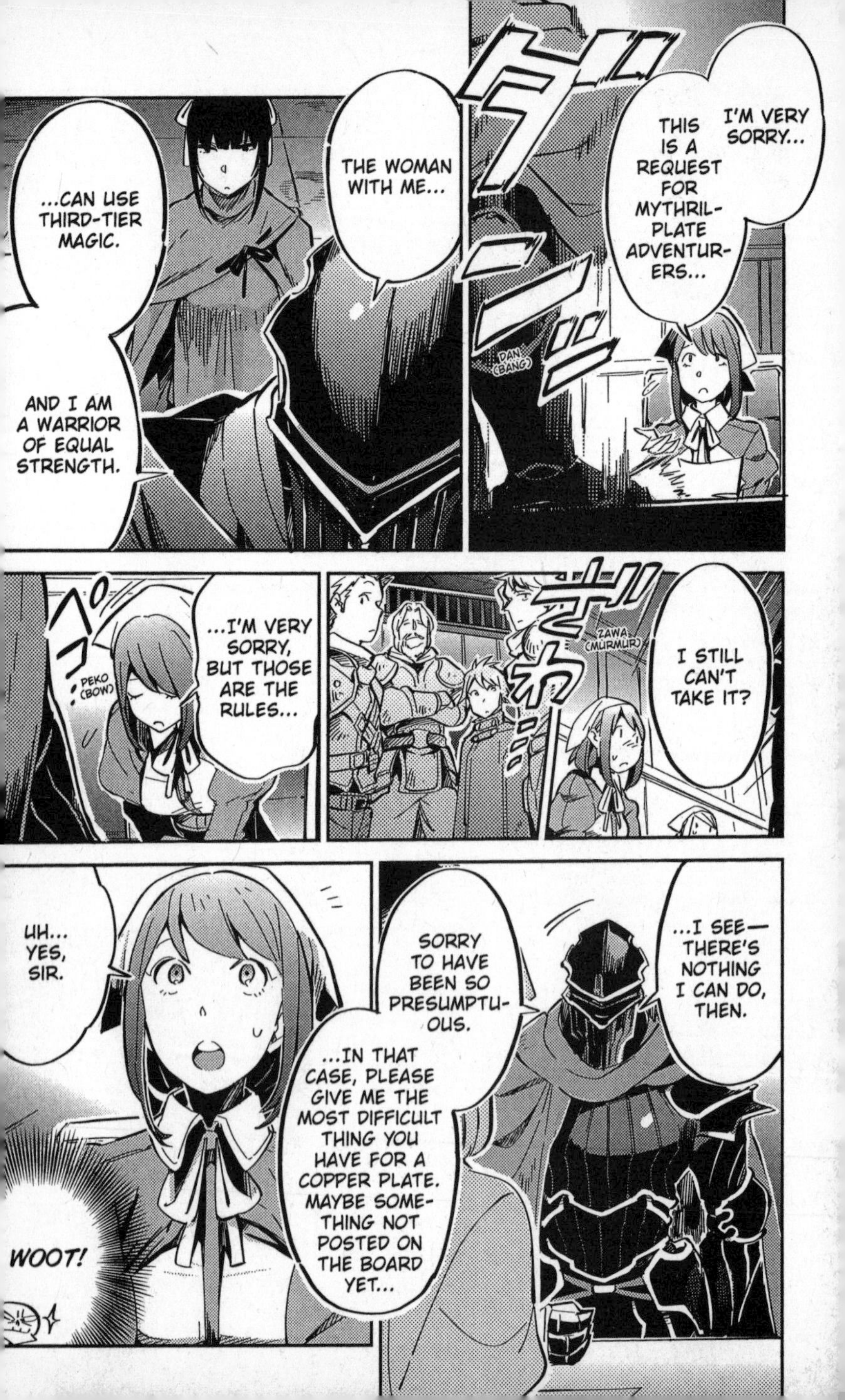
I'M VERY SORRY...
THIS IS A REQUEST FOR MYTHRIL-PLATE ADVENTURERS...
DAN (BANG)
THE WOMAN WITH ME...
...CAN USE THIRD-TIER MAGIC.
AND I AM A WARRIOR OF EQUAL STRENGTH.
I STILL CAN'T TAKE IT?
ZAWA (MURMUR)
...I'M VERY SORRY, BUT THOSE ARE THE RULES...
PEKO (BOW)
...I SEE— THERE'S NOTHING I CAN DO, THEN.
SORRY TO HAVE BEEN SO PRESUMPTUOUS.
...IN THAT CASE, PLEASE GIVE ME THE MOST DIFFICULT THING YOU HAVE FOR A COPPER PLATE. MAYBE SOMETHING NOT POSTED ON THE BOARD YET...
UH... YES, SIR.
WOOT!

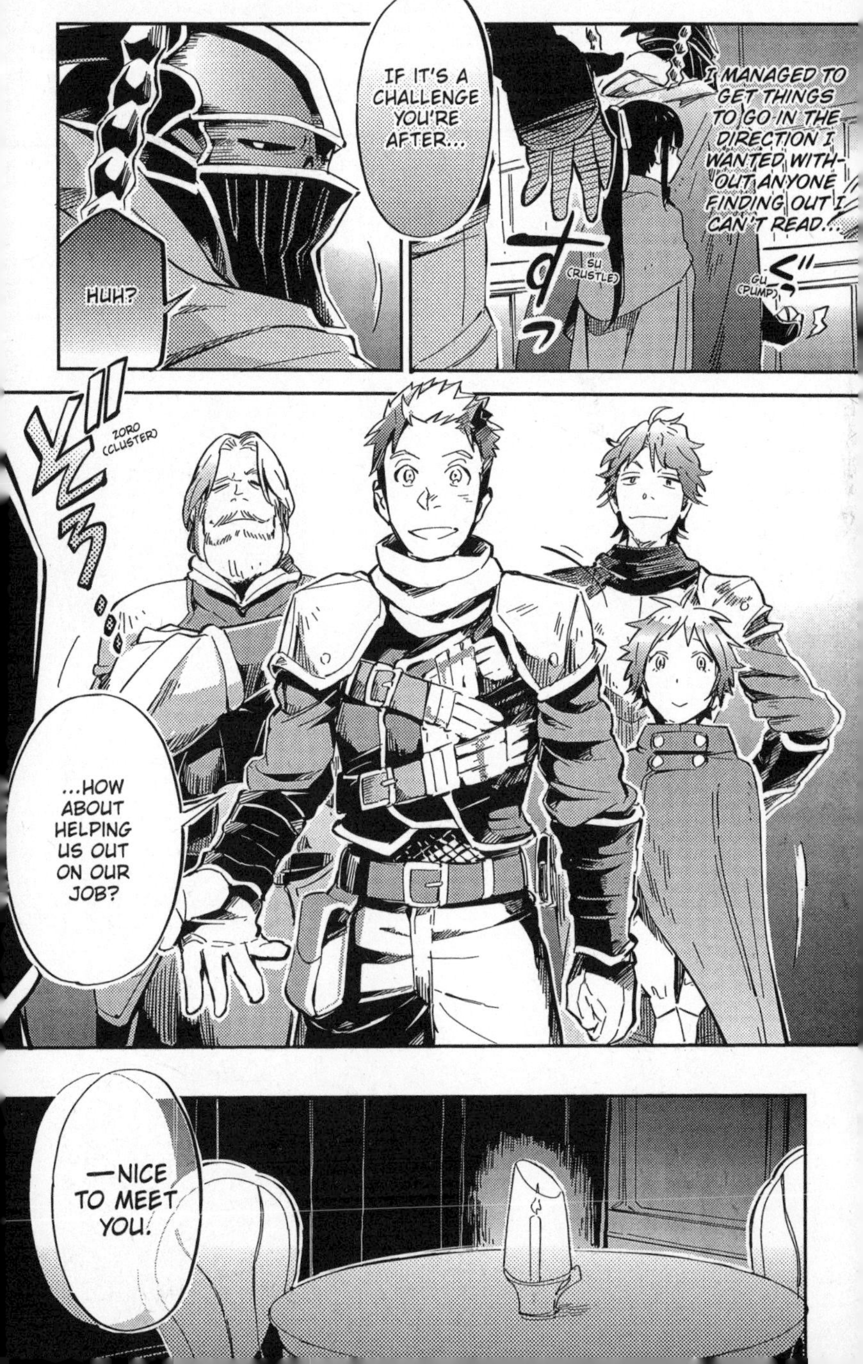
I MANAGED TO GET THINGS TO GO IN THE DIRECTION I WANTED WITHOUT ANYONE FINDING OUT I CAN'T READ...
SU (RUSTLE)
GU (PUMP)
IF IT'S A CHALLENGE YOU'RE AFTER...
HUH?
ZORO (CLUSTER)
...HOW ABOUT HELPING US OUT ON OUR JOB?
—NICE TO MEET YOU.

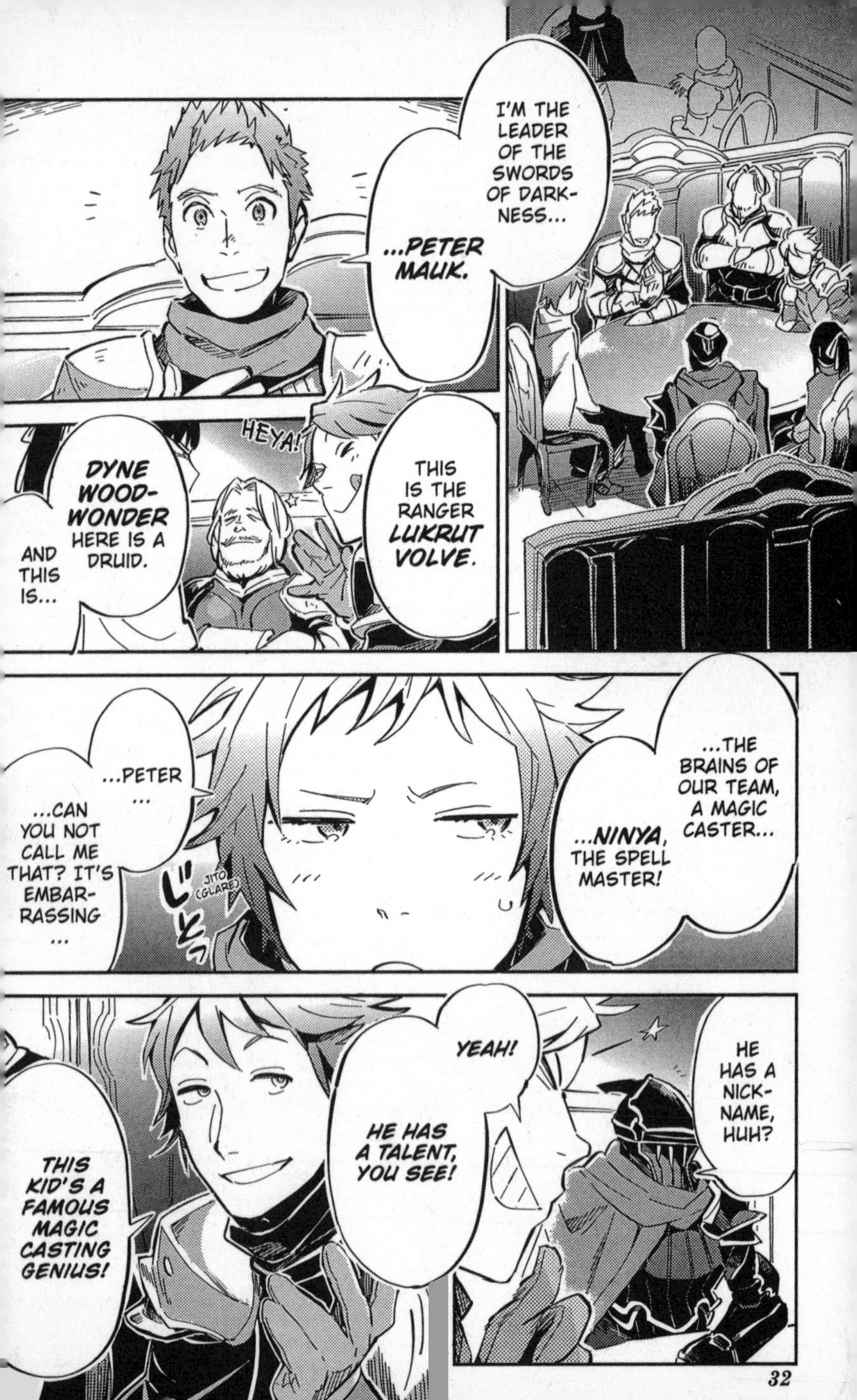

I'M THE LEADER OF THE SWORDS OF DARKNESS...
...PETER MAUK.
HEYA!
THIS IS THE RANGER LUKRUT VOLVE.
DYNE WOODWONDER HERE IS A DRUID.
AND THIS IS...
...THE BRAINS OF OUR TEAM, A MAGIC CASTER...
...NINYA, THE SPELL MASTER!
JITO (GLARE)
...PETER...
...CAN YOU NOT CALL ME THAT? IT'S EMBARRASSING...
HE HAS A NICKNAME, HUH?
YEAH!
HE HAS A TALENT, YOU SEE!
THIS KID'S A FAMOUS MAGIC CASTING GENIUS!

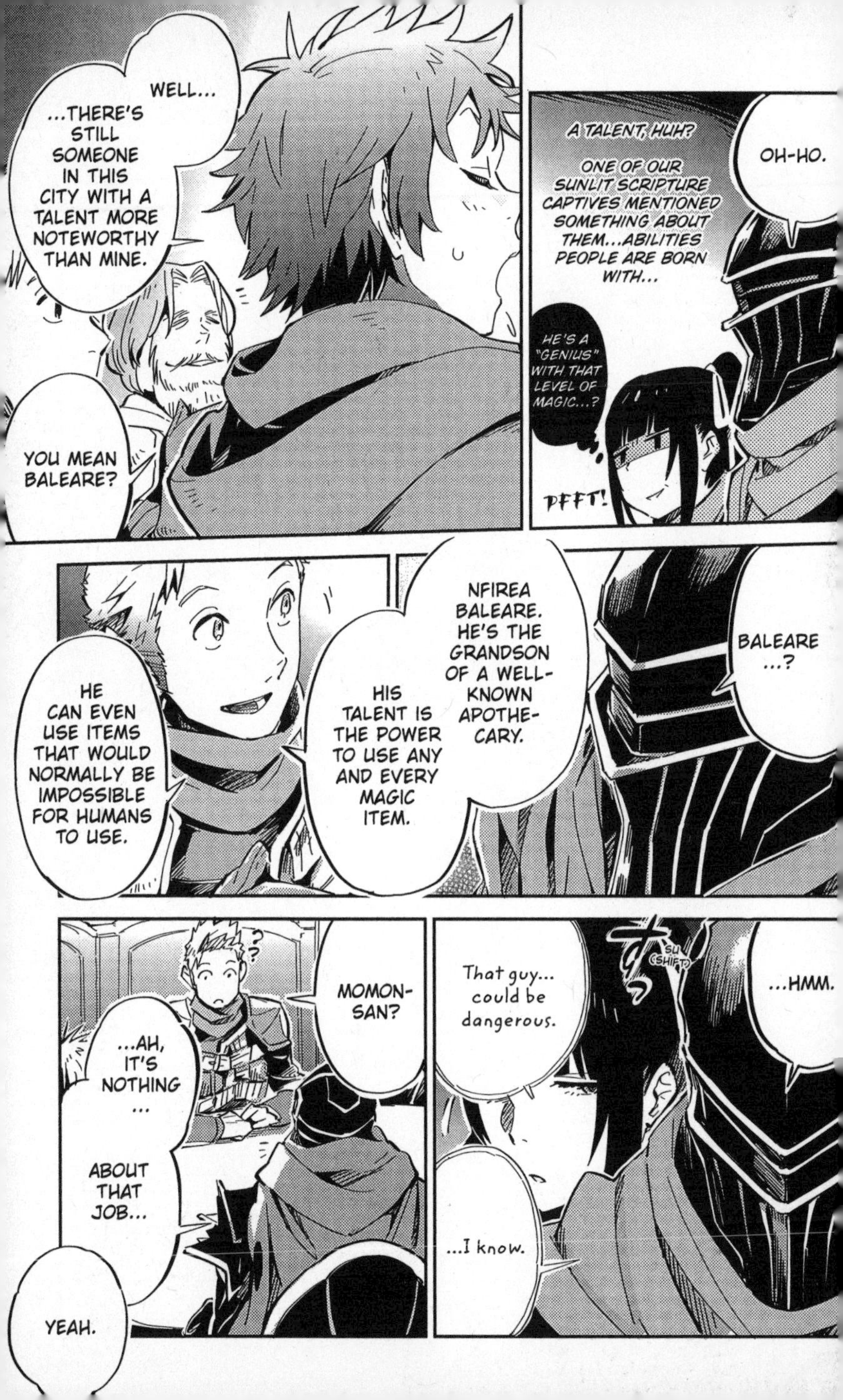
OH-HO.
A TALENT, HUH?
ONE OF OUR SUNLIT SCRIPTURE CAPTIVES MENTIONED SOMETHING ABOUT THEM...ABILITIES PEOPLE ARE BORN WITH...
HE'S A "GENIUS" WITH THAT LEVEL OF MAGIC...?
PFFT!
WELL...
...THERE'S STILL SOMEONE IN THIS CITY WITH A TALENT MORE NOTEWORTHY THAN MINE.
YOU MEAN BALEARE?
BALEARE ...?
NFIREA BALEARE. HE'S THE GRANDSON OF A WELL-KNOWN APOTHECARY.
HIS TALENT IS THE POWER TO USE ANY AND EVERY MAGIC ITEM.
HE CAN EVEN USE ITEMS THAT WOULD NORMALLY BE IMPOSSIBLE FOR HUMANS TO USE.
...HMM.
SU (SHIFT)
That guy... could be dangerous.
...I know.
MOMON-SAN?
...AH, IT'S NOTHING...
ABOUT THAT JOB...
YEAH.

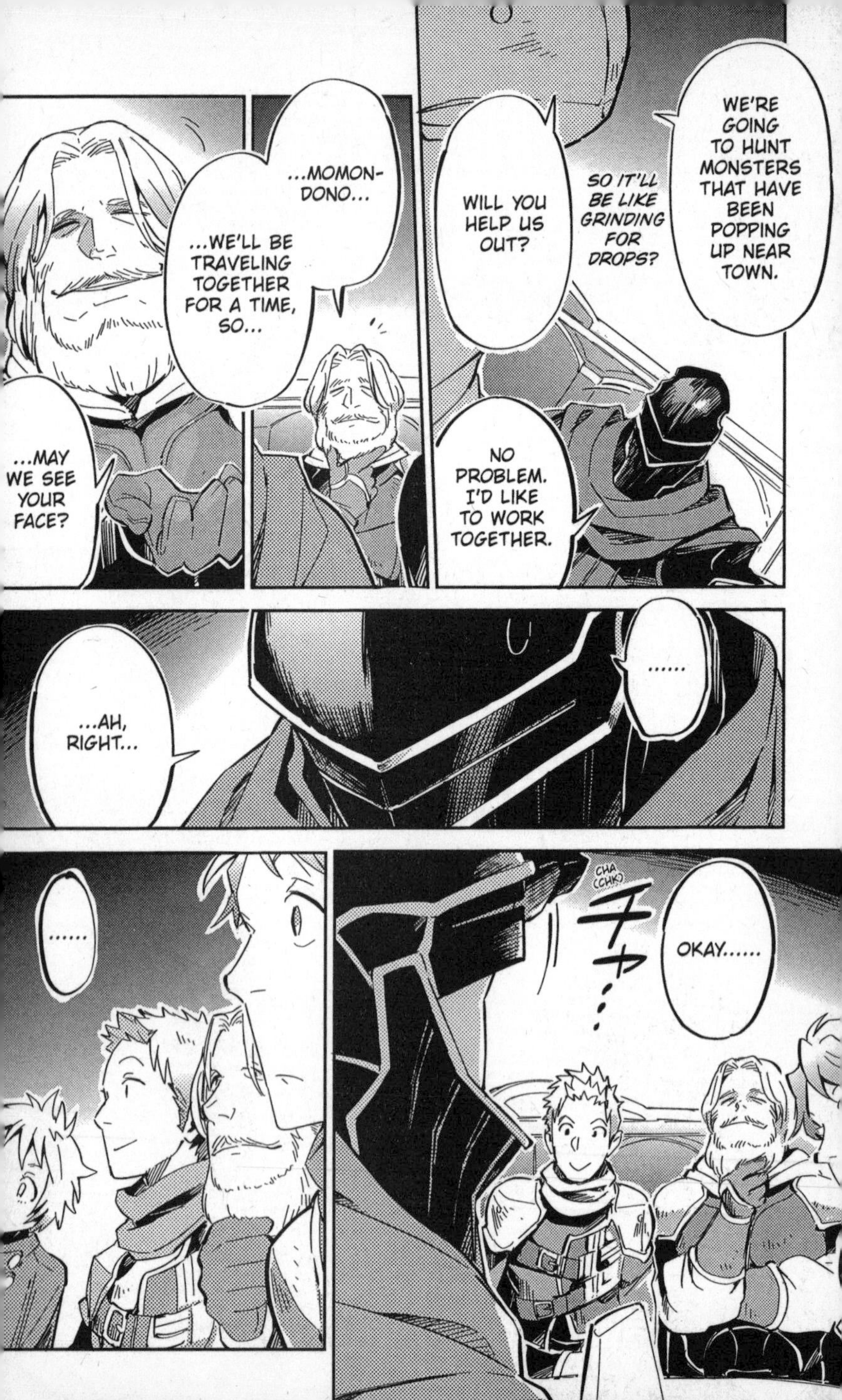
WE'RE GOING TO HUNT MONSTERS THAT HAVE BEEN POPPING UP NEAR TOWN.
SO IT'LL BE LIKE GRINDING FOR DROPS?
WILL YOU HELP US OUT?
NO PROBLEM. I'D LIKE TO WORK TOGETHER.
...MOMON-DONO...
...WE'LL BE TRAVELING TOGETHER FOR A TIME, SO...
...MAY WE SEE YOUR FACE?
......
...AH, RIGHT...
CHA (CHK)
チャ…
OKAY......
......

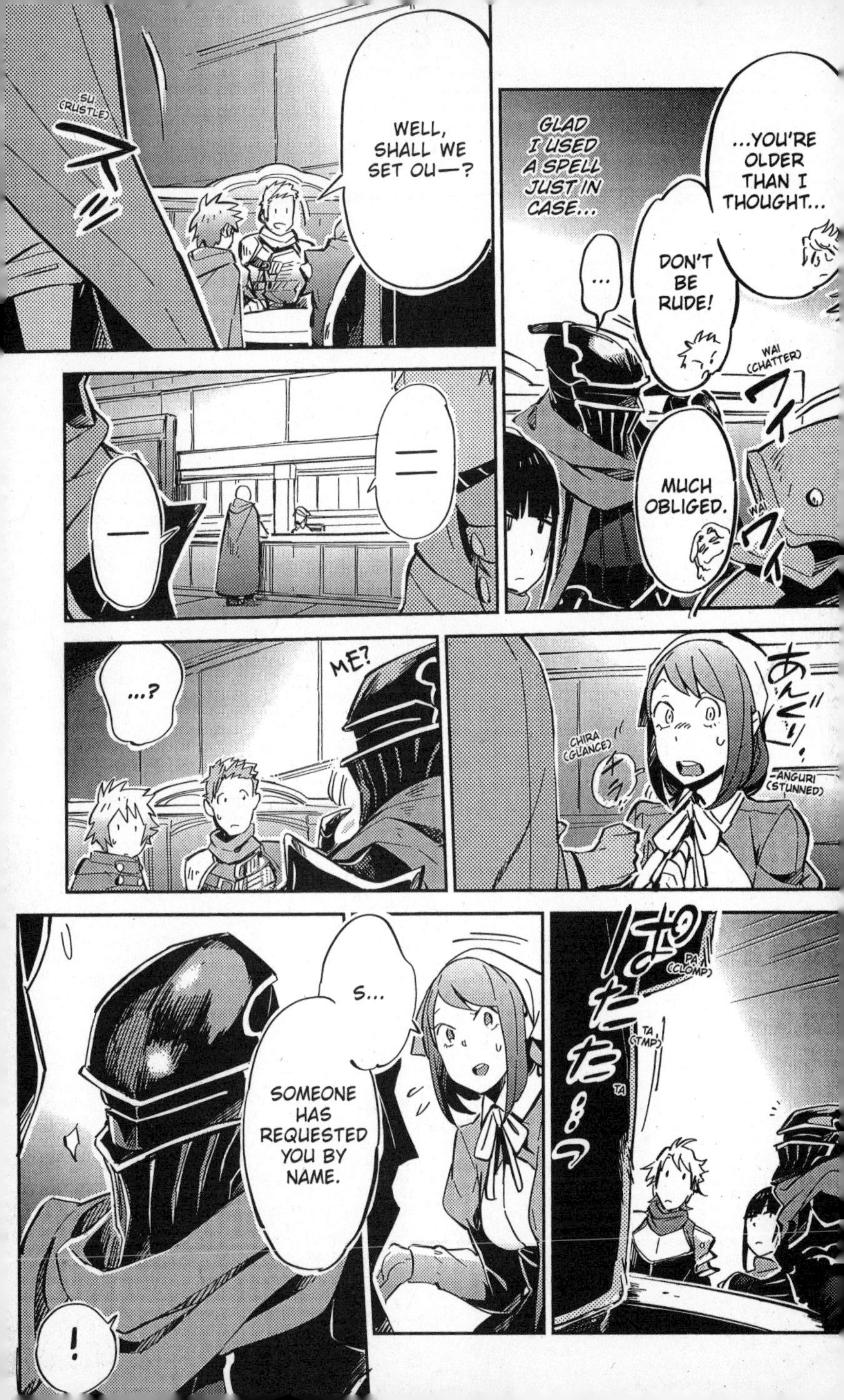
...YOU'RE OLDER THAN I THOUGHT...
GLAD I USED A SPELL JUST IN CASE...
DON'T BE RUDE!
...
WAI (CHATTER)
MUCH OBLIGED.
WAI
SU (RUSTLE)
WELL, SHALL WE SET OU—?
—
—
ANGURI (STUNNED)
CHIRA (GLANCE)
ME?
...?
PA (CLOMP)
TA (TMP)
TA
S...
SOMEONE HAS REQUESTED YOU BY NAME.
!

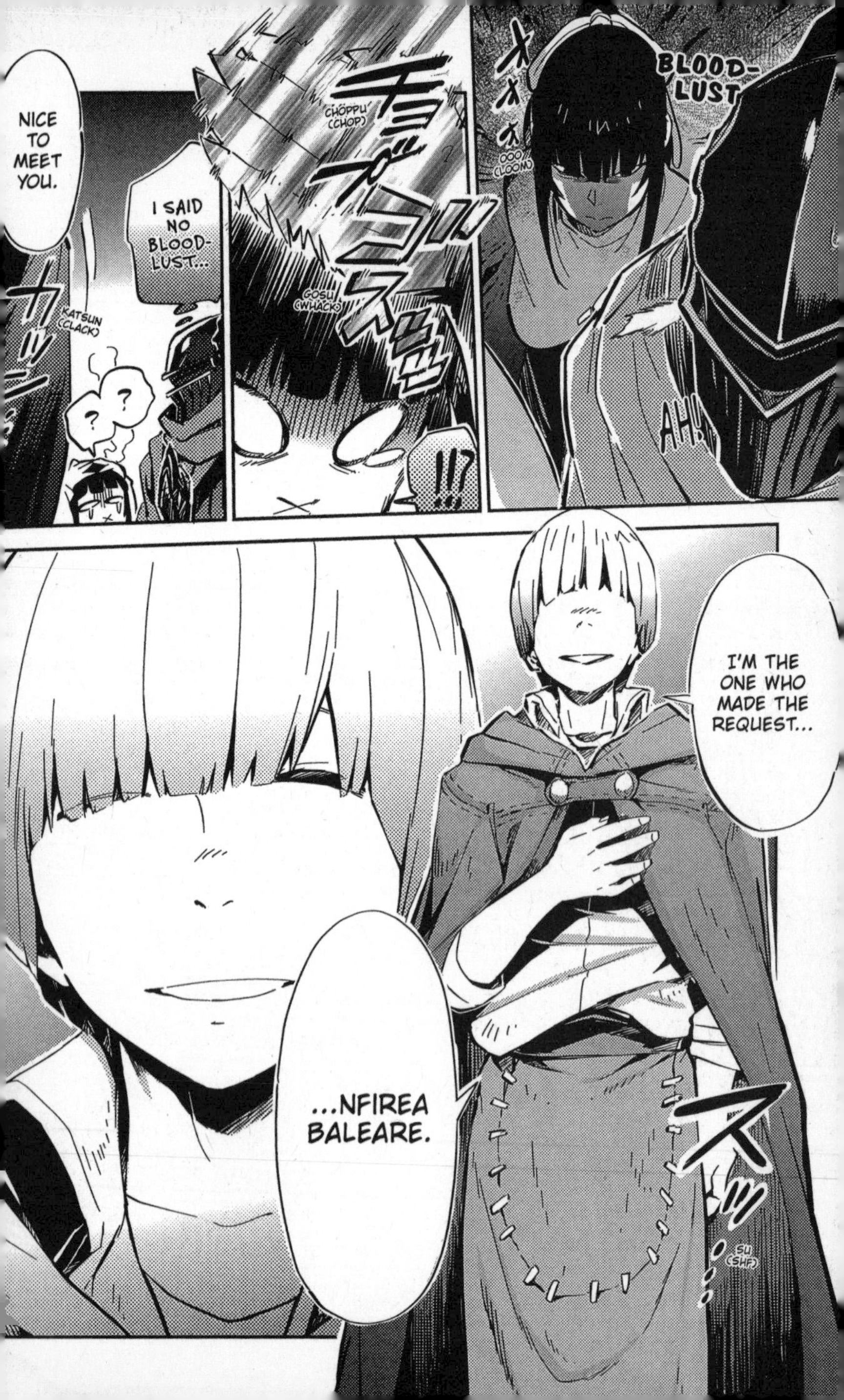
BLOOD-LUST
OOO (LOOM)
AH!
CHOPPU (CHOP)
GOSU (WHACK)
!!?
I SAID NO BLOOD-LUST...
KATSUN (CLACK)
? ?
NICE TO MEET YOU.
I'M THE ONE WHO MADE THE REQUEST...
SU (SHF)
...NFIREA BALEARE.

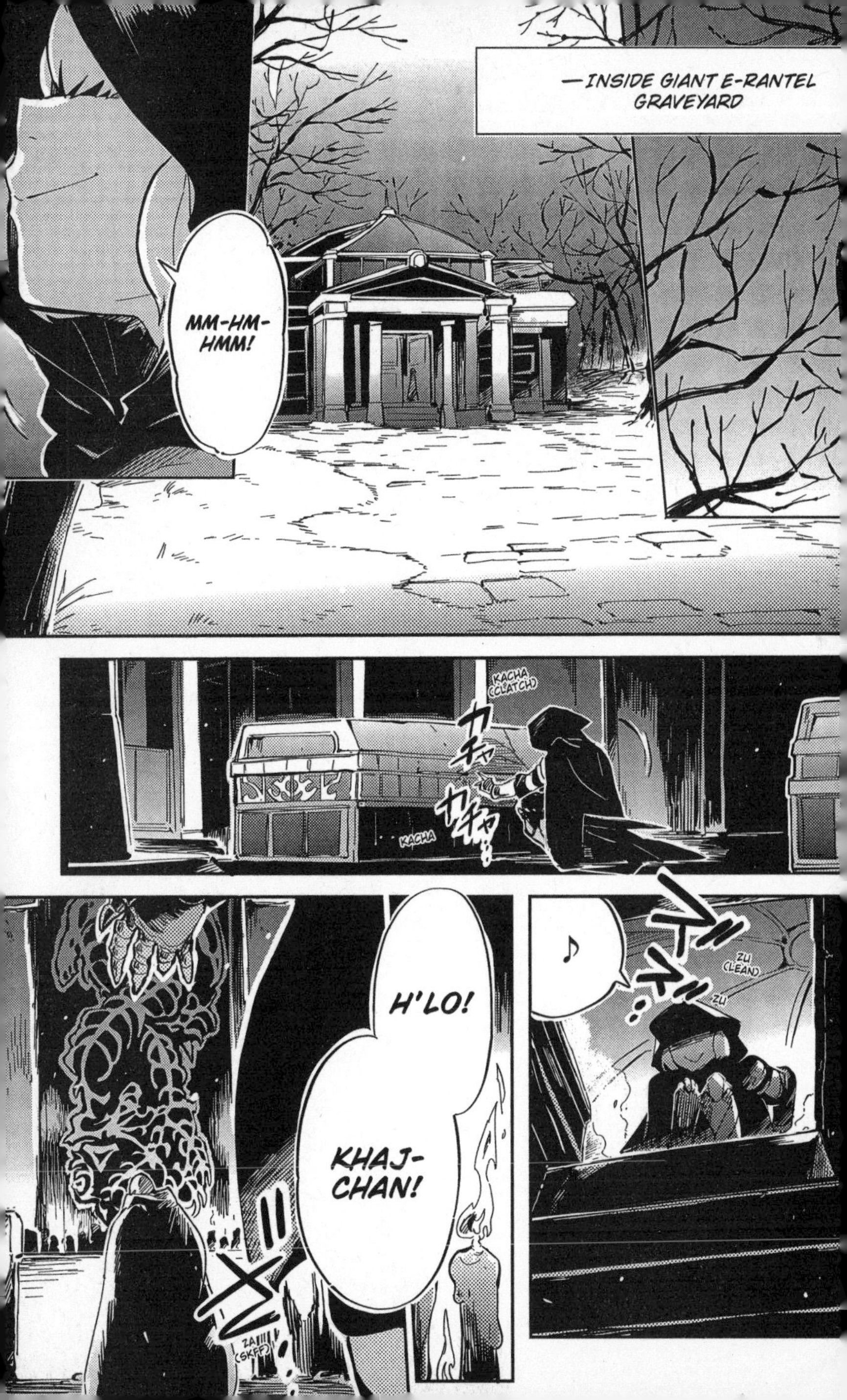
—INSIDE GIANT E-RANTEL GRAVEYARD
MM-HM-HMM!
KACHA (CLATCH)
KACHA
♪
ZU (LEAN)
ZU
H'LO!
KHAJ-CHAN!
ZA (SKFF)

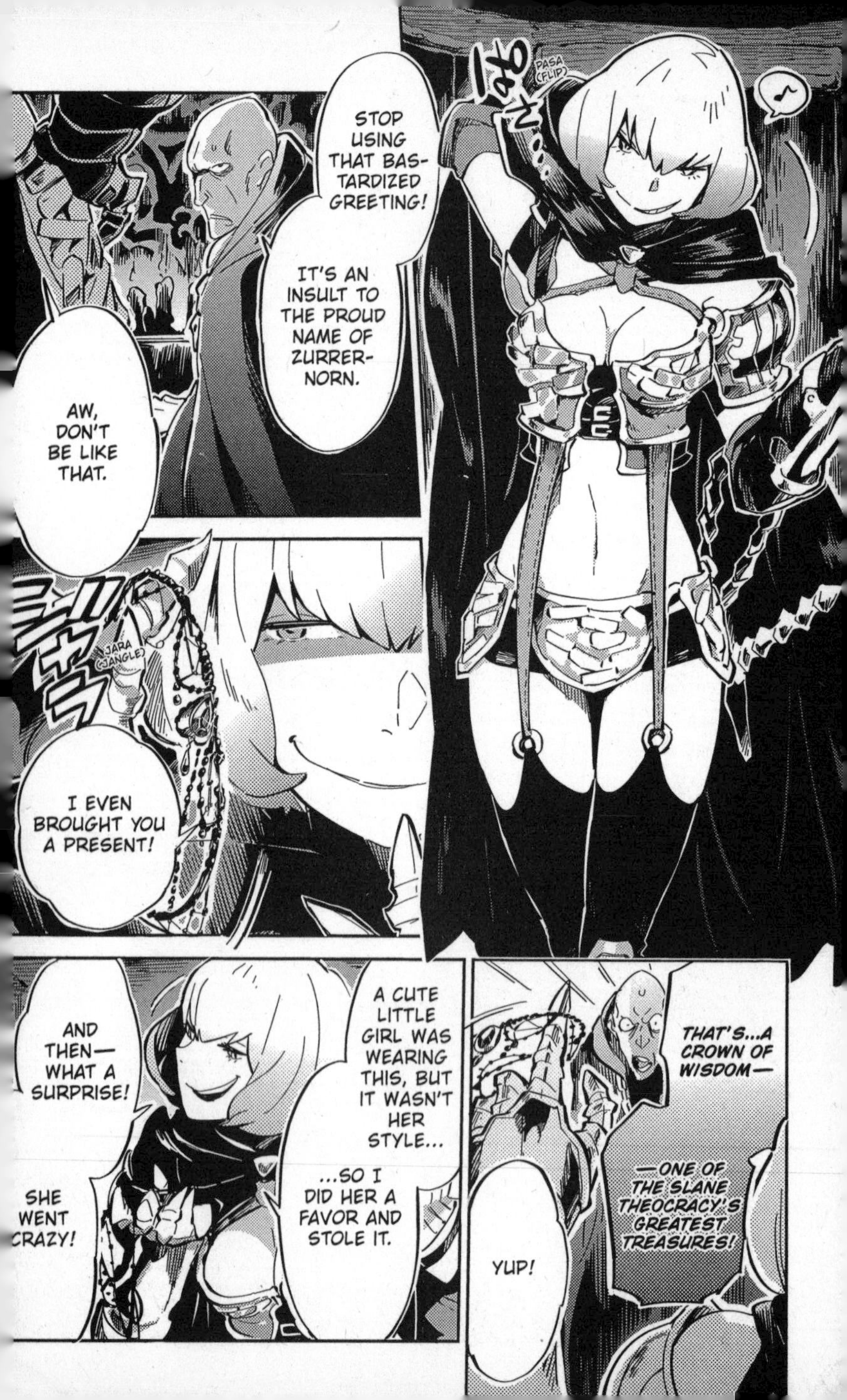
PASA (FLIP)
♪
STOP USING THAT BASTARDIZED GREETING!
IT'S AN INSULT TO THE PROUD NAME OF ZURRERNORN.
AW, DON'T BE LIKE THAT.
JARA (JANGLE)
I EVEN BROUGHT YOU A PRESENT!
THAT'S...A CROWN OF WISDOM—
—ONE OF THE SLANE THEOCRACY'S GREATEST TREASURES!
YUP!
A CUTE LITTLE GIRL WAS WEARING THIS, BUT IT WASN'T HER STYLE...
AND THEN—WHAT A SURPRISE!
...SO I DID HER A FAVOR AND STOLE IT.
SHE WENT CRAZY!

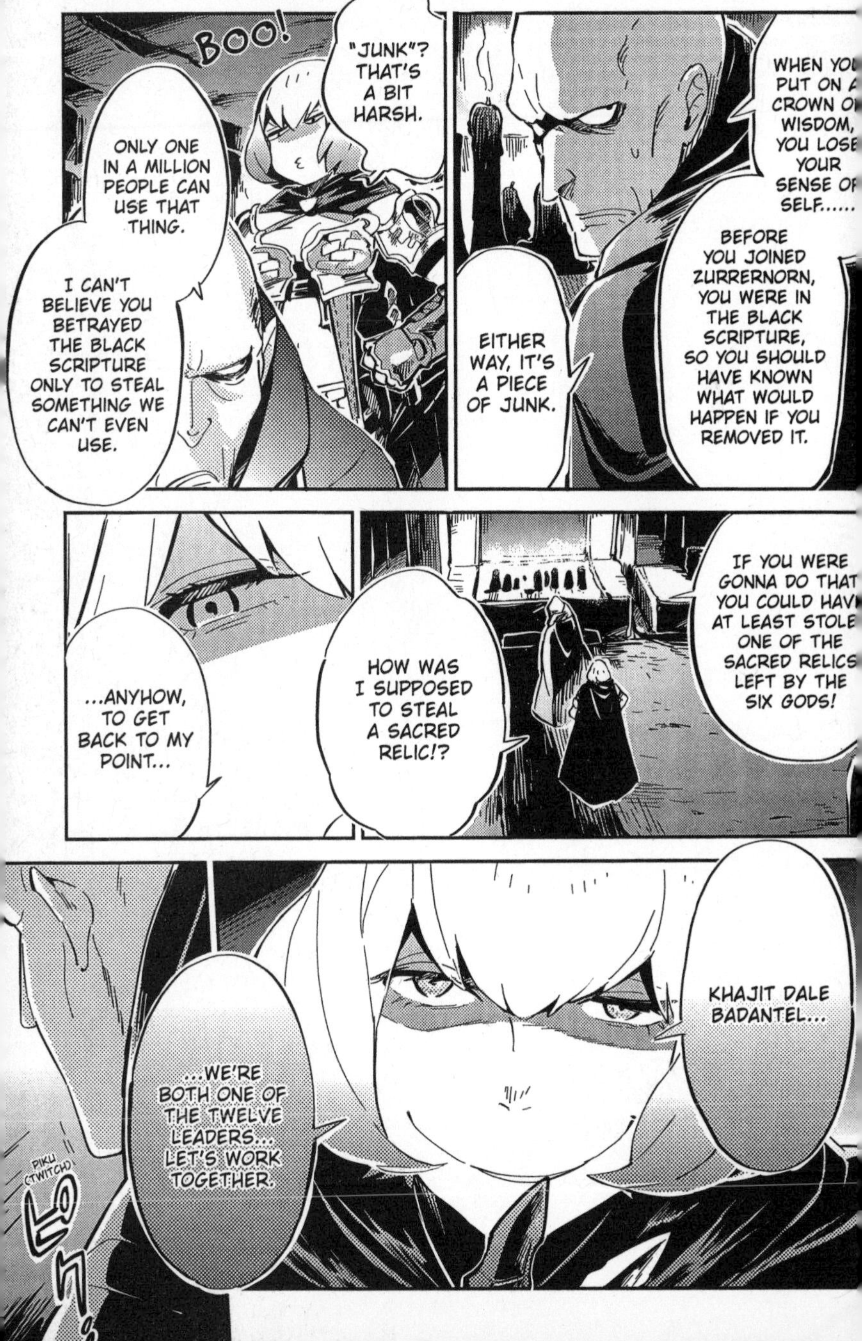
WHEN YOU PUT ON A CROWN OF WISDOM, YOU LOSE YOUR SENSE OF SELF......
BEFORE YOU JOINED ZURRERNORN, YOU WERE IN THE BLACK SCRIPTURE, SO YOU SHOULD HAVE KNOWN WHAT WOULD HAPPEN IF YOU REMOVED IT.
EITHER WAY, IT'S A PIECE OF JUNK.
"JUNK"? THAT'S A BIT HARSH.
BOO!
ONLY ONE IN A MILLION PEOPLE CAN USE THAT THING.
I CAN'T BELIEVE YOU BETRAYED THE BLACK SCRIPTURE ONLY TO STEAL SOMETHING WE CAN'T EVEN USE.
IF YOU WERE GONNA DO THAT YOU COULD HAVE AT LEAST STOLEN ONE OF THE SACRED RELICS LEFT BY THE SIX GODS!
HOW WAS I SUPPOSED TO STEAL A SACRED RELIC!?
...ANYHOW, TO GET BACK TO MY POINT...
KHAJIT DALE BADANTEL...
...WE'RE BOTH ONE OF THE TWELVE LEADERS... LET'S WORK TOGETHER.
PIKU (TWITCH)

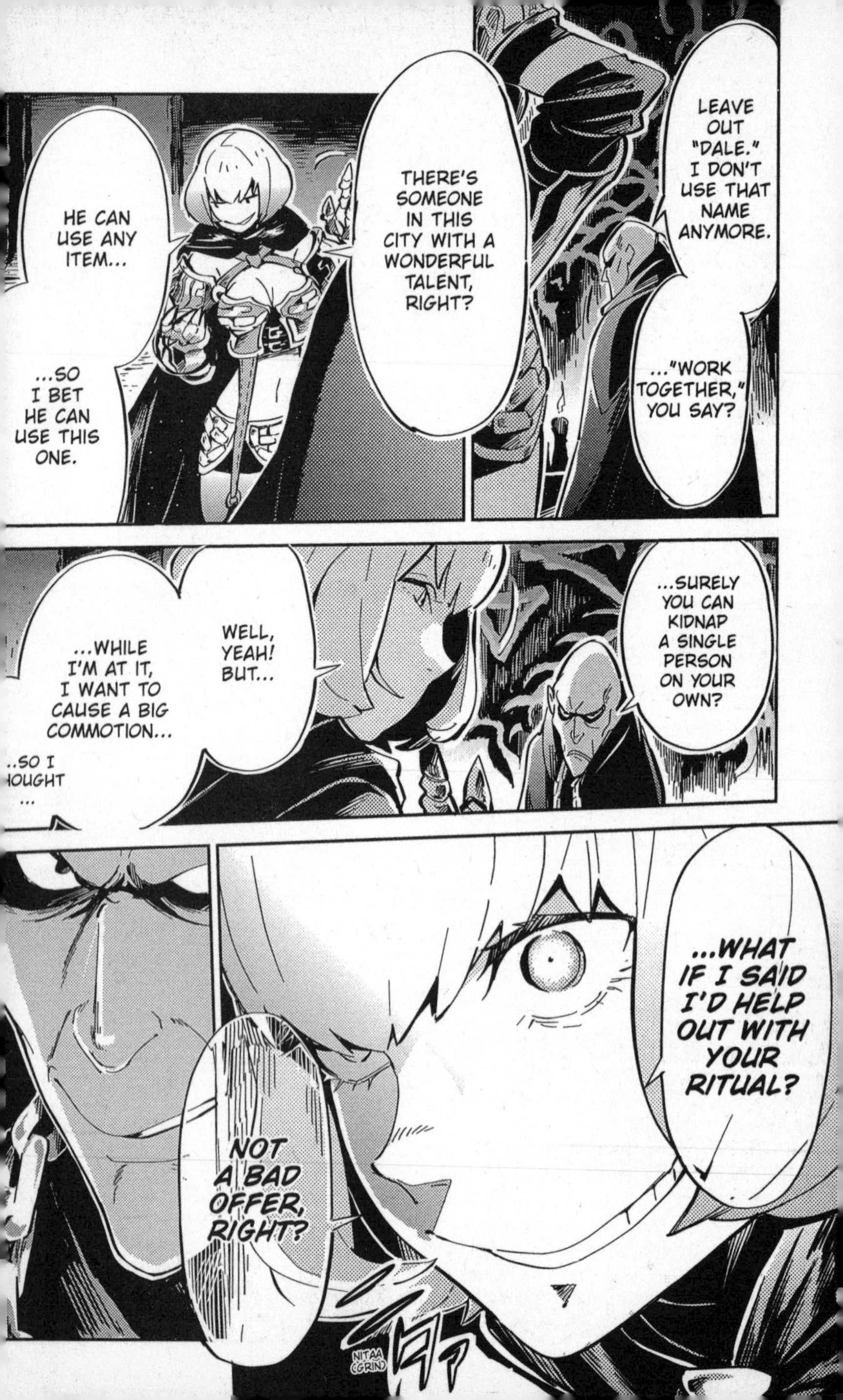
LEAVE OUT "DALE." I DON'T USE THAT NAME ANYMORE.
..."WORK TOGETHER," YOU SAY?
THERE'S SOMEONE IN THIS CITY WITH A WONDERFUL TALENT, RIGHT?
HE CAN USE ANY ITEM...
...SO I BET HE CAN USE THIS ONE.
...SURELY YOU CAN KIDNAP A SINGLE PERSON ON YOUR OWN?
WELL, YEAH! BUT...
...WHILE I'M AT IT, I WANT TO CAUSE A BIG COMMOTION...
..SO I HOUGHT ...
...WHAT IF I SAID I'D HELP OUT WITH YOUR RITUAL?
NOT A BAD OFFER, RIGHT?
NITAA (GRIN)

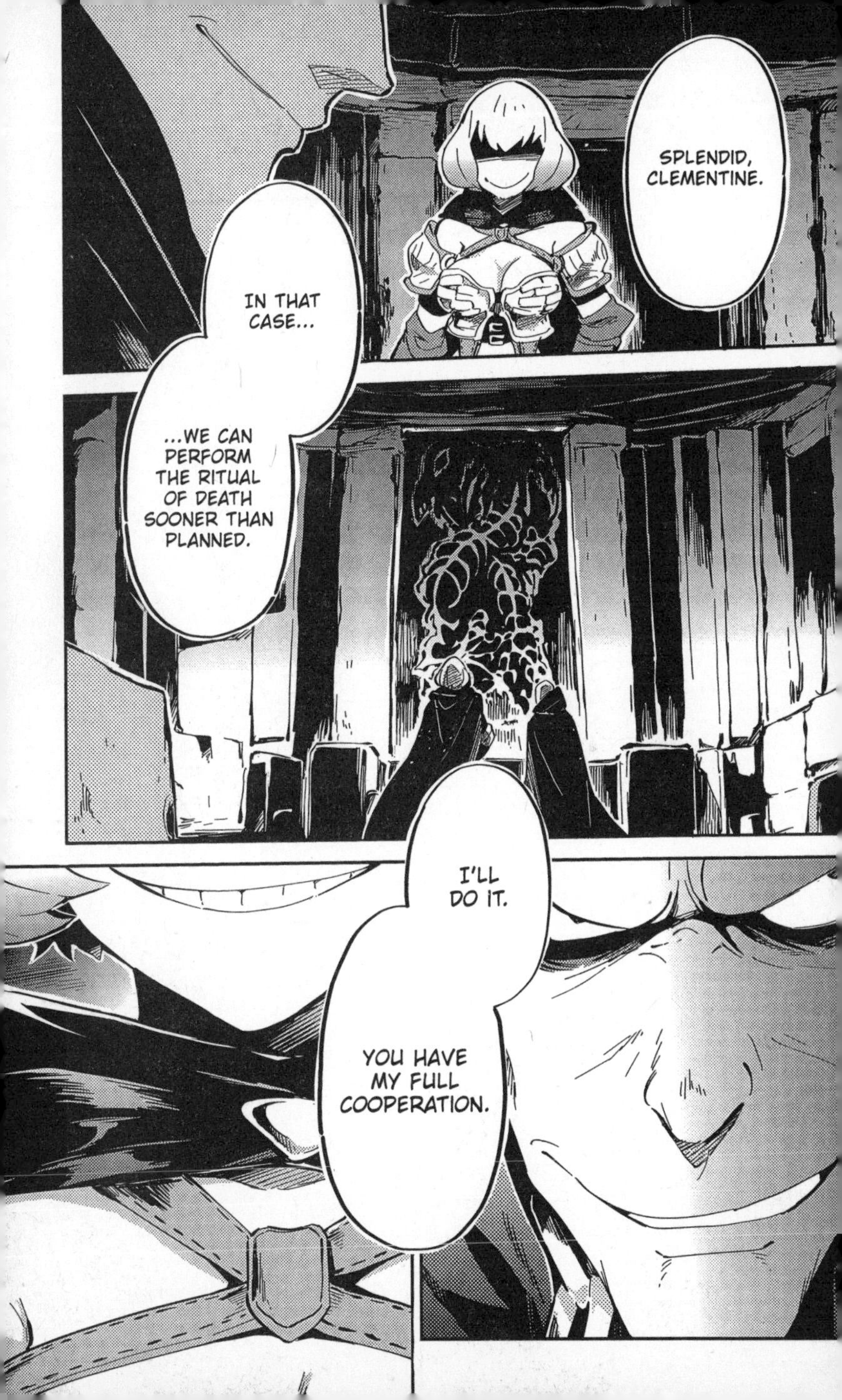
SPLENDID, CLEMENTINE.
IN THAT CASE...
...WE CAN PERFORM THE RITUAL OF DEATH SOONER THAN PLANNED.
I'LL DO IT.
YOU HAVE MY FULL COOPERATION.

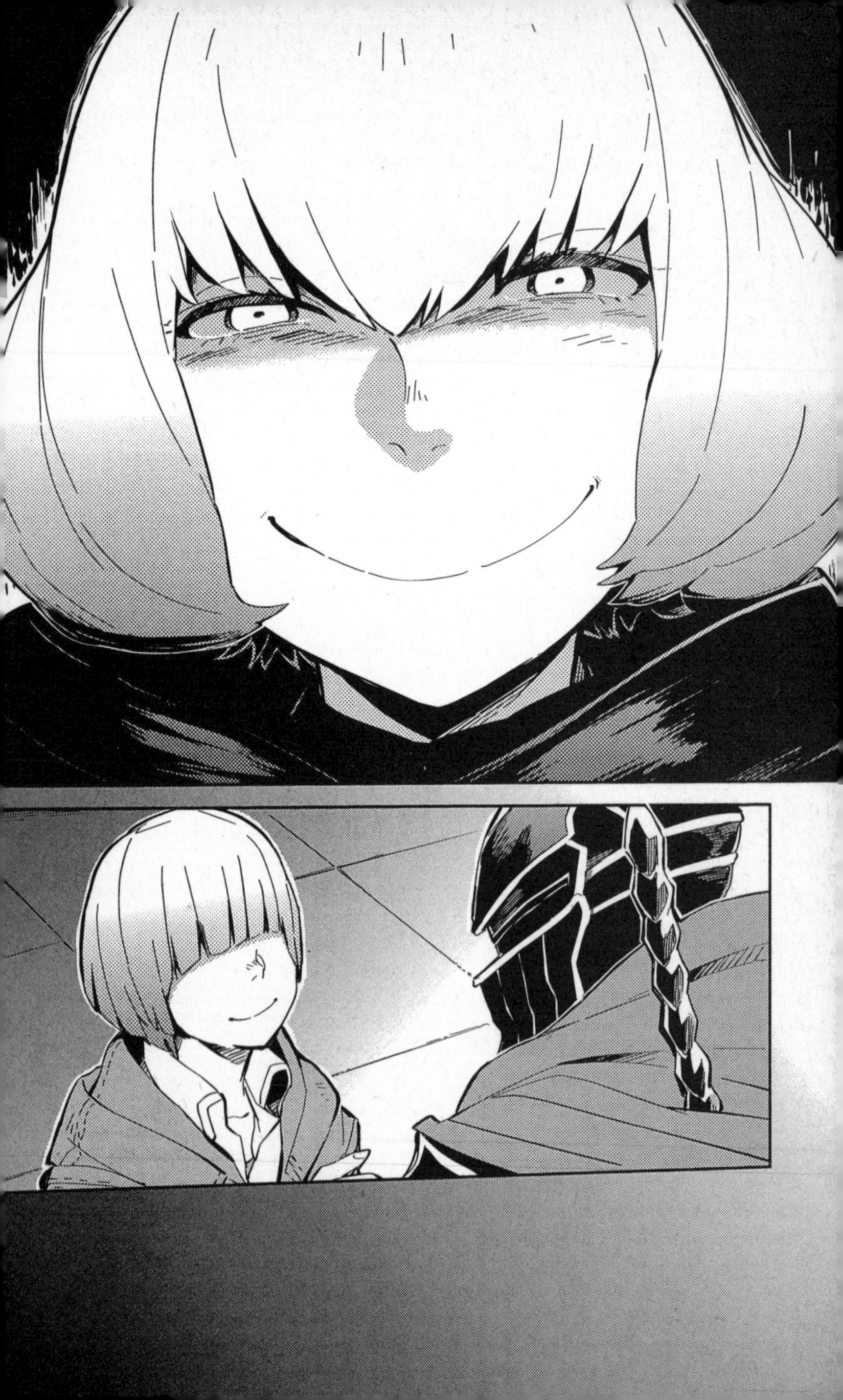

Interpretive notes of the OVERLORD Chapter 5

Adventurers

Adventurers are anti-monster mercenaries. As the name implies, they also venture into ruins and unexplored regions, but most of their work involves exterminating monsters. To be an adventurer, one must register at an adventurer guild.

Adventurer Ranks

A dog tag–like plate is given to all who register at an adventurer guild. The material one's plate is made out of depends on one's rank. All new registrees are given copper plates, but as an adventurer's rank increases, they acquire iron, silver, gold, platinum, mythril, orichalcum, and, finally, adamantite plates.

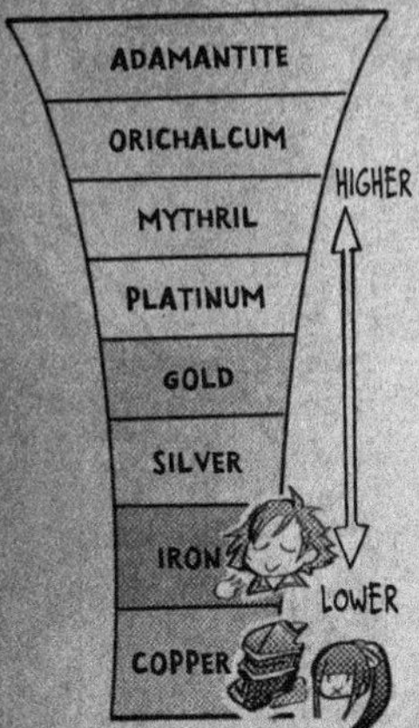
ADAMANTITE
ORICHALCUM
MYTHRIL
PLATINUM
GOLD
SILVER
IRON
COPPER
HIGHER
LOWER

High-ranking adventurers can take on more difficult missions (with better compensation). This system was created so that people don't lose their lives attempting missions beyond their ability.

Parties

Monsters have various special abilities depending on their type. In order to face as many kinds of monsters as possible, adventurers normally form parties of people with different skills.

As seen previously, low-ranking adventurers cannot work higher-level jobs, so parties are generally formed by adventurers of similar ranks. For financial and other reasons, low-ranking adventurers tend to cluster at certain inns, while high-ranking adventurers cluster at others, so that makes it easy for adventurers to find compatible party members in the places where they're staying.

Social Standing

High-ranking adventurers earn incomes that match their ranks, but no matter how much an adventurer makes, they have a hard time earning people's respect. Of course, there are instances when someone receives gratitude for a job they've done, but that seems to be more directed at the individual who performed the service rather than them as an adventurer. If regularly employed soldiers are like full-time employees, then adventurers are like temp workers.

Since adventurer power is a threat to rulers, adventurers are rarely praised by their nations. In countries where the army has the capacity to take care of monsters themselves, adventurer status is even lower. There are no adventurers in the Slane Theocracy, and the standing of adventurers in the Baharuth Empire has been falling ever since the current emperor came to power.

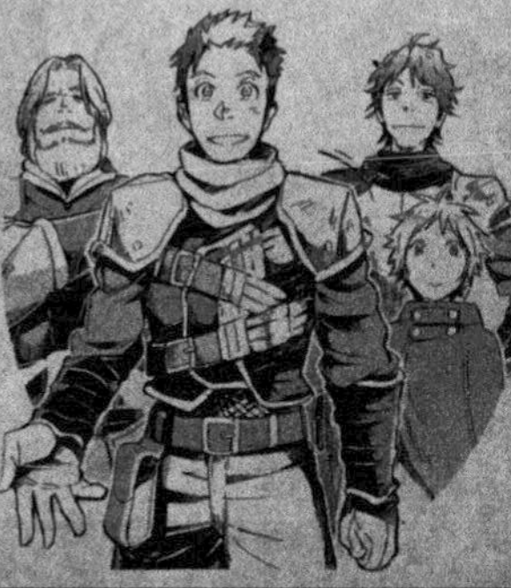

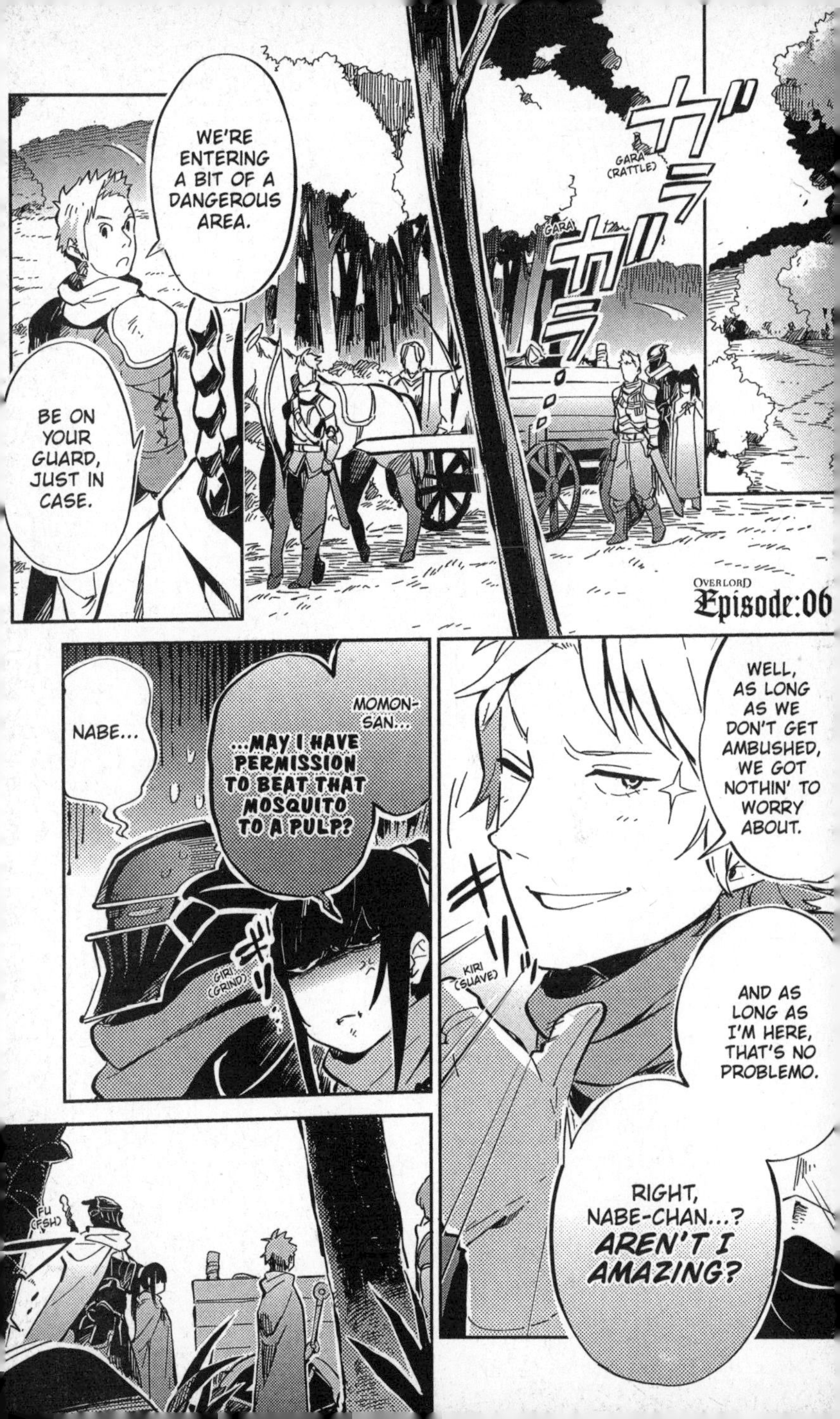
GARA (RATTLE)
GARA
OVERLORD
Episode:06
WE'RE ENTERING A BIT OF A DANGEROUS AREA.
BE ON YOUR GUARD, JUST IN CASE.
WELL, AS LONG AS WE DON'T GET AMBUSHED, WE GOT NOTHIN' TO WORRY ABOUT.
KIRI (SUAVE)
AND AS LONG AS I'M HERE, THAT'S NO PROBLEMO.
RIGHT, NABE-CHAN...? AREN'T I AMAZING?
MOMON-SAN...
...MAY I HAVE PERMISSION TO BEAT THAT MOSQUITO TO A PULP?
NABE...
GIRI (GRIND)
FU (FSH)

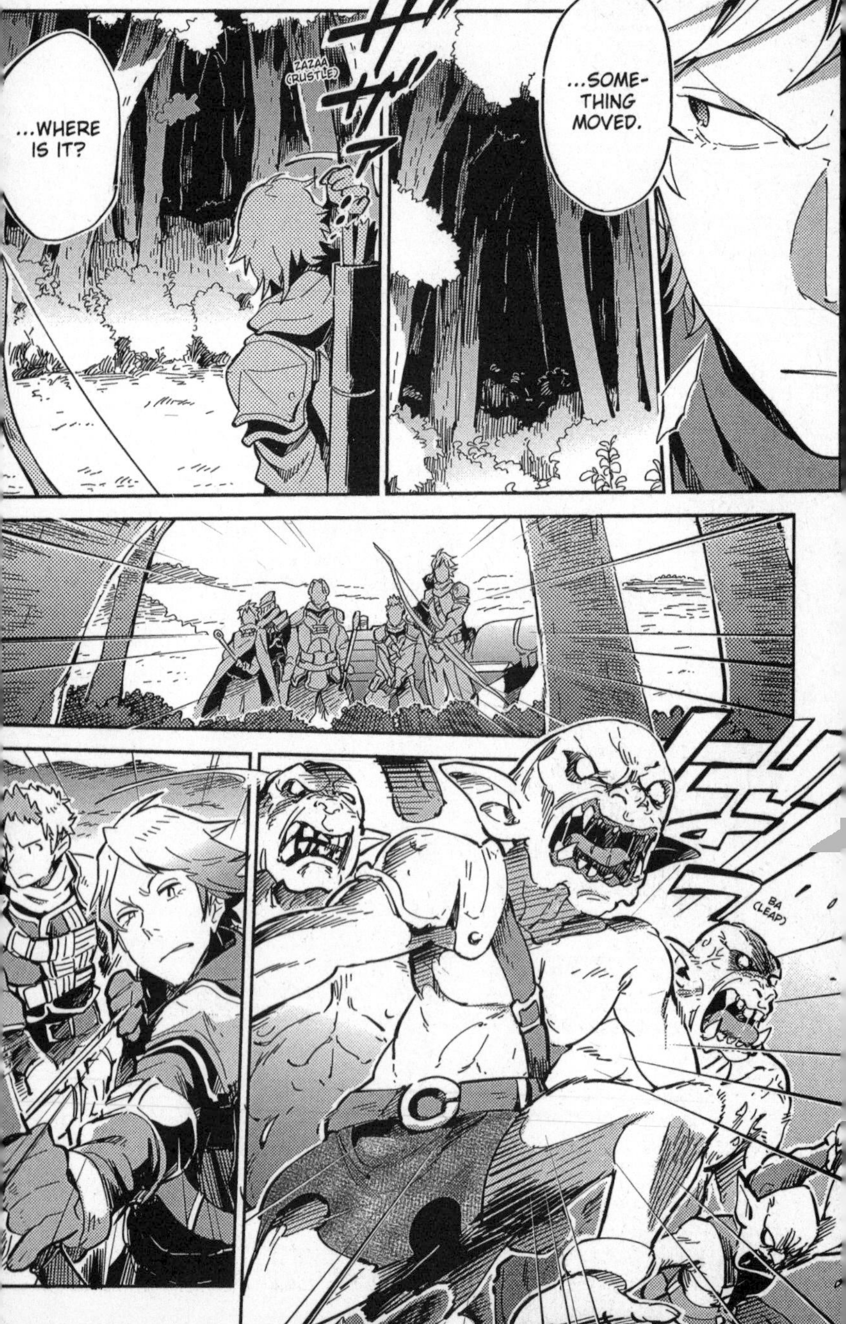
...SOME-THING MOVED.
ZAZAA (RUSTLE)
...WHERE IS IT?
BA (LEAP)

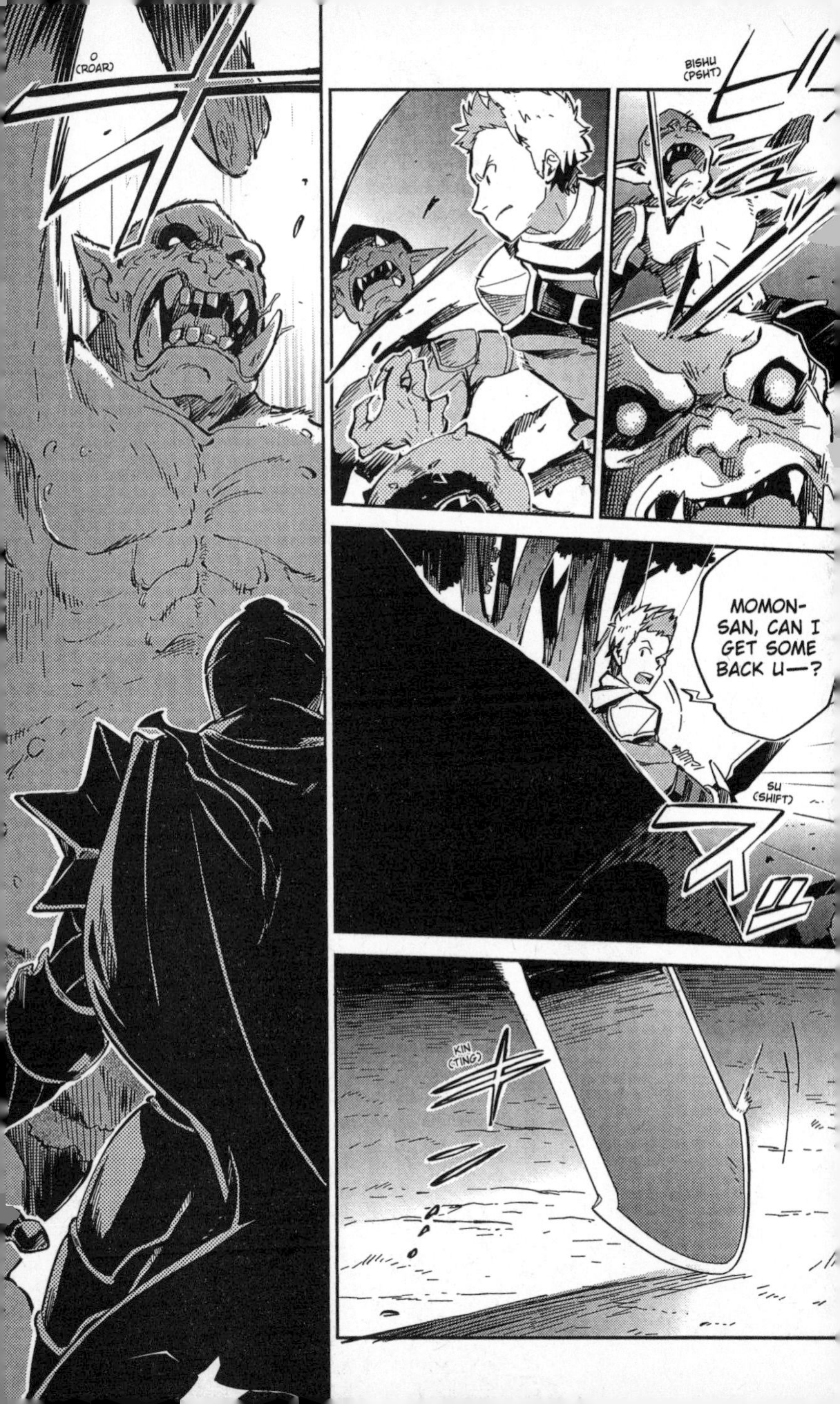
BISHU (PSHT)
MOMON-SAN, CAN I GET SOME BACK U—?
SU (SHIFT)
KIN (TING)
O (ROAR)

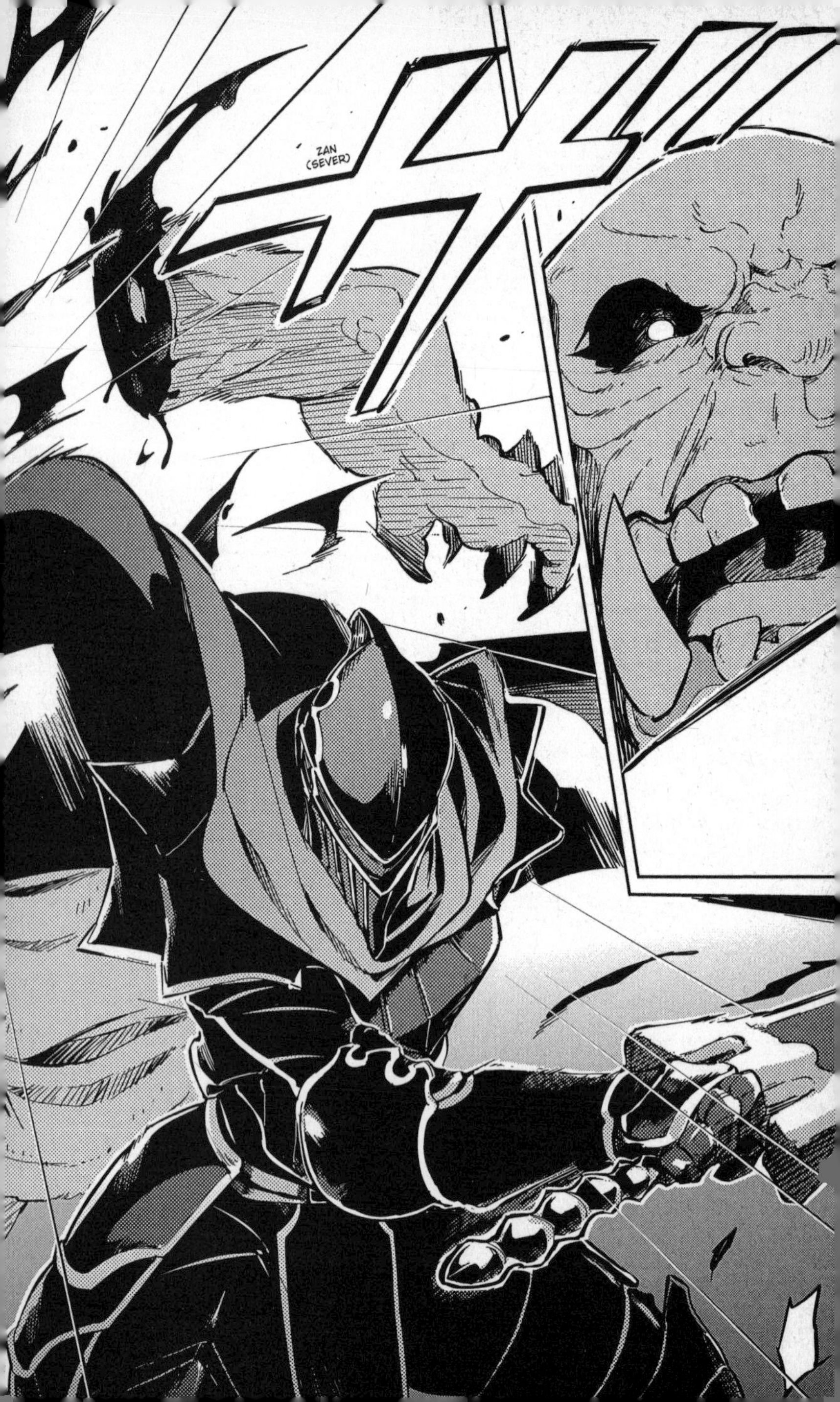
ZAN
(SEVER)

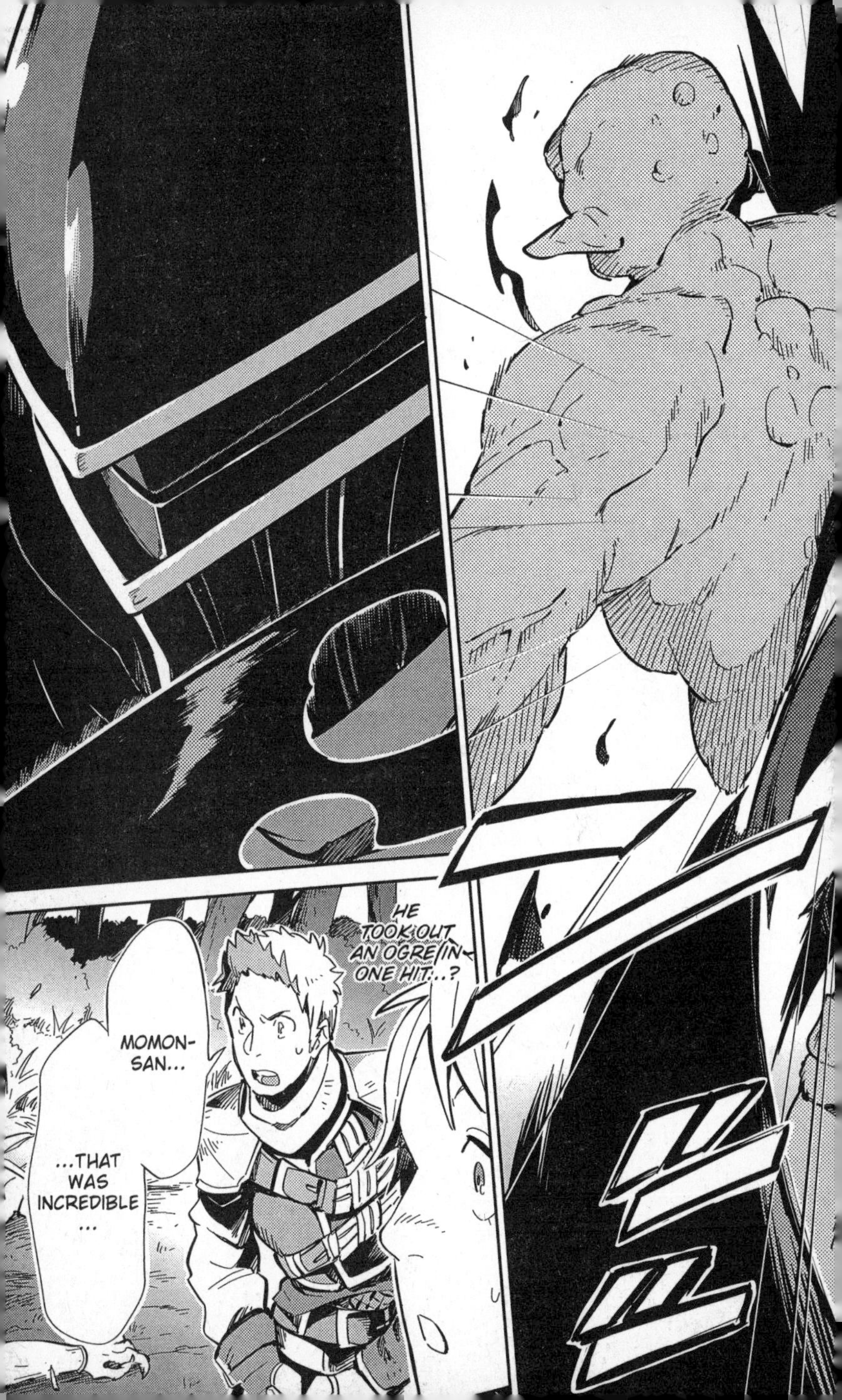
HE TOOK OUT AN OGRE IN ONE HIT...?
MOMON-SAN...
...THAT WAS INCREDIBLE ...

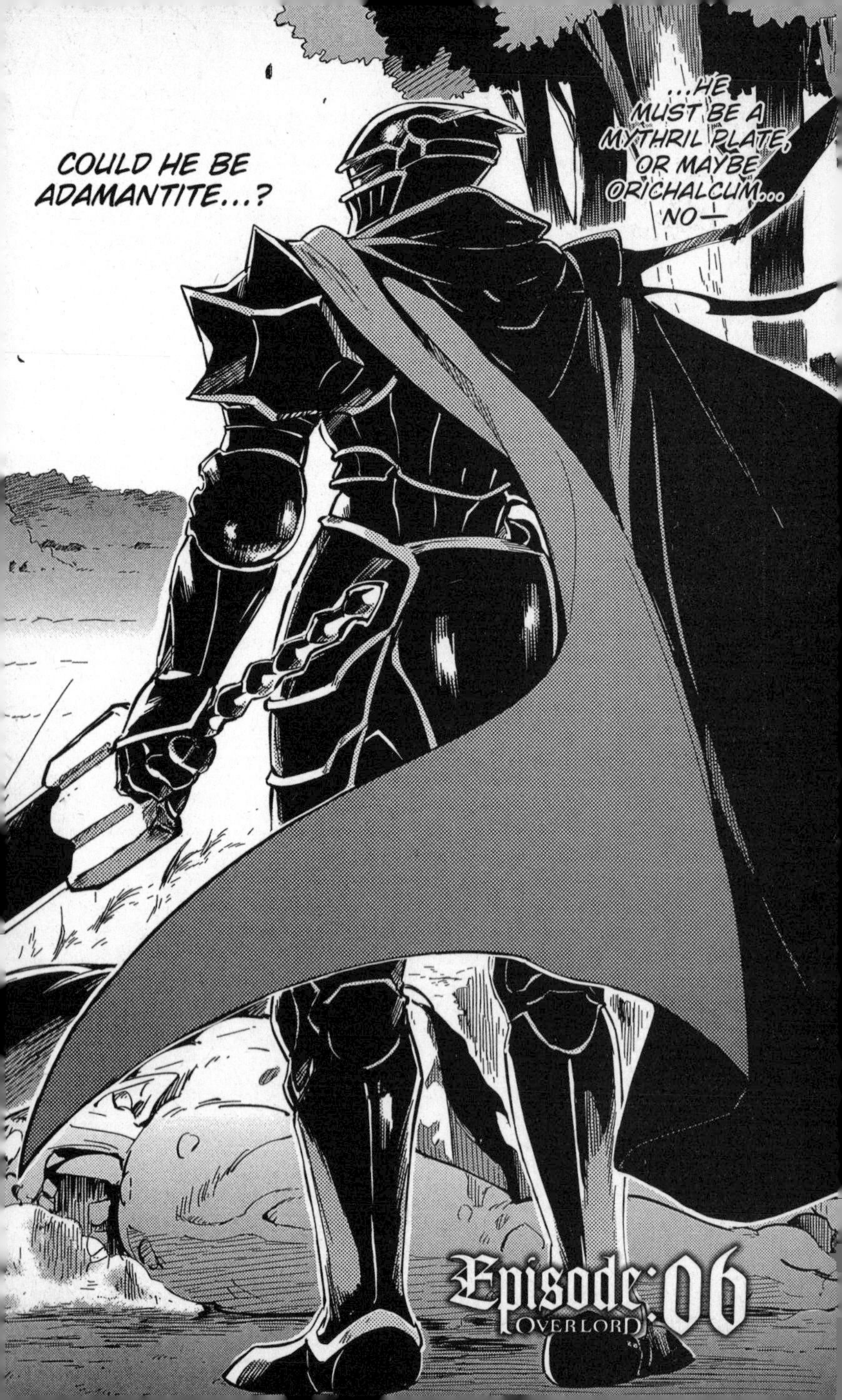
...HE MUST BE A MYTHRIL PLATE, OR MAYBE ORICHALCUM... NO—
COULD HE BE ADAMANTITE...?
Episode:06
OVERLORD

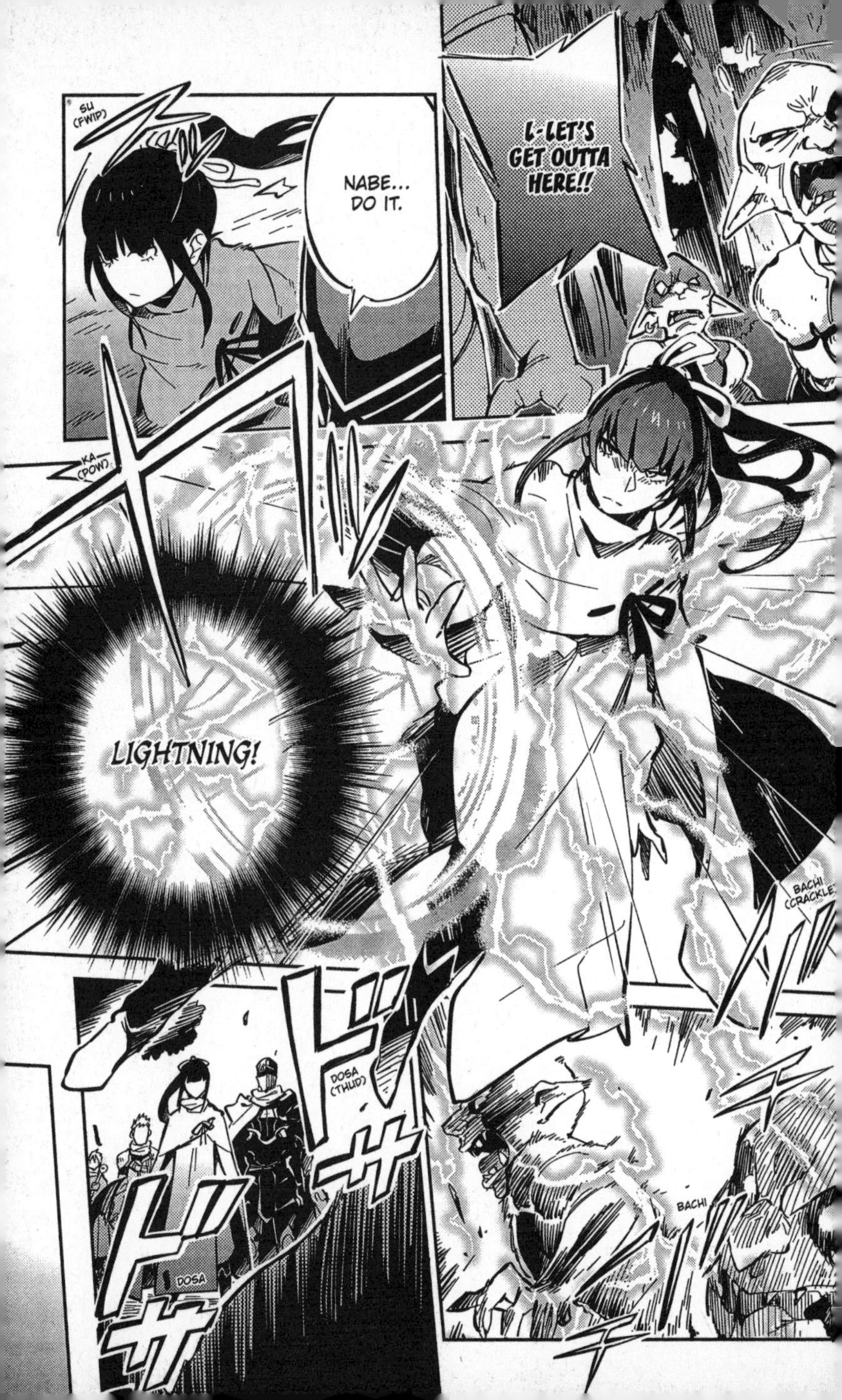

L-LET'S GET OUTTA HERE!!
SU (FWIP)
NABE... DO IT.
KA (POW)
LIGHTNING!
BACHI (CRACKLE)
BACHI
DOSA (THUD)
DOSA

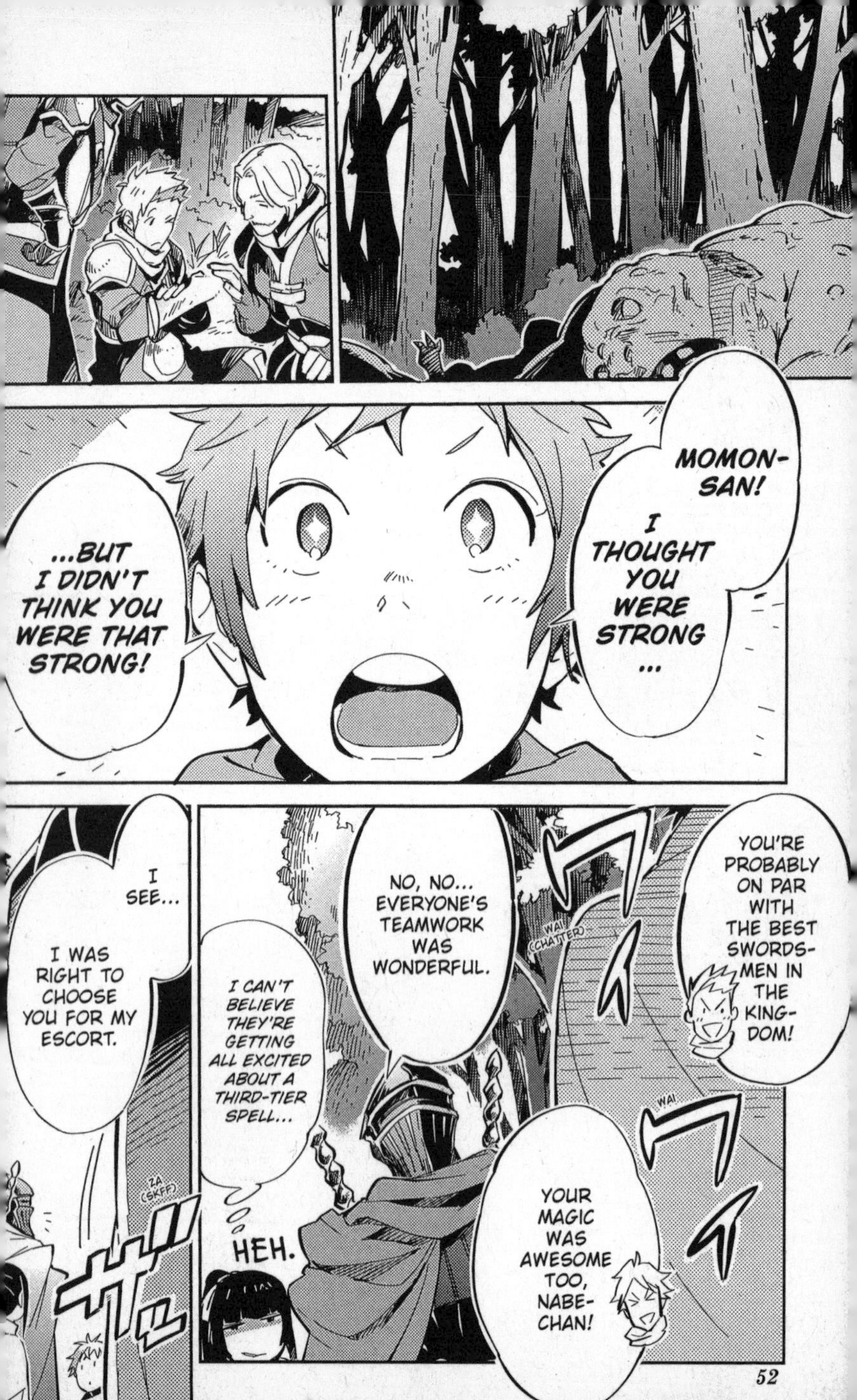
MOMON-SAN!
I THOUGHT YOU WERE STRONG...
...BUT I DIDN'T THINK YOU WERE THAT STRONG!
YOU'RE PROBABLY ON PAR WITH THE BEST SWORDSMEN IN THE KINGDOM!
WAI (CHATTER)
NO, NO... EVERYONE'S TEAMWORK WAS WONDERFUL.
WAI
YOUR MAGIC WAS AWESOME TOO, NABE-CHAN!
I CAN'T BELIEVE THEY'RE GETTING ALL EXCITED ABOUT A THIRD-TIER SPELL...
HEH.
I SEE...
I WAS RIGHT TO CHOOSE YOU FOR MY ESCORT.
ZA (SKFF)

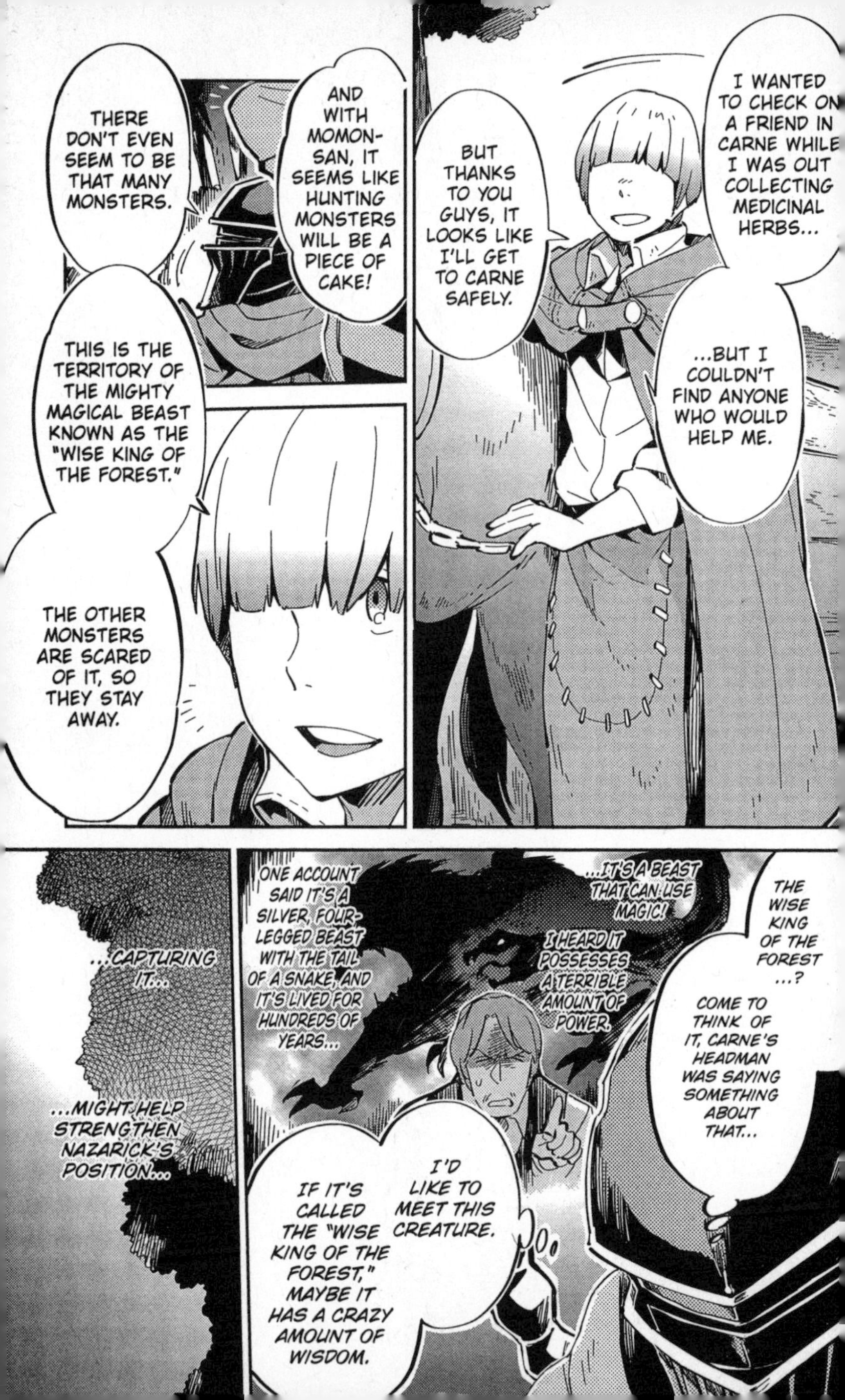
I WANTED TO CHECK ON A FRIEND IN CARNE WHILE I WAS OUT COLLECTING MEDICINAL HERBS...
...BUT I COULDN'T FIND ANYONE WHO WOULD HELP ME.
BUT THANKS TO YOU GUYS, IT LOOKS LIKE I'LL GET TO CARNE SAFELY.
AND WITH MOMON-SAN, IT SEEMS LIKE HUNTING MONSTERS WILL BE A PIECE OF CAKE!
THERE DON'T EVEN SEEM TO BE THAT MANY MONSTERS.
THIS IS THE TERRITORY OF THE MIGHTY MAGICAL BEAST KNOWN AS THE "WISE KING OF THE FOREST."
THE OTHER MONSTERS ARE SCARED OF IT, SO THEY STAY AWAY.
THE WISE KING OF THE FOREST ...?
COME TO THINK OF IT, CARNE'S HEADMAN WAS SAYING SOMETHING ABOUT THAT...
...IT'S A BEAST THAT CAN USE MAGIC!
I HEARD IT POSSESSES A TERRIBLE AMOUNT OF POWER.
ONE ACCOUNT SAID IT'S A SILVER, FOUR-LEGGED BEAST WITH THE TAIL OF A SNAKE, AND IT'S LIVED FOR HUNDREDS OF YEARS...
I'D LIKE TO MEET THIS CREATURE.
IF IT'S CALLED THE "WISE KING OF THE FOREST," MAYBE IT HAS A CRAZY AMOUNT OF WISDOM.
...CAPTURING IT...
...MIGHT HELP STRENGTHEN NAZARICK'S POSITION...

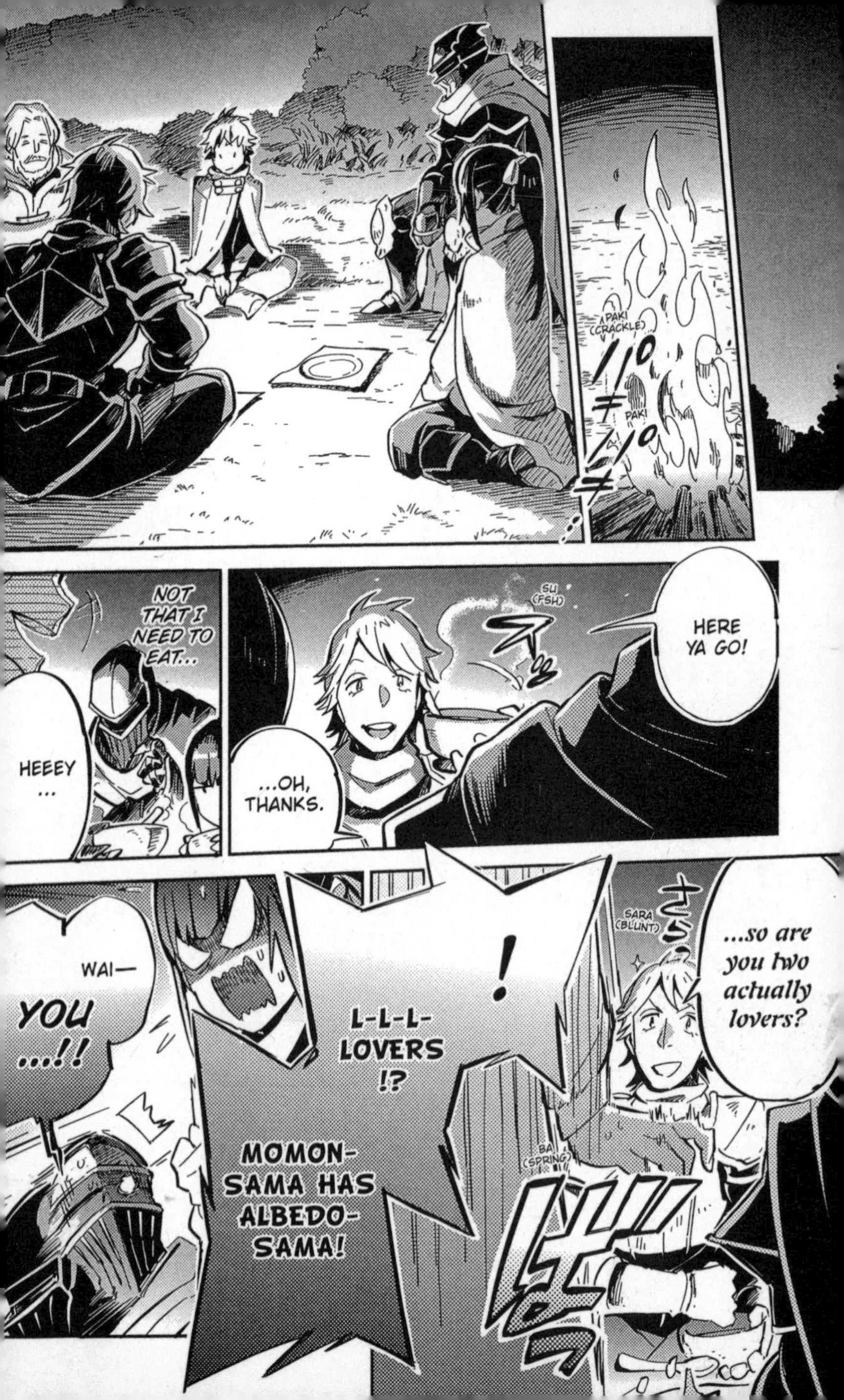
PAKI (CRACKLE)
PAKI
HERE YA GO!
SU (FSH)
...OH, THANKS.
NOT THAT I NEED TO EAT...
HEEEY ...
...so are you two actually lovers?
SARA (BLUNT)
!
BA (SPRING)
L-L-L-LOVERS !?
MOMON-SAMA HAS ALBEDO-SAMA!
WAI—
YOU ...!!

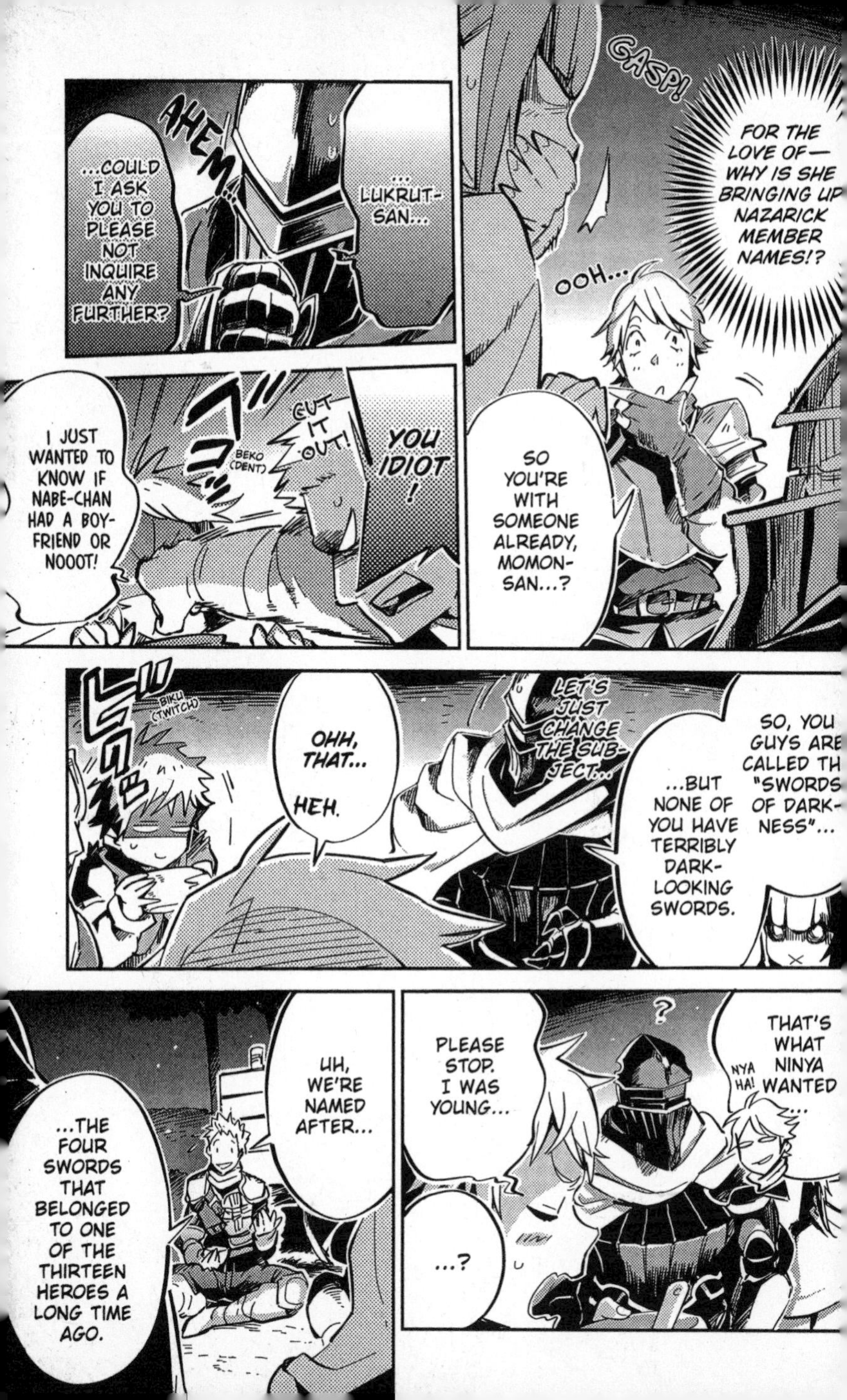
GASP!
FOR THE LOVE OF—WHY IS SHE BRINGING UP NAZARICK MEMBER NAMES!?
OOH...
SO YOU'RE WITH SOMEONE ALREADY, MOMON-SAN...?
AHEM
...LUKRUT-SAN...
...COULD I ASK YOU TO PLEASE NOT INQUIRE ANY FURTHER?
YOU IDIOT!
CUT IT OUT!
BEKO (DENT)
I JUST WANTED TO KNOW IF NABE-CHAN HAD A BOY-FRIEND OR NOOOT!
SO, YOU GUYS ARE CALLED TH "SWORDS OF DARK-NESS"...
...BUT NONE OF YOU HAVE TERRIBLY DARK-LOOKING SWORDS.
LET'S JUST CHANGE THE SUB-JECT...
OHH, THAT...
HEH.
BIKU (TWITCH)
THAT'S WHAT NINYA WANTED...
NYA HA!
?
PLEASE STOP. I WAS YOUNG...
...?
UH, WE'RE NAMED AFTER...
...THE FOUR SWORDS THAT BELONGED TO ONE OF THE THIRTEEN HEROES A LONG TIME AGO.

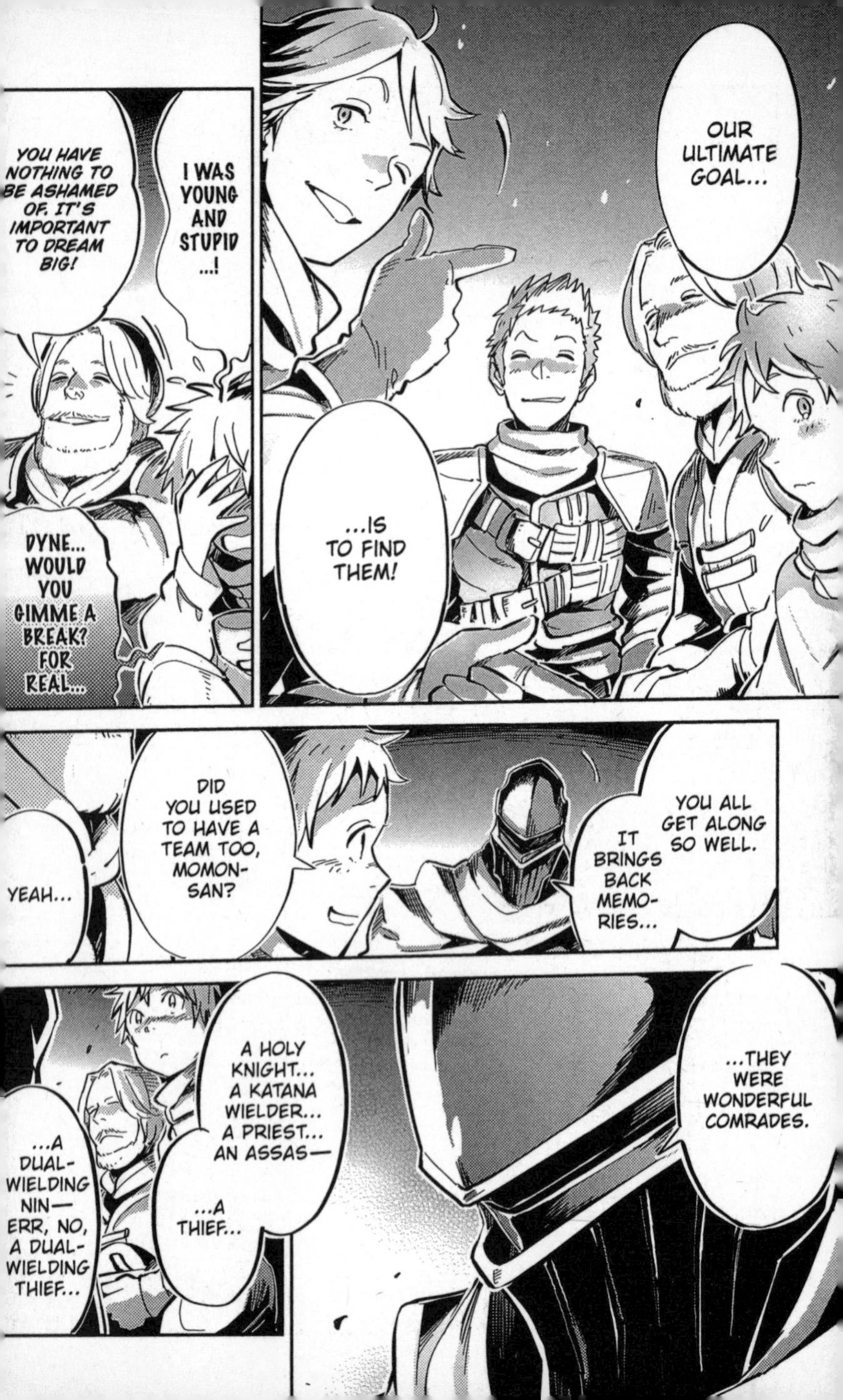
OUR ULTIMATE GOAL...
...IS TO FIND THEM!
I WAS YOUNG AND STUPID ...!
YOU HAVE NOTHING TO BE ASHAMED OF. IT'S IMPORTANT TO DREAM BIG!
DYNE... WOULD YOU GIMME A BREAK? FOR REAL...
YOU ALL GET ALONG SO WELL.
IT BRINGS BACK MEMORIES...
DID YOU USED TO HAVE A TEAM TOO, MOMON-SAN?
YEAH...
...THEY WERE WONDERFUL COMRADES.
A HOLY KNIGHT... A KATANA WIELDER... A PRIEST... AN ASSAS—
...A THIEF...
...A DUAL-WIELDING NIN— ERR, NO, A DUAL-WIELDING THIEF...

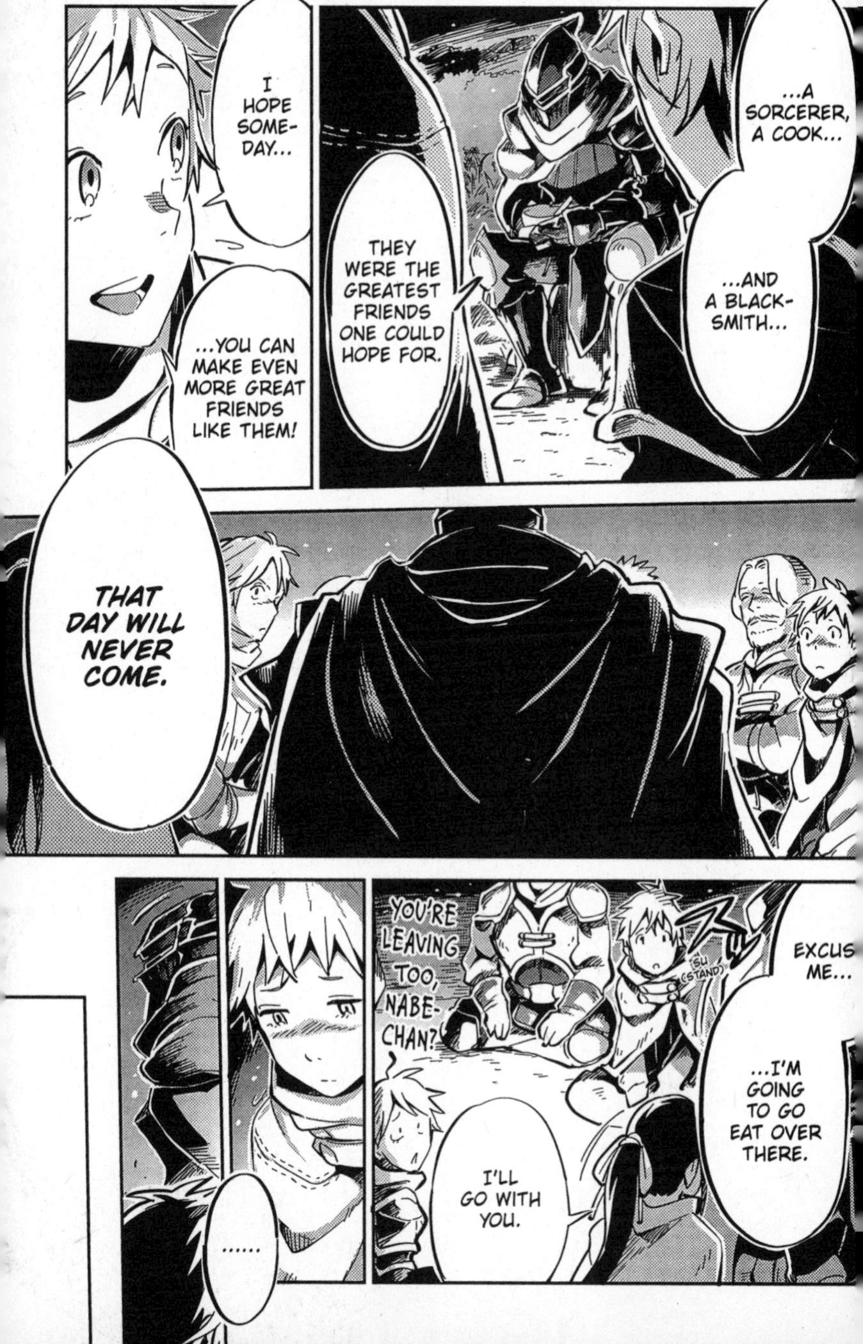
...A SORCERER, A COOK...
...AND A BLACKSMITH...
THEY WERE THE GREATEST FRIENDS ONE COULD HOPE FOR.
I HOPE SOMEDAY...
...YOU CAN MAKE EVEN MORE GREAT FRIENDS LIKE THEM!
THAT DAY WILL NEVER COME.
EXCUSE ME...
SU (STAND)
...I'M GOING TO GO EAT OVER THERE.
YOU'RE LEAVING TOO, NABE-CHAN?
I'LL GO WITH YOU.
......

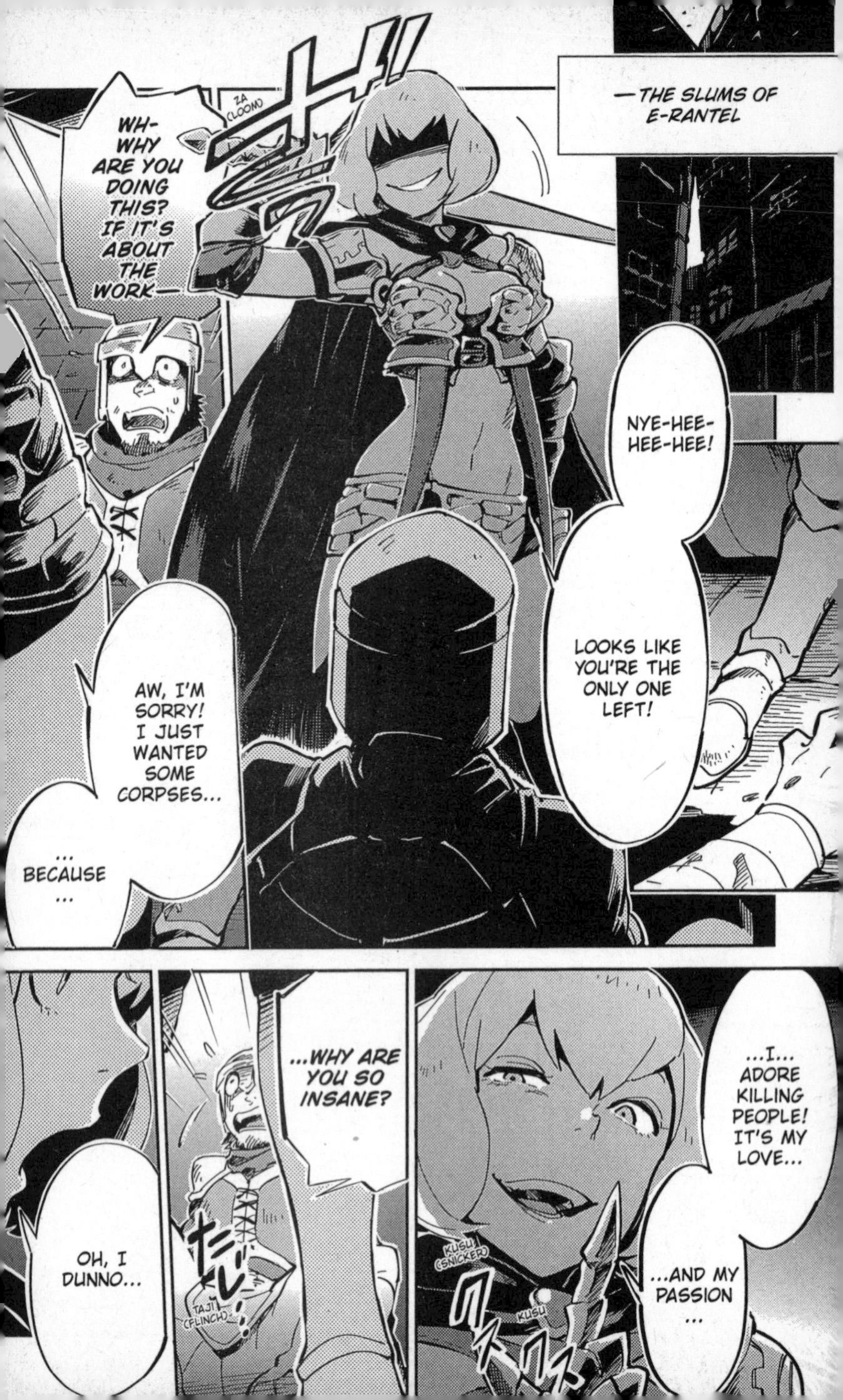
—THE SLUMS OF E-RANTEL
NYE-HEE-HEE-HEE!
LOOKS LIKE YOU'RE THE ONLY ONE LEFT!
ZA (LOOM)
WH-WHY ARE YOU DOING THIS? IF IT'S ABOUT THE WORK—
AW, I'M SORRY! I JUST WANTED SOME CORPSES...
... BECAUSE ...
...I... ADORE KILLING PEOPLE! IT'S MY LOVE...
KUSU (SNICKER)
KUSU
...AND MY PASSION ...
...WHY ARE YOU SO INSANE?
TAJI (FLINCH)
OH, I DUNNO...

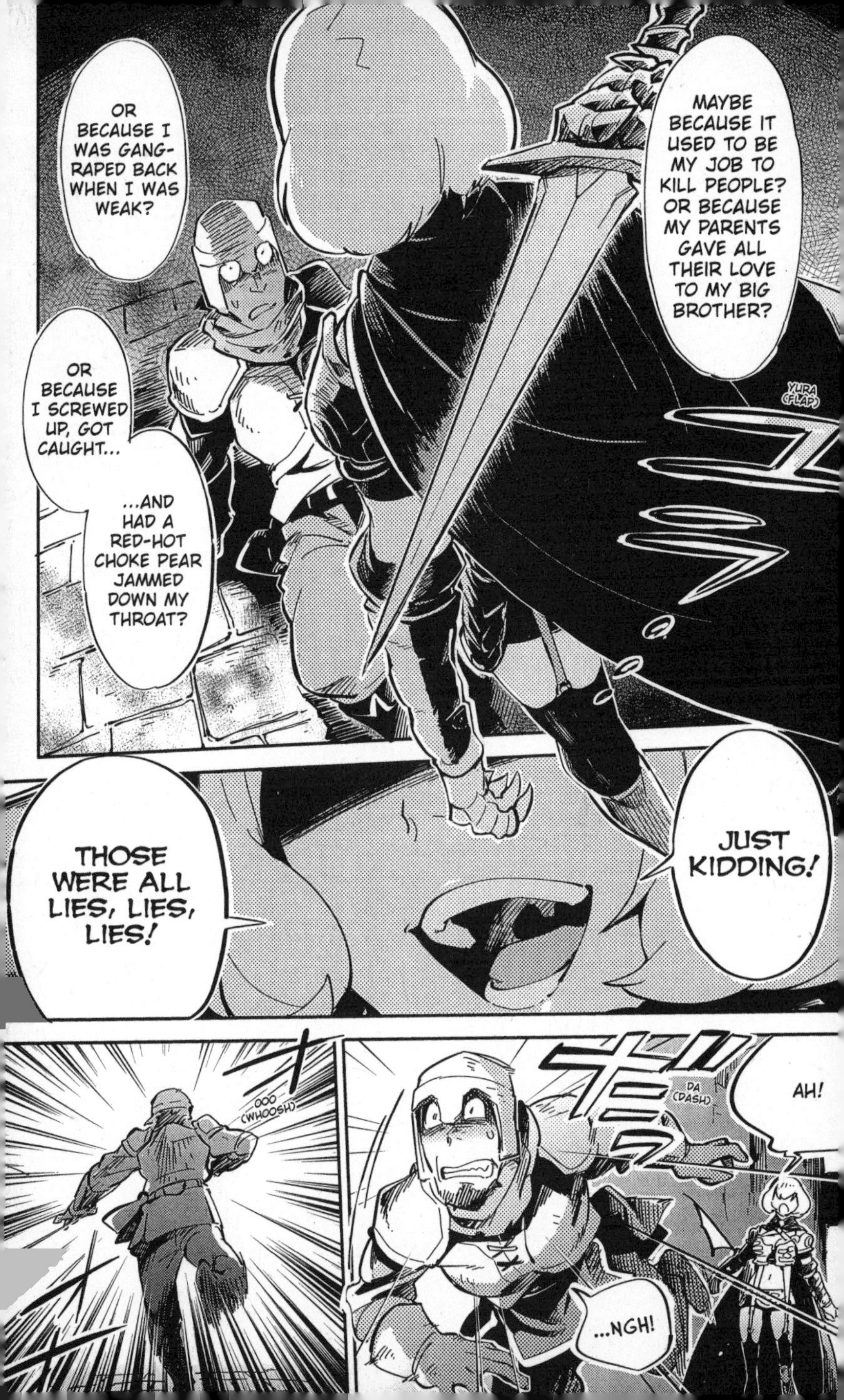
MAYBE BECAUSE IT USED TO BE MY JOB TO KILL PEOPLE? OR BECAUSE MY PARENTS GAVE ALL THEIR LOVE TO MY BIG BROTHER?
OR BECAUSE I WAS GANG-RAPED BACK WHEN I WAS WEAK?
YURA (FLAP)
OR BECAUSE I SCREWED UP, GOT CAUGHT...
...AND HAD A RED-HOT CHOKE PEAR JAMMED DOWN MY THROAT?
JUST KIDDING!
THOSE WERE ALL LIES, LIES, LIES!
AH!
DA (DASH)
...NGH!
OOO (WHOOSH)

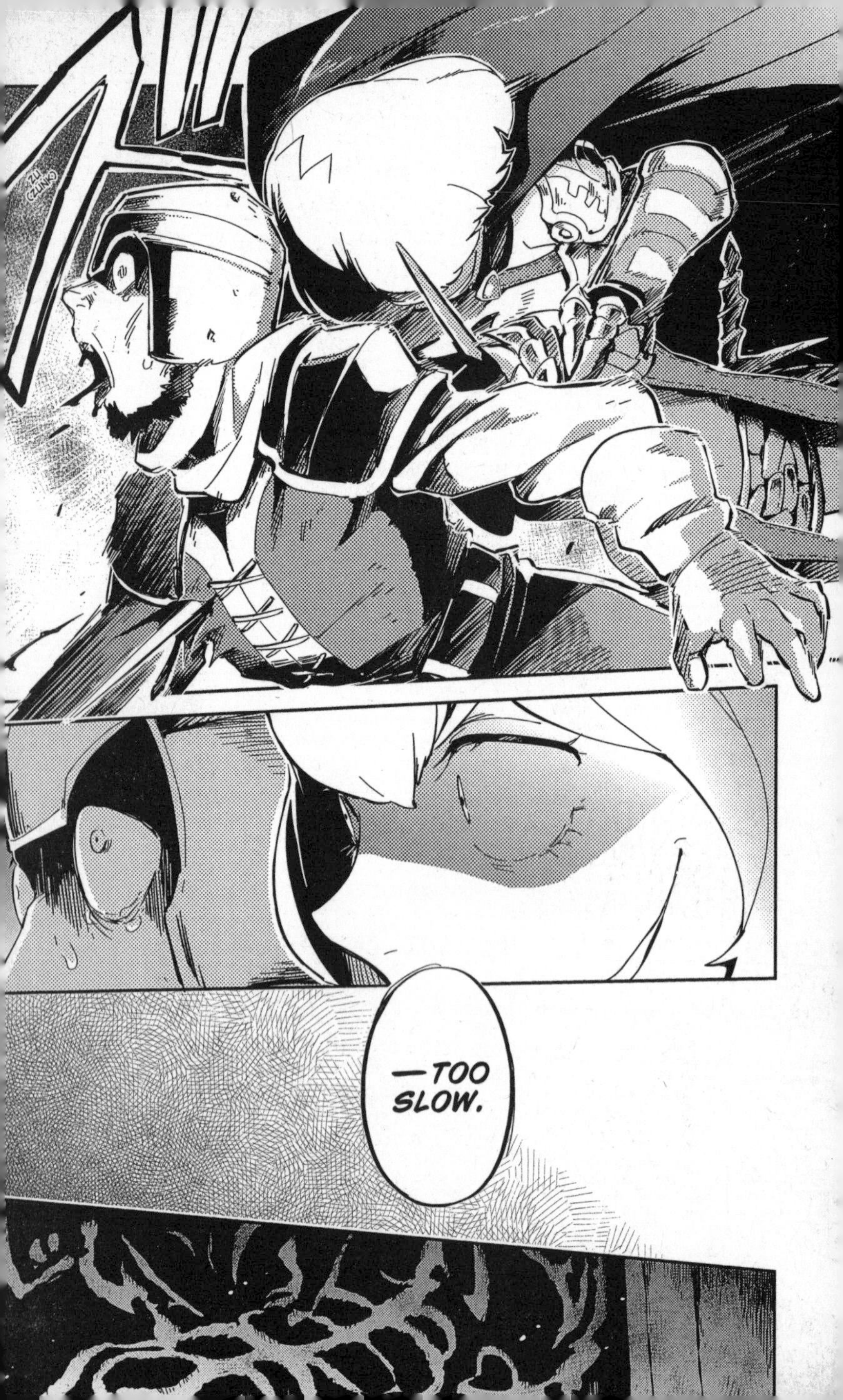
ZU
(ZUNK)
—TOO SLOW.

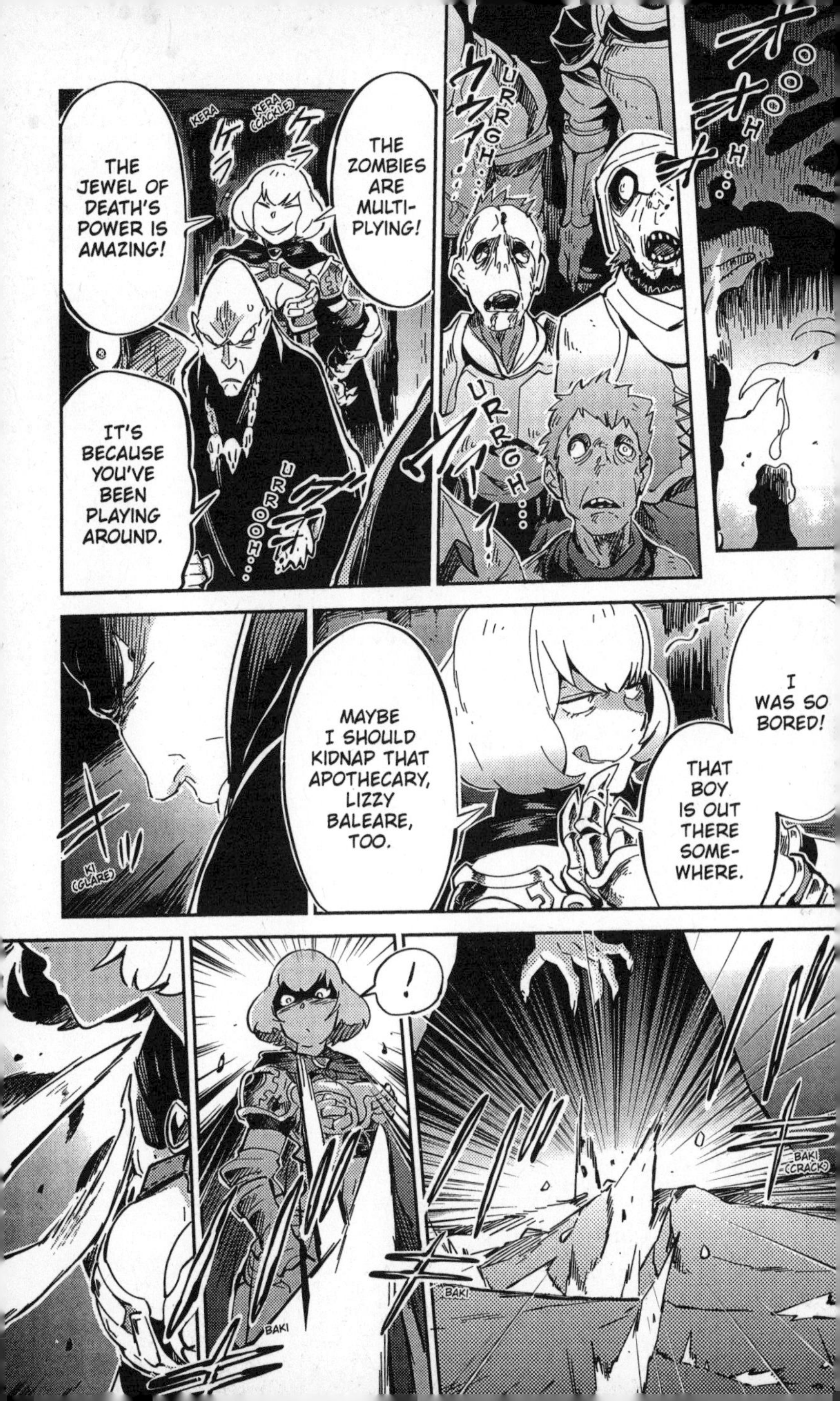

OOOOHH...
URRGH...
URRGH...
KERA KERA (CACKLE)
THE ZOMBIES ARE MULTI-PLYING!
THE JEWEL OF DEATH'S POWER IS AMAZING!
IT'S BECAUSE YOU'VE BEEN PLAYING AROUND.
URROOH...
I WAS SO BORED!
THAT BOY IS OUT THERE SOME-WHERE.
MAYBE I SHOULD KIDNAP THAT APOTHECARY, LIZZY BALEARE, TOO.
KI (GLARE)
BAKI (CRACK)
BAKI
!
BAKI

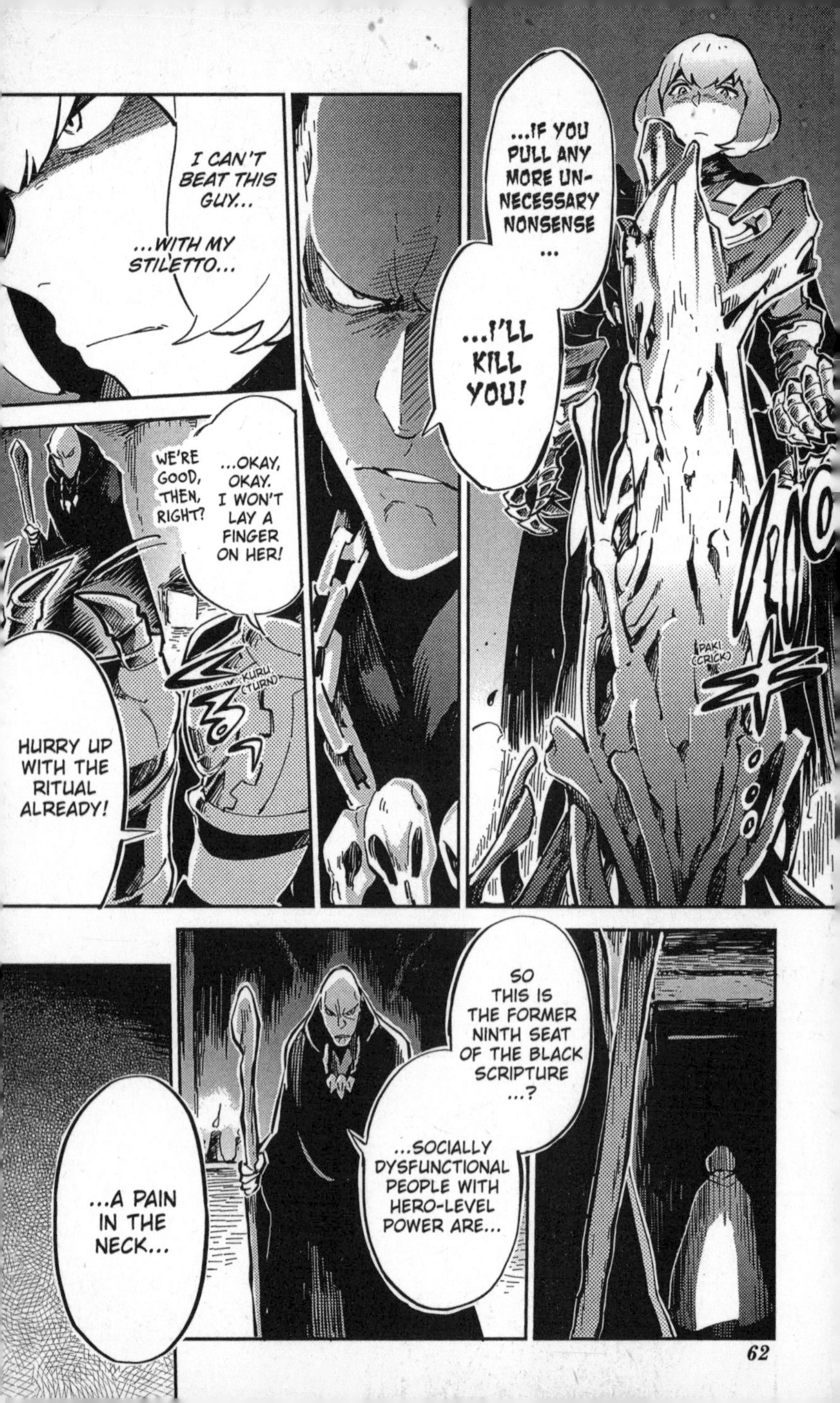

...IF YOU PULL ANY MORE UN-NECESSARY NONSENSE...
...I'LL KILL YOU!
PAKI (CRICK)
I CAN'T BEAT THIS GUY...
...WITH MY STILETTO...
...OKAY, OKAY. I WON'T LAY A FINGER ON HER!
WE'RE GOOD, THEN, RIGHT?
KURU (TURN)
HURRY UP WITH THE RITUAL ALREADY!
SO THIS IS THE FORMER NINTH SEAT OF THE BLACK SCRIPTURE...?
...SOCIALLY DYSFUNCTIONAL PEOPLE WITH HERO-LEVEL POWER ARE...
...A PAIN IN THE NECK...

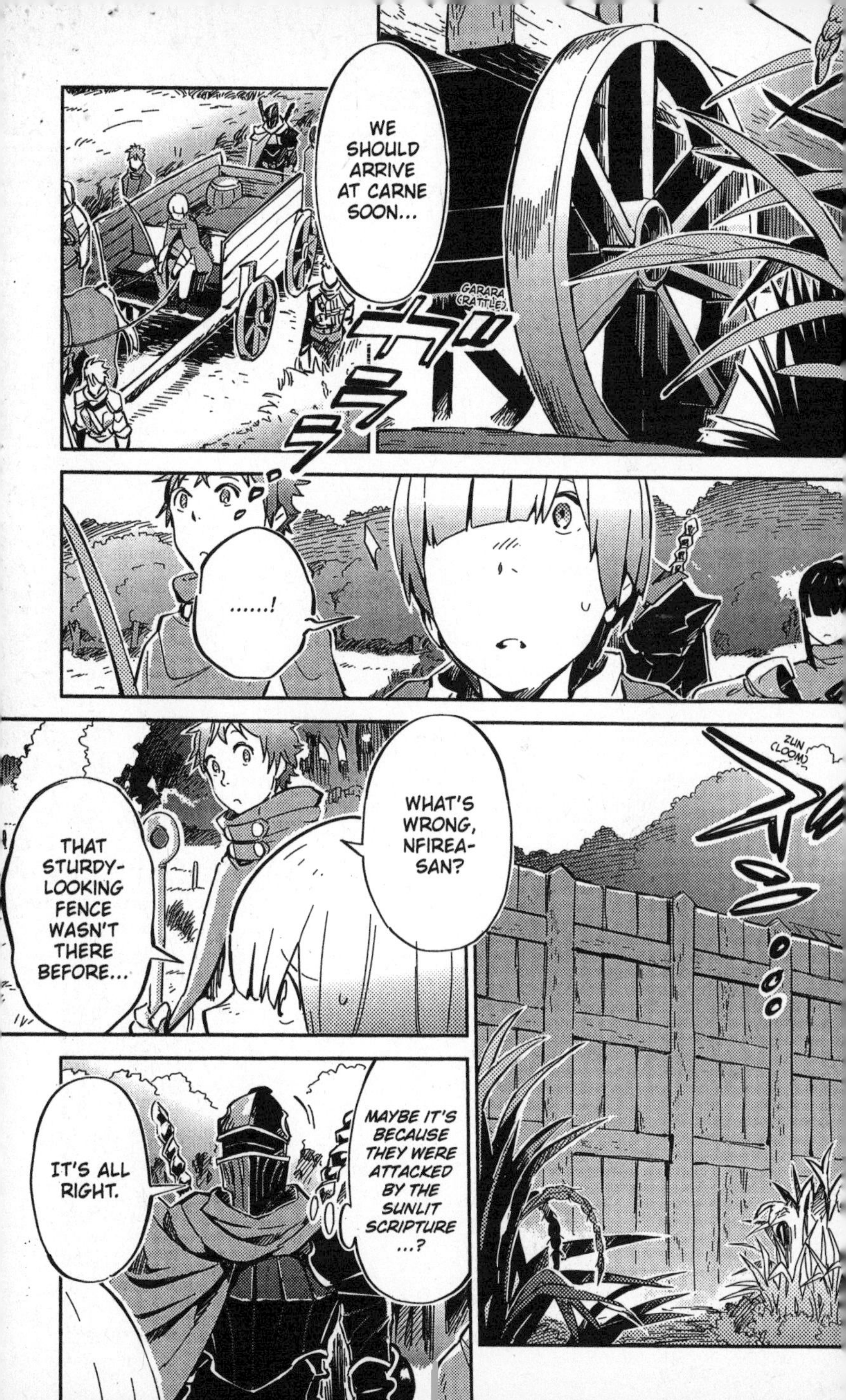
WE SHOULD ARRIVE AT CARNE SOON...
GARARA (RATTLE)
......!
ZUN (LOOM)
WHAT'S WRONG, NFIREA-SAN?
THAT STURDY-LOOKING FENCE WASN'T THERE BEFORE...
MAYBE IT'S BECAUSE THEY WERE ATTACKED BY THE SUNLIT SCRIPTURE ...?
IT'S ALL RIGHT.

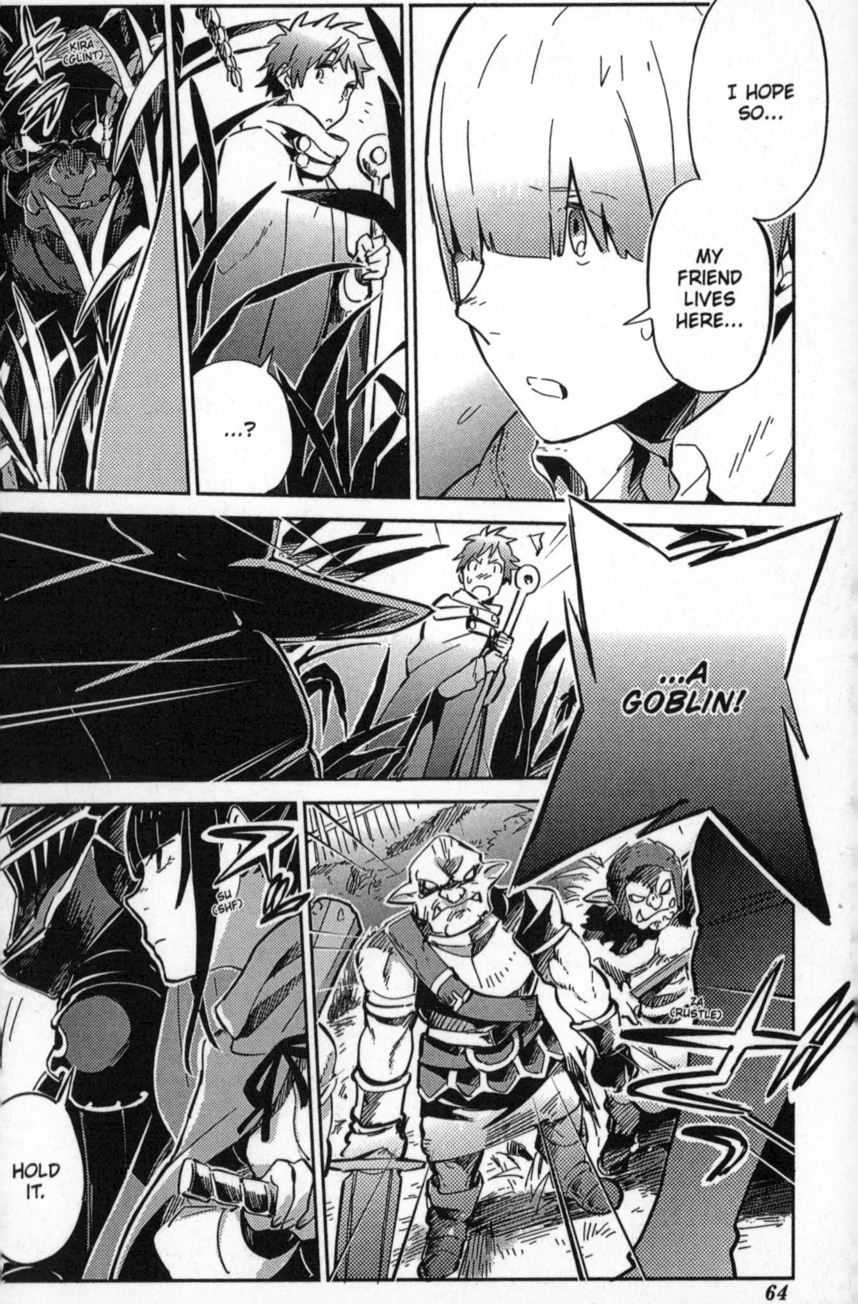
I HOPE SO...
MY FRIEND LIVES HERE...
...?
KIRA (GLINT)
...A GOBLIN!
ZA (RUSTLE)
SU (SHF)
HOLD IT.

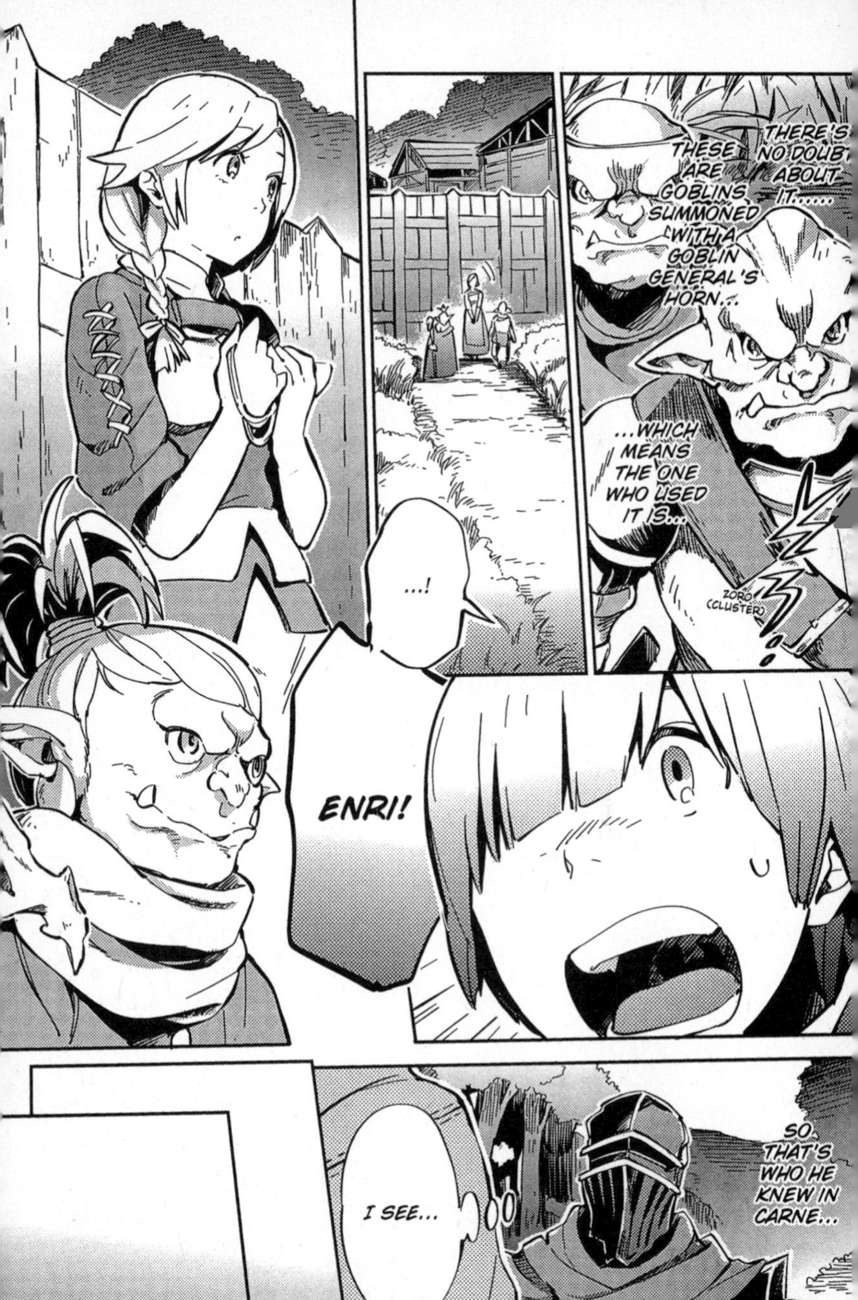

THERE'S NO DOUBT ABOUT IT.....
THESE ARE GOBLINS SUMMONED WITH A GOBLIN GENERAL'S HORN...
...WHICH MEANS THE ONE WHO USED IT IS...
ZORO (CLUSTER)
...!
ENRI!
SO THAT'S WHO HE KNEW IN CARNE...
I SEE...

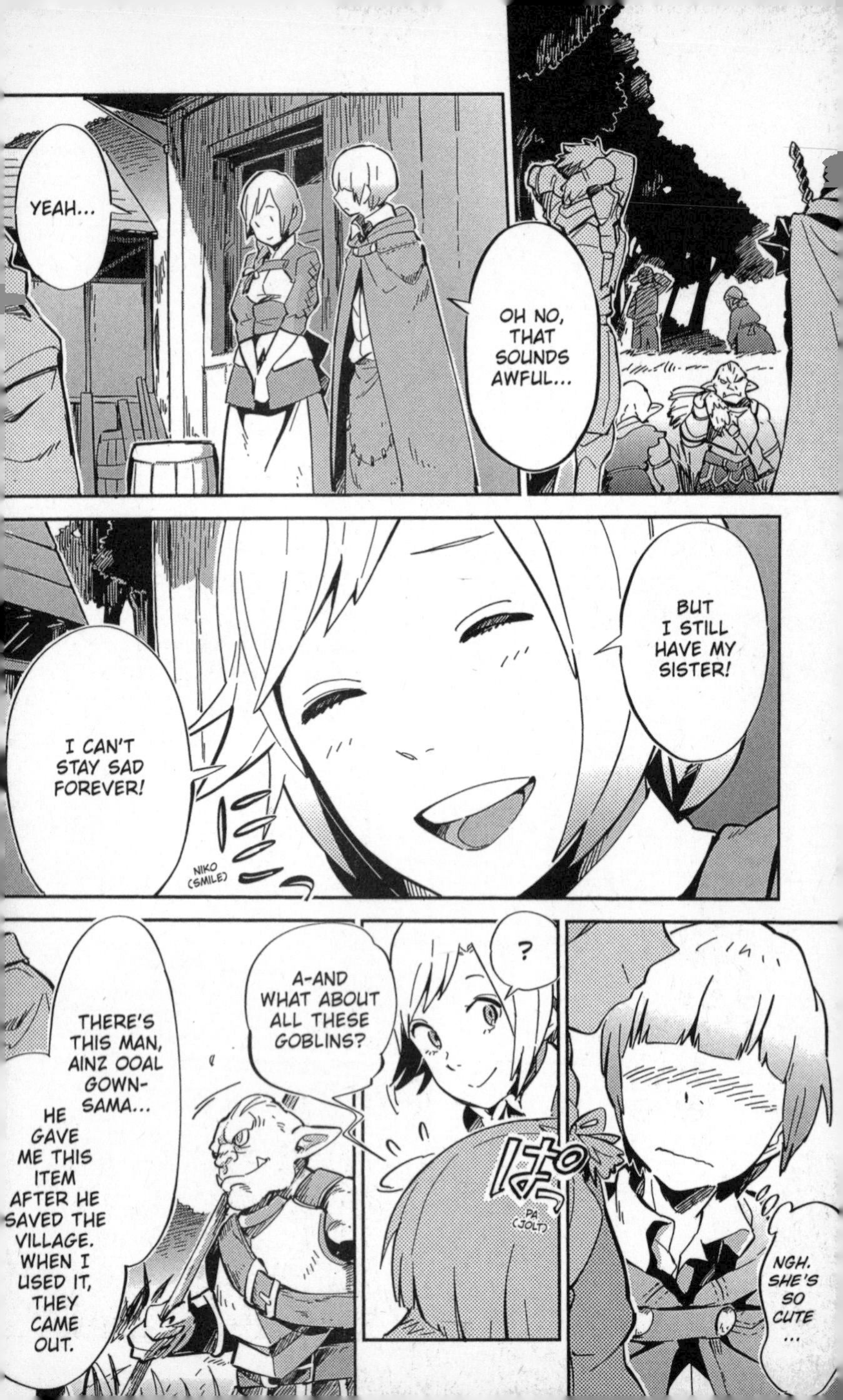
OH NO, THAT SOUNDS AWFUL...
YEAH...
BUT I STILL HAVE MY SISTER!
I CAN'T STAY SAD FOREVER!
NIKO (SMILE)
ぱっ
PA (JOLT)
NGH. SHE'S SO CUTE...
?
A-AND WHAT ABOUT ALL THESE GOBLINS?
THERE'S THIS MAN, AINZ OOAL GOWN-SAMA...
HE GAVE ME THIS ITEM AFTER HE SAVED THE VILLAGE. WHEN I USED IT, THEY CAME OUT.

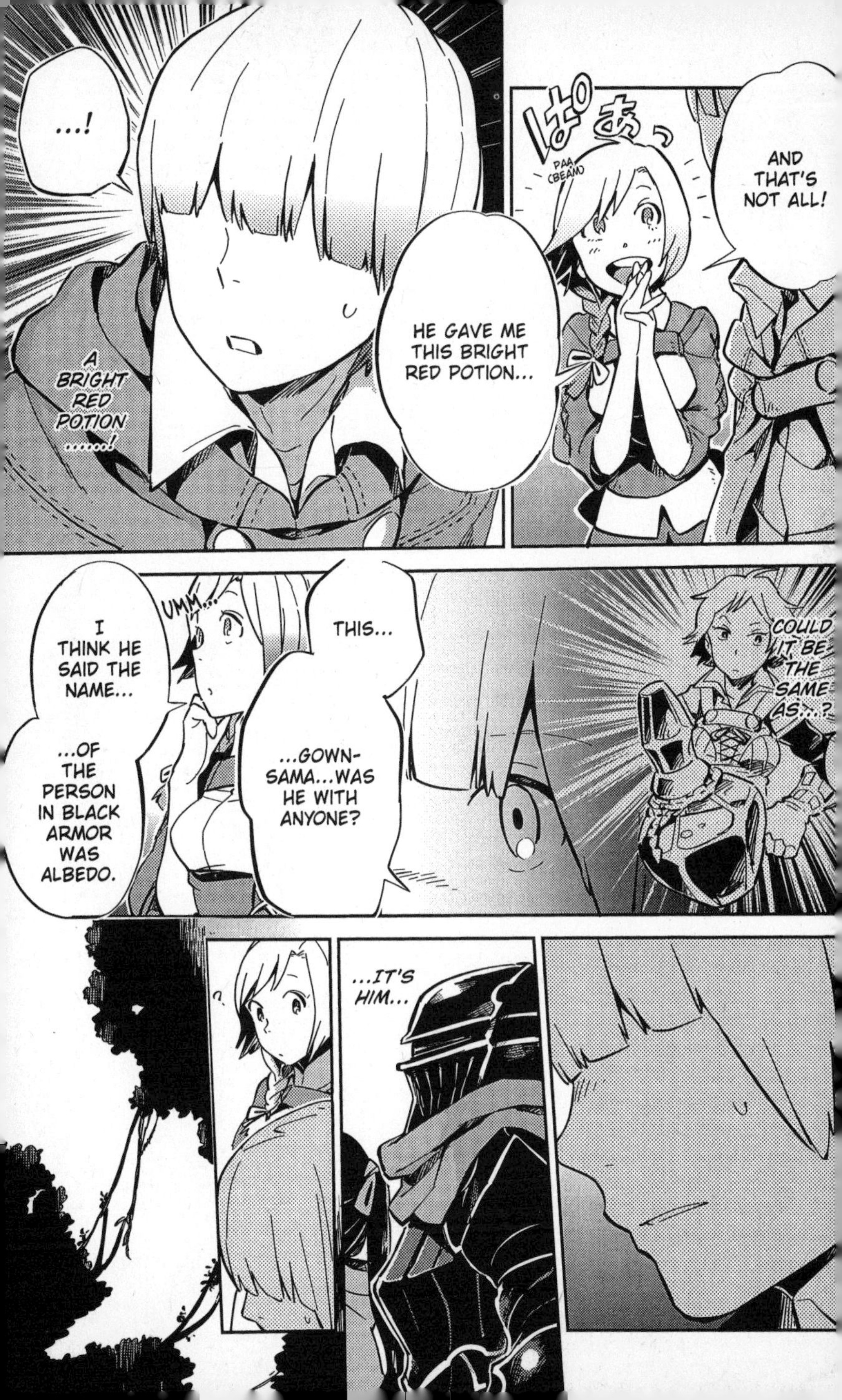
ぱあっ
PAA (BEAM)
AND THAT'S NOT ALL!
HE GAVE ME THIS BRIGHT RED POTION...
...!
A BRIGHT RED POTION.......!
COULD IT BE THE SAME AS...?
THIS...
...GOWN-SAMA...WAS HE WITH ANYONE?
UMM...
I THINK HE SAID THE NAME...
...OF THE PERSON IN BLACK ARMOR WAS ALBEDO.
...IT'S HIM...
?

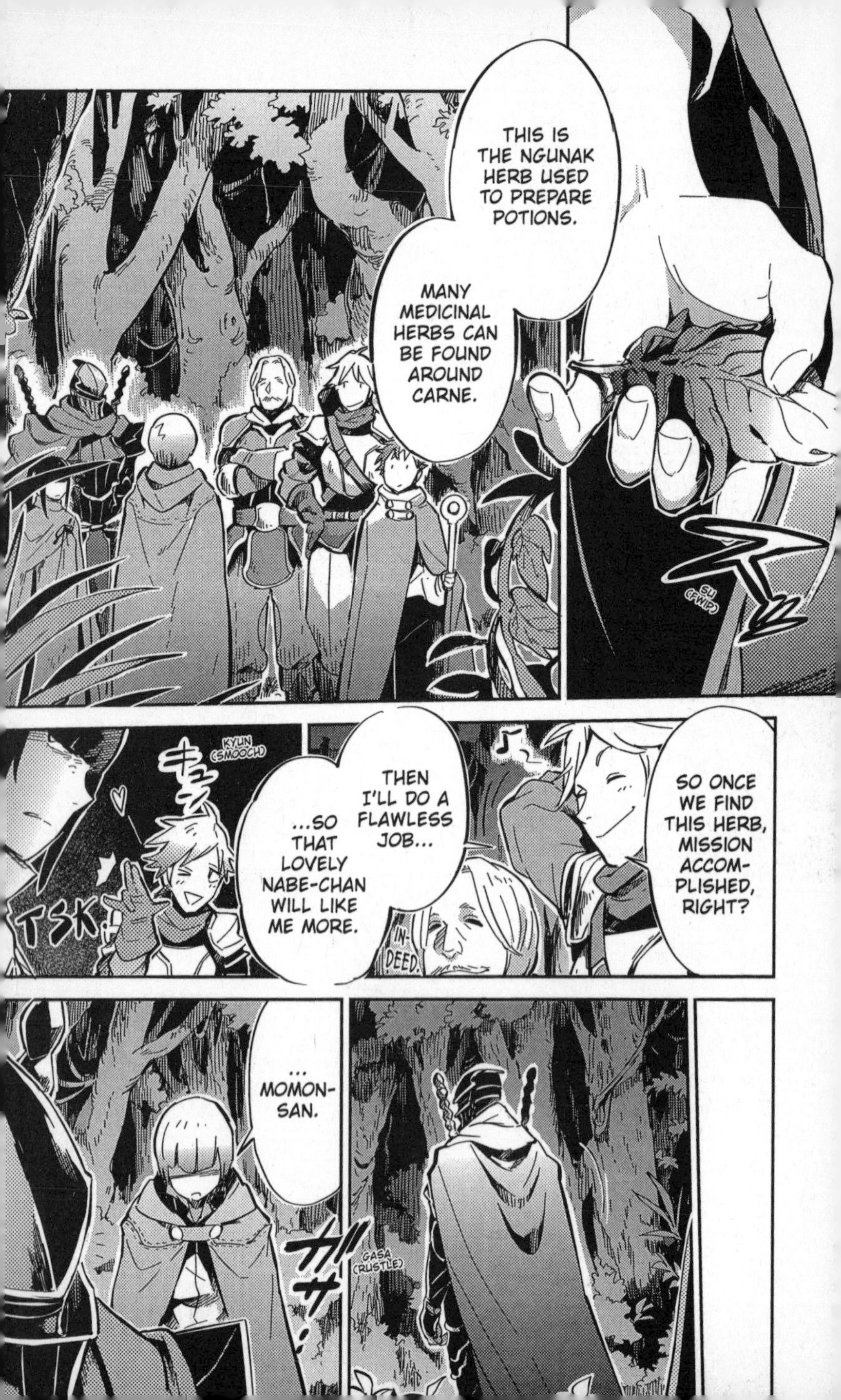

THIS IS THE NGUNAK HERB USED TO PREPARE POTIONS.
MANY MEDICINAL HERBS CAN BE FOUND AROUND CARNE.
SU (FWIP)
SO ONCE WE FIND THIS HERB, MISSION ACCOM-PLISHED, RIGHT?
IN-DEED.
THEN I'LL DO A FLAWLESS JOB...
...SO THAT LOVELY NABE-CHAN WILL LIKE ME MORE.
KYUN (SMOOCH)
TSK
GASA (RUSTLE)
... MOMON-SAN.

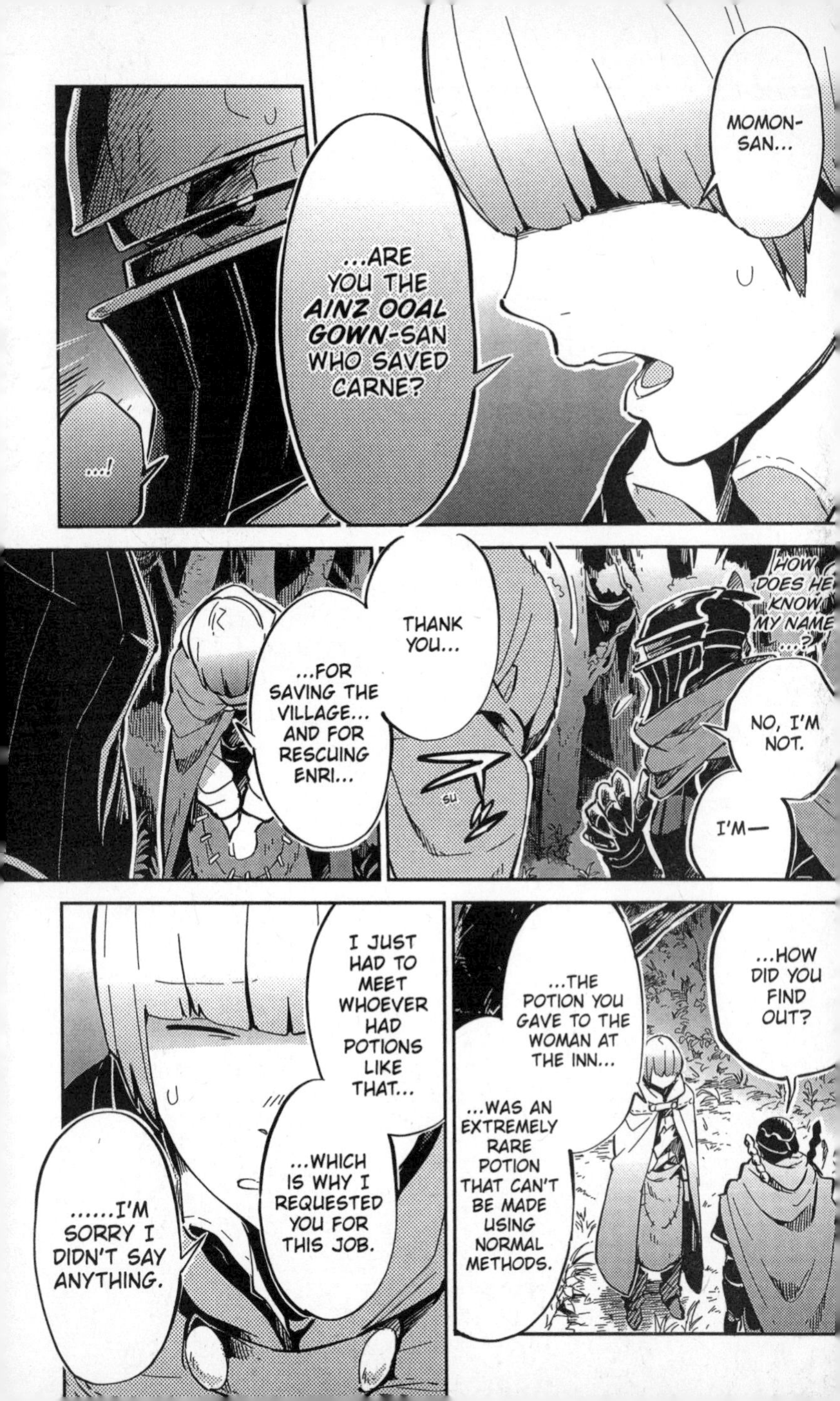
MOMON-SAN...
...ARE YOU THE AINZ OOAL GOWN-SAN WHO SAVED CARNE?
...!
HOW DOES HE KNOW MY NAME ...?
NO, I'M NOT.
I'M—
SU
THANK YOU...
...FOR SAVING THE VILLAGE... AND FOR RESCUING ENRI...
...HOW DID YOU FIND OUT?
...THE POTION YOU GAVE TO THE WOMAN AT THE INN...
...WAS AN EXTREMELY RARE POTION THAT CAN'T BE MADE USING NORMAL METHODS.
I JUST HAD TO MEET WHOEVER HAD POTIONS LIKE THAT...
...WHICH IS WHY I REQUESTED YOU FOR THIS JOB.
......I'M SORRY I DIDN'T SAY ANYTHING.

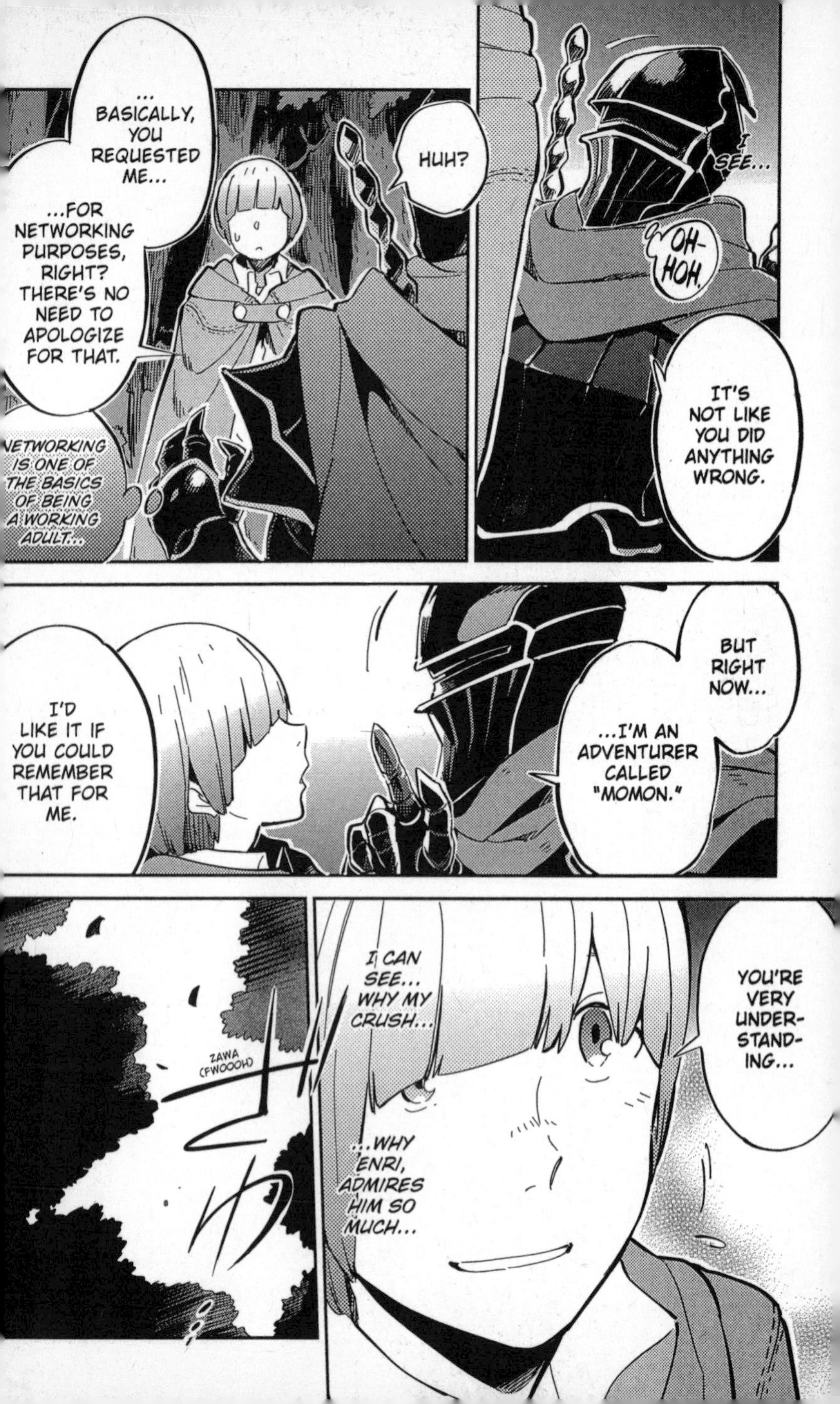
I SEE...
OH-HOH.
IT'S NOT LIKE YOU DID ANYTHING WRONG.
...BASICALLY, YOU REQUESTED ME...
HUH?
...FOR NETWORKING PURPOSES, RIGHT? THERE'S NO NEED TO APOLOGIZE FOR THAT.
NETWORKING IS ONE OF THE BASICS OF BEING A WORKING ADULT...
BUT RIGHT NOW...
...I'M AN ADVENTURER CALLED "MOMON."
I'D LIKE IT IF YOU COULD REMEMBER THAT FOR ME.
YOU'RE VERY UNDER-STAND-ING...
I CAN SEE... WHY MY CRUSH...
...WHY ENRI, ADMIRES HIM SO MUCH...
ZAWA (FWOOOH)

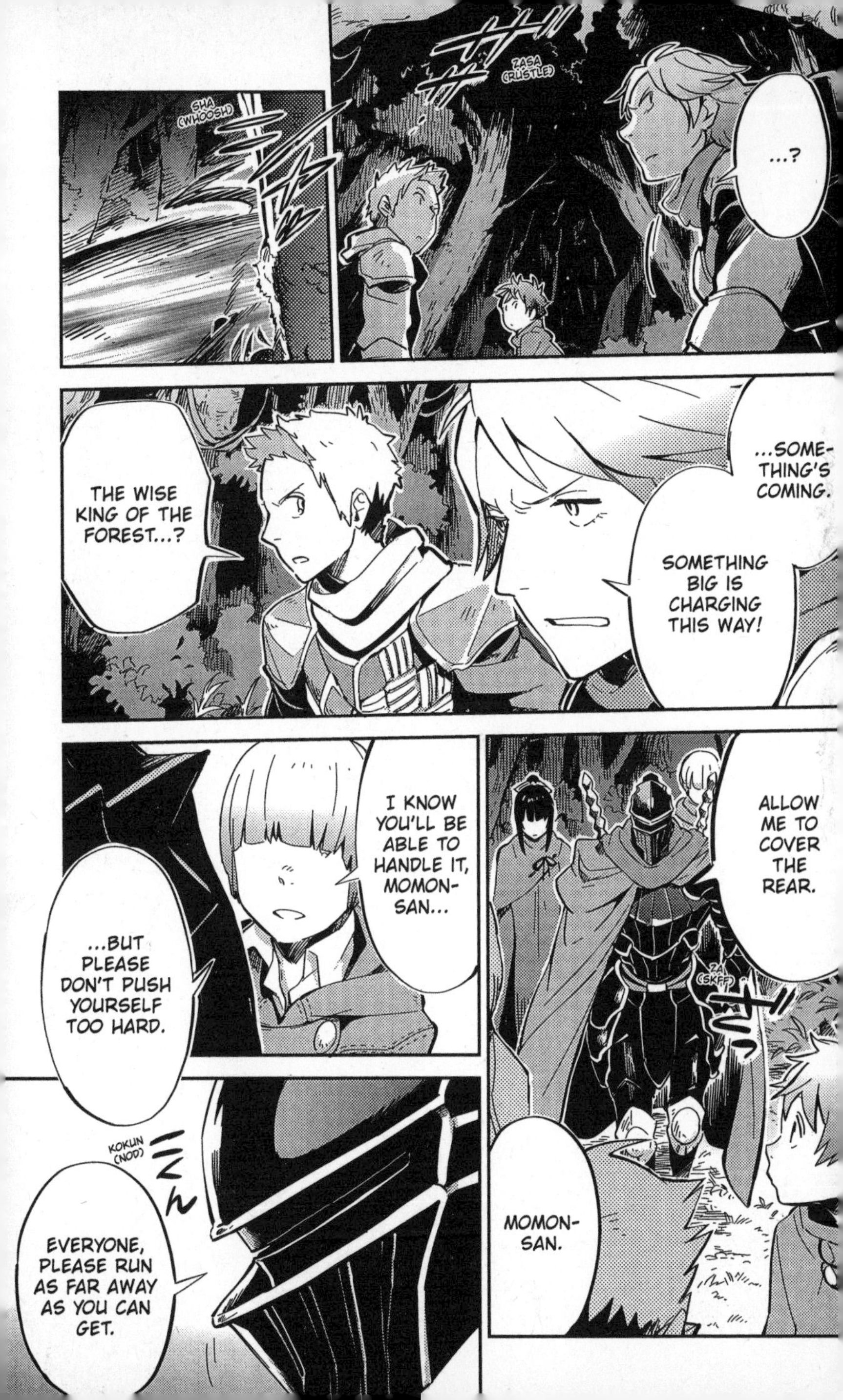
ZASA (RUSTLE)
...?
SHA (WHOOSH)
...SOMETHING'S COMING.
SOMETHING BIG IS CHARGING THIS WAY!
THE WISE KING OF THE FOREST...?
ALLOW ME TO COVER THE REAR.
ZA (SKFF)
MOMON-SAN.
I KNOW YOU'LL BE ABLE TO HANDLE IT, MOMON-SAN...
...BUT PLEASE DON'T PUSH YOURSELF TOO HARD.
KOKUN (NOD)
EVERYONE, PLEASE RUN AS FAR AWAY AS YOU CAN GET.

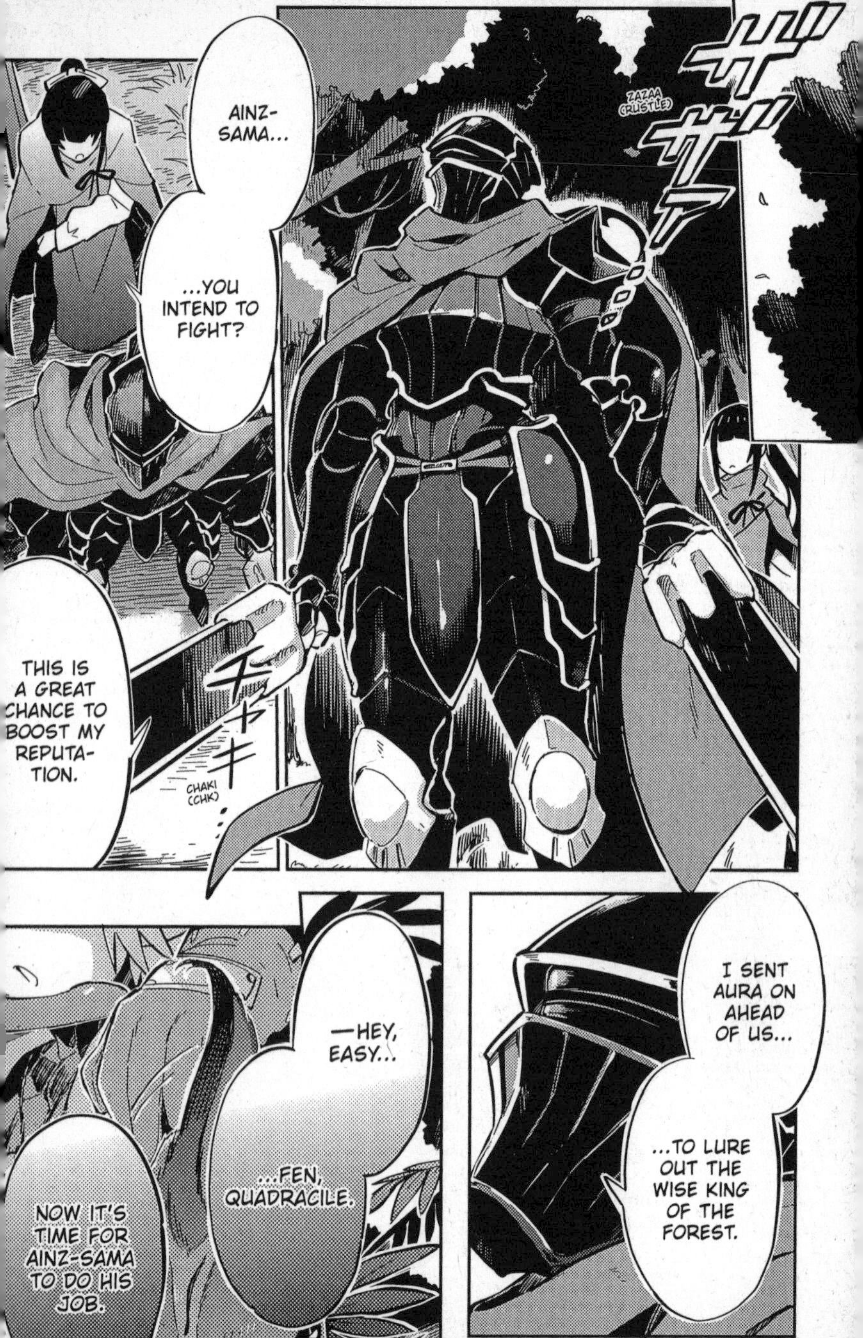

ザザァ
ZAZAA (RUSTLE)
AINZ-SAMA...
...YOU INTEND TO FIGHT?
チャキ
CHAKI (CHK)
THIS IS A GREAT CHANCE TO BOOST MY REPUTATION.
I SENT AURA ON AHEAD OF US...
...TO LURE OUT THE WISE KING OF THE FOREST.
—HEY, EASY...
...FEN, QUADRACILE.
NOW IT'S TIME FOR AINZ-SAMA TO DO HIS JOB.

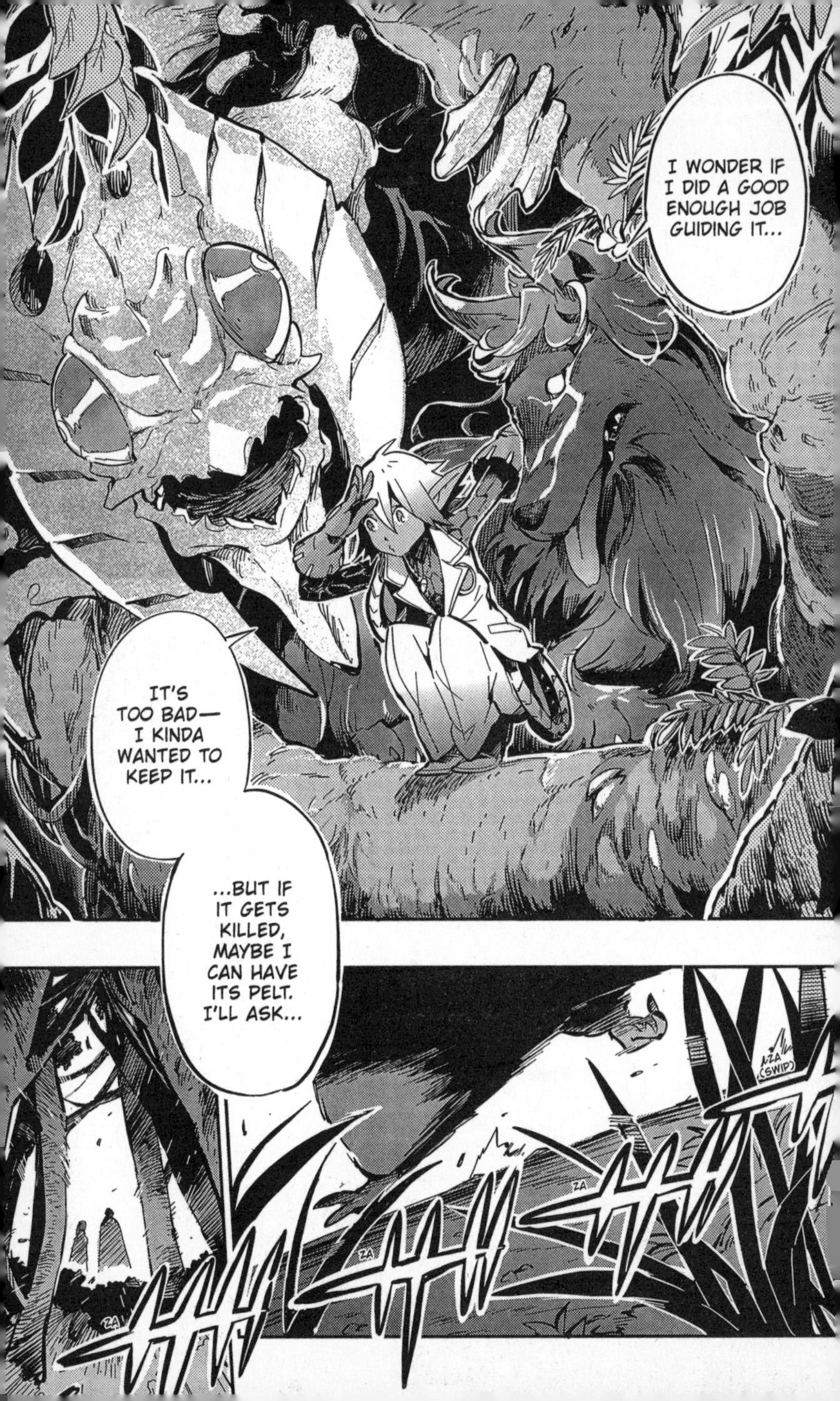
I WONDER IF I DID A GOOD ENOUGH JOB GUIDING IT...
IT'S TOO BAD— I KINDA WANTED TO KEEP IT...
...BUT IF IT GETS KILLED, MAYBE I CAN HAVE ITS PELT. I'LL ASK...
ZA (SWIP)
ZA
ZA
ZA

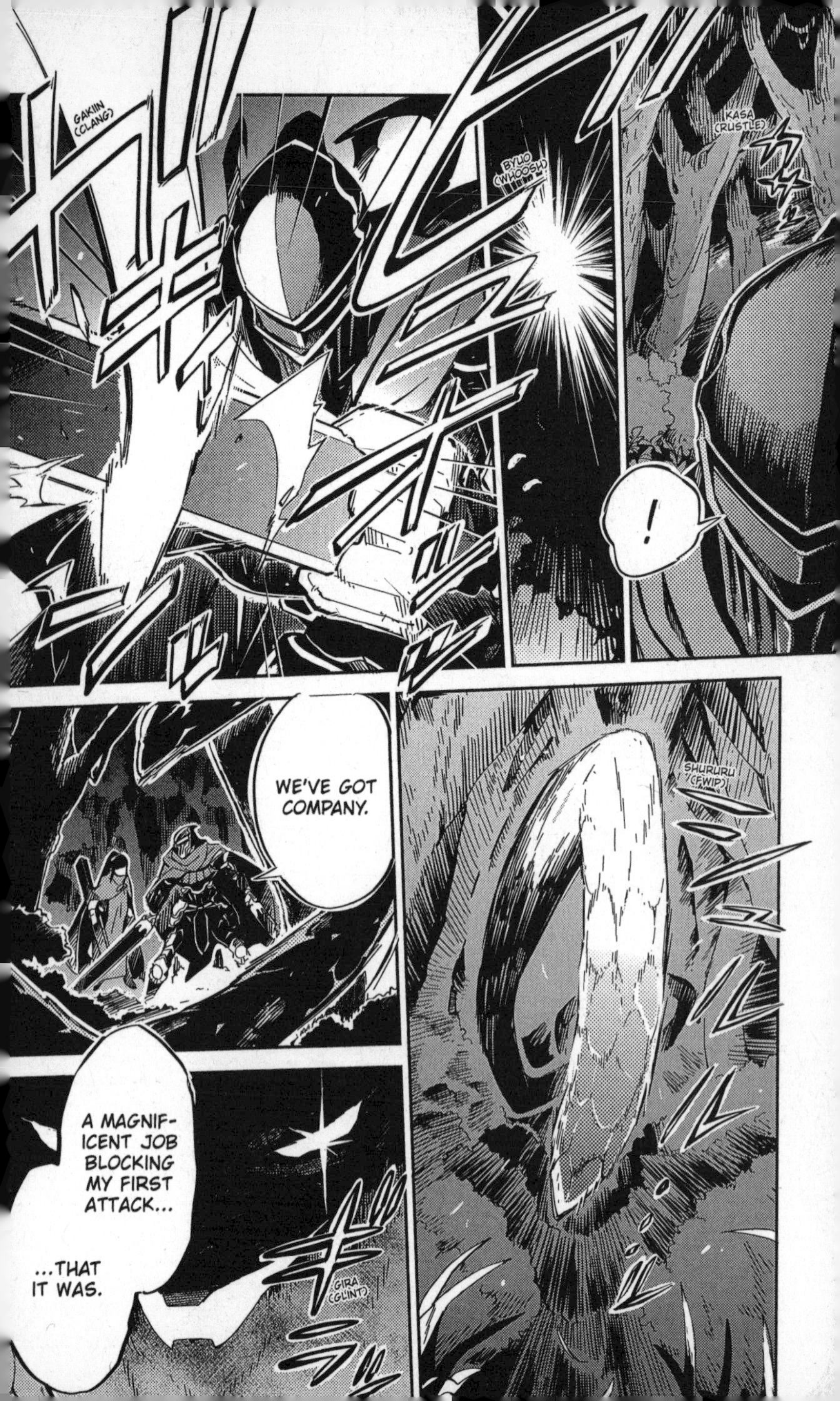
KASA (RUSTLE)
!
BYUO (WHOOSH)
GAKIIN (CLANG)
SHURURU (FWIP)
WE'VE GOT COMPANY.
A MAGNIFICENT JOB BLOCKING MY FIRST ATTACK...
...THAT IT WAS.
GIRA (GLINT)

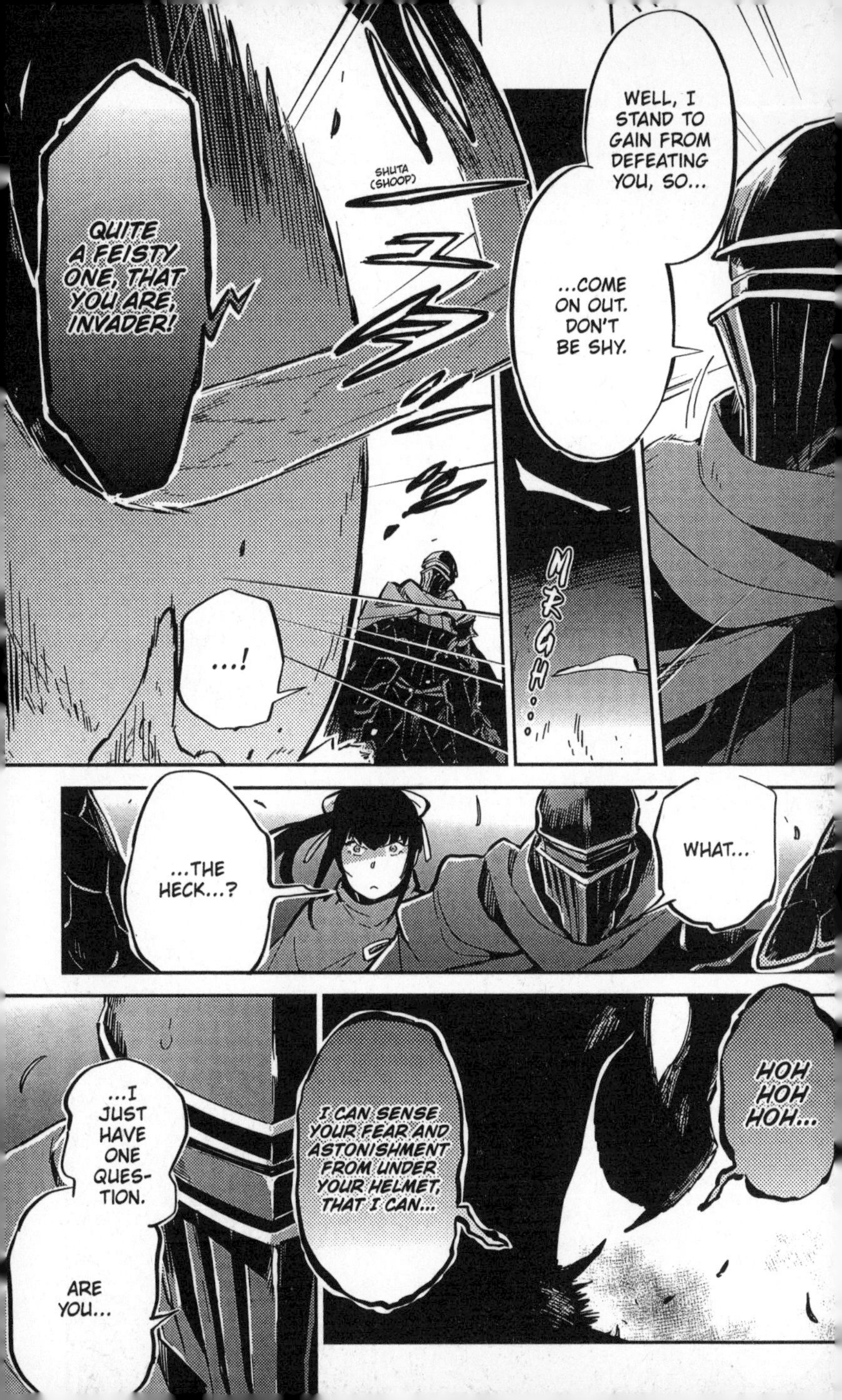
WELL, I STAND TO GAIN FROM DEFEATING YOU, SO...
...COME ON OUT. DON'T BE SHY.
SHUTA (SHOOP)
QUITE A FEISTY ONE, THAT YOU ARE, INVADER!
MRGH...
...!
WHAT...
...THE HECK...?
HOH HOH HOH...
I CAN SENSE YOUR FEAR AND ASTONISHMENT FROM UNDER YOUR HELMET, THAT I CAN...
...I JUST HAVE ONE QUES-TION.
ARE YOU...

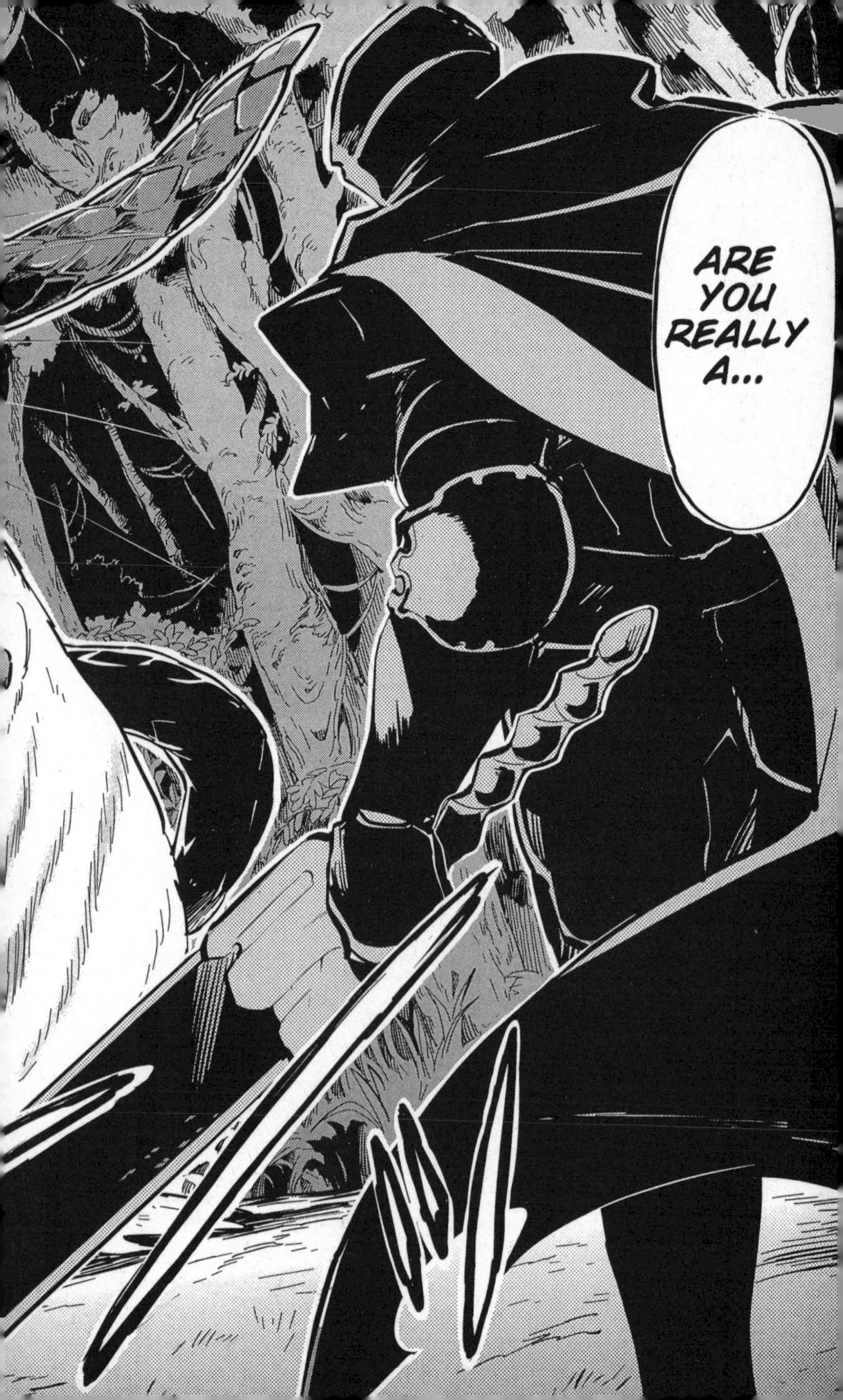
ARE YOU REALLY A...

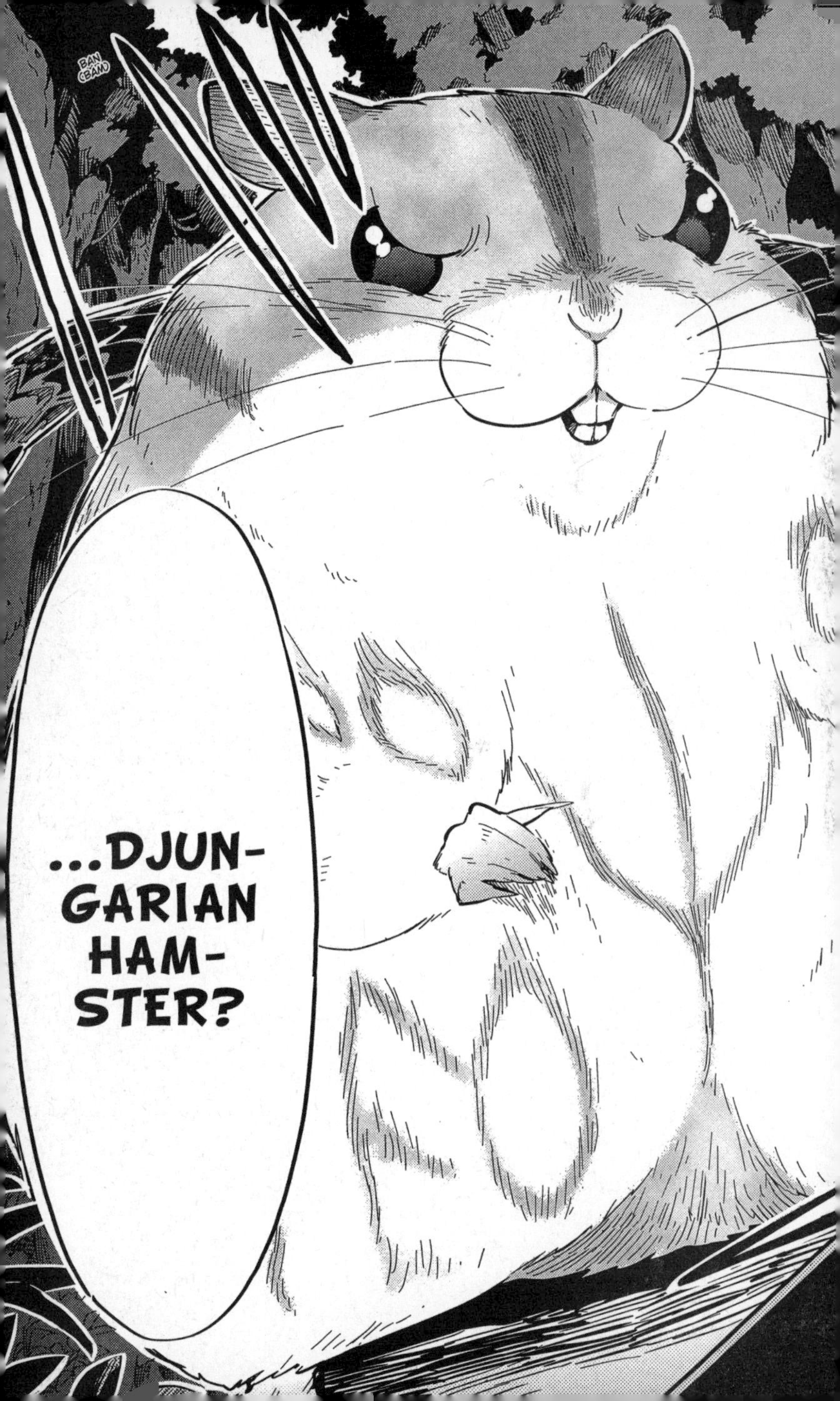
BAN (BAM)
...DJUN-
GARIAN
HAM-
STER?

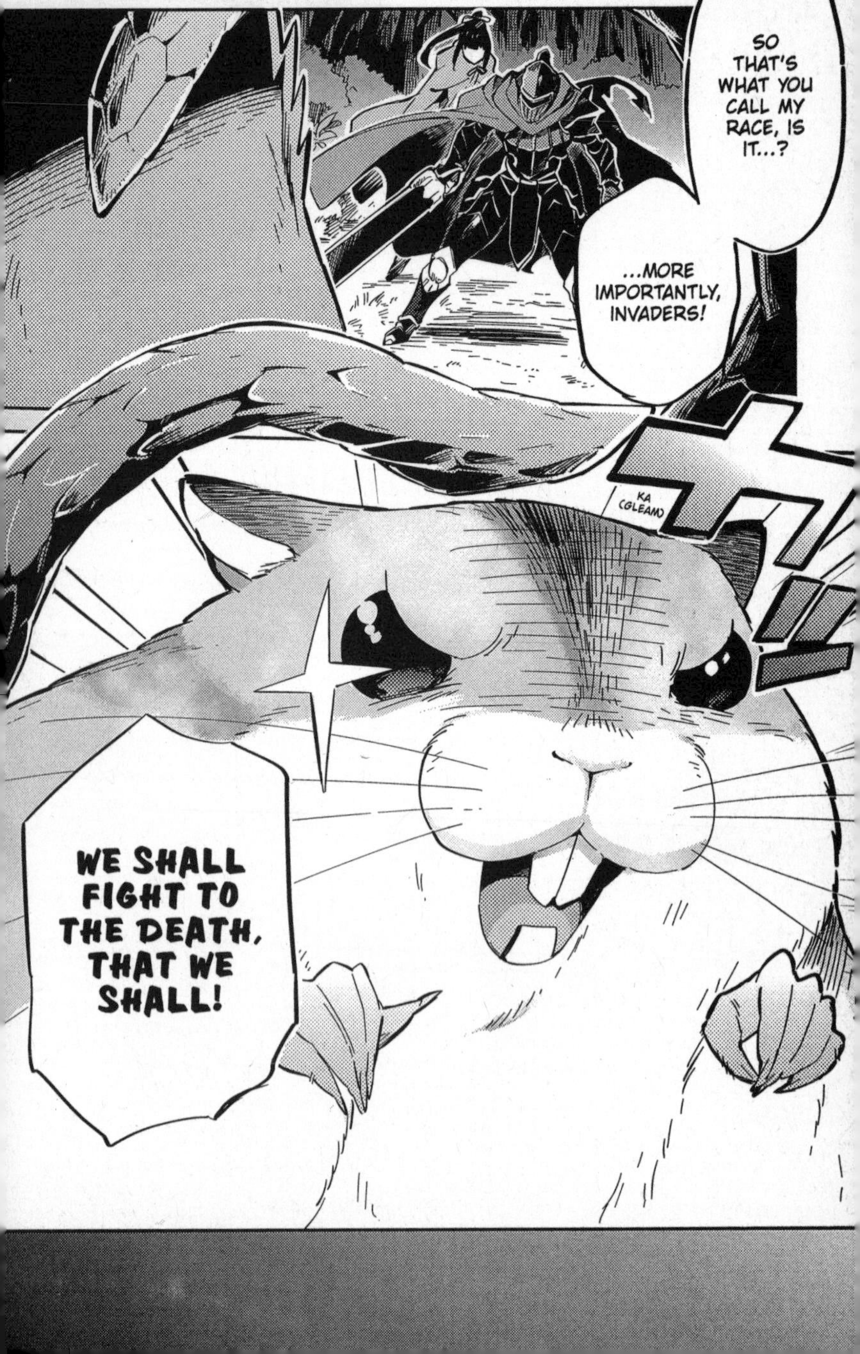
SO THAT'S WHAT YOU CALL MY RACE, IS IT...?
...MORE IMPORTANTLY, INVADERS!
KA (GLEAM)
WE SHALL FIGHT TO THE DEATH, THAT WE SHALL!

Interpretive notes of the OVERLORD

Chapter 6

Healing Potions

Medicine that heals wounds. When a tiny scrape could make the difference between life and death, potions are one type of item that adventurers think is worthwhile to live frugally for. There are three major types, depending on the ingredients: healing potions made of herbs, healing potions made of both herbs and magic, and healing potions made solely of magic.

•Healing potions made with herbs don't have instantaneous effects, but they are cheap and heal wounds by enhancing the natural healing processes.

•Healing potions made with herbs and magic take effect more quickly than potions made with herbs alone. This is generally the type of potion adventurers drink after a battle.

•Healing potions that use only magic are made by infusing alchemical solutions with magic, and they take effect immediately. It takes a good command of high-level alchemy to produce these, so they cost quite a lot. Since no herbs are used, nothing settles to the bottom of the bottle.

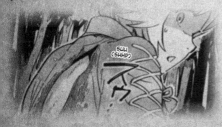

SUU
(SHHP)

Gods' Blood

A legendary red healing potion. Normal healing potions always end up turning blue during the production process—red ones are very, very rare. Many apothecaries have tried to produce Gods' Blood, but none have succeeded, so people joke that "The gods are actually blue-blooded!"

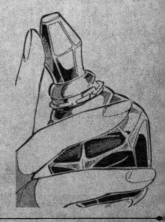

The alchemical solution used to make regular healing potions degrades over time. To maintain quality, Preservation is cast on them, but Gods' Blood doesn't degrade and, as a result, doesn't require a spell.

Without factoring in added value, Gods' Blood sells for eight gold pieces. If the added value is considered, the item becomes so valuable it wouldn't be strange if someone possessing a bottle of it were targeted by thieves.

Lizzy Baleare offered thirty-two gold pieces for that Gods' Blood potion. In this world, that amount could provide modest support for a family of three for three years.

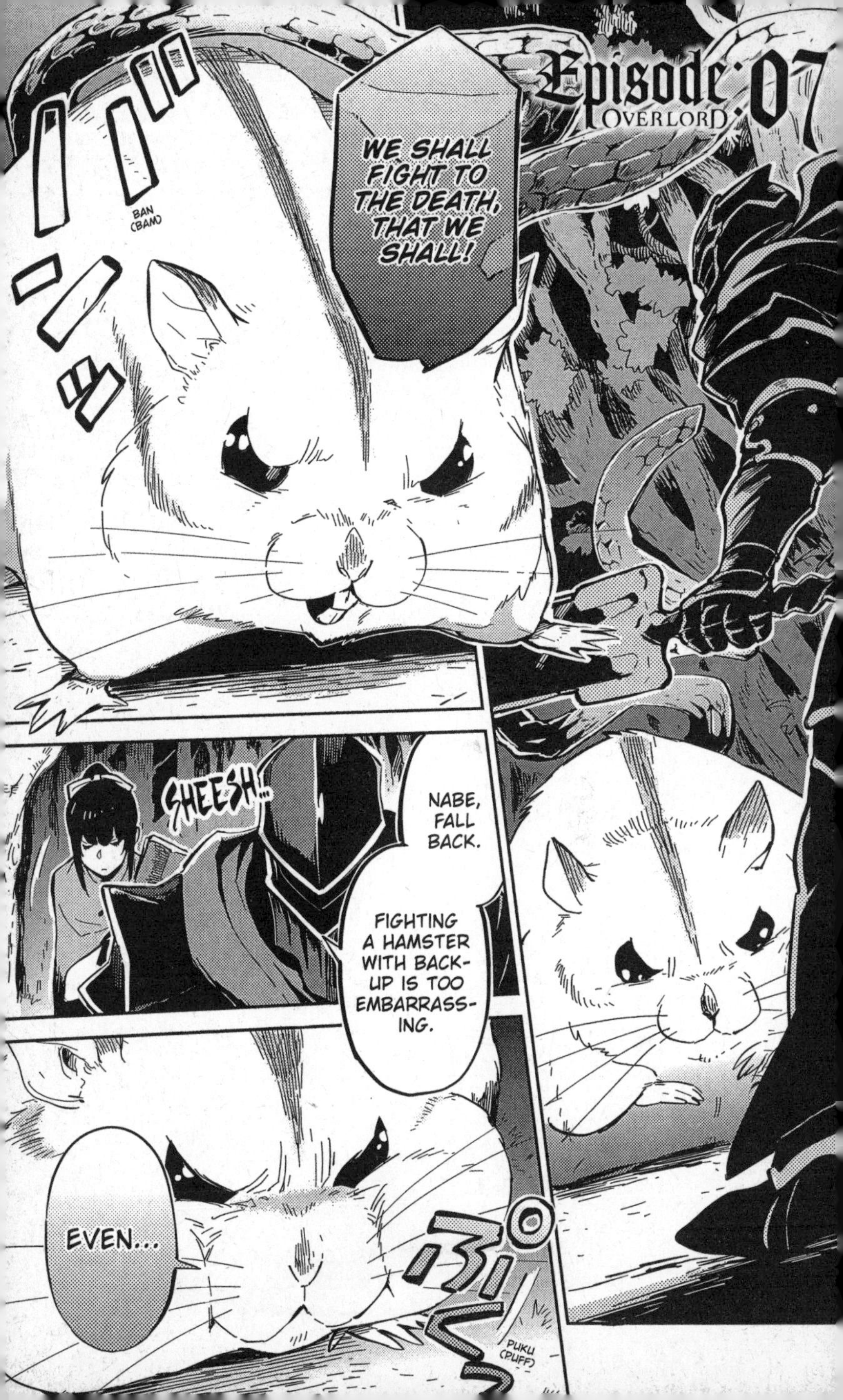
Episode: 07
OVERLORD
WE SHALL FIGHT TO THE DEATH, THAT WE SHALL!
BAN (BAM)
NABE, FALL BACK.
FIGHTING A HAMSTER WITH BACK-UP IS TOO EMBARRASS-ING.
SHEESH...
EVEN...
PUKU (PUFF)

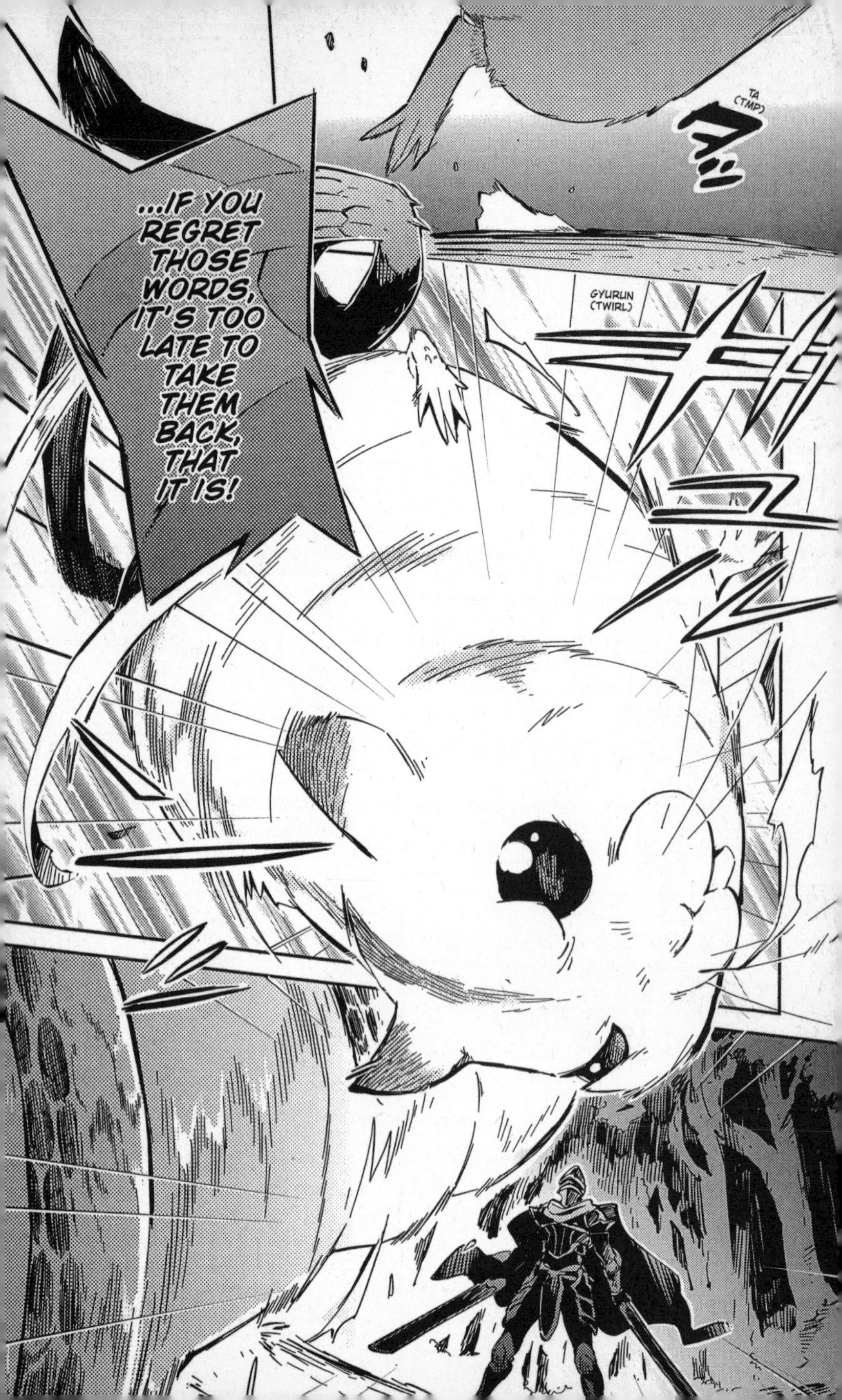
TA (TMP)
...IF YOU REGRET THOSE WORDS, IT'S TOO LATE TO TAKE THEM BACK, THAT IT IS!
GYURUN (TWIRL)

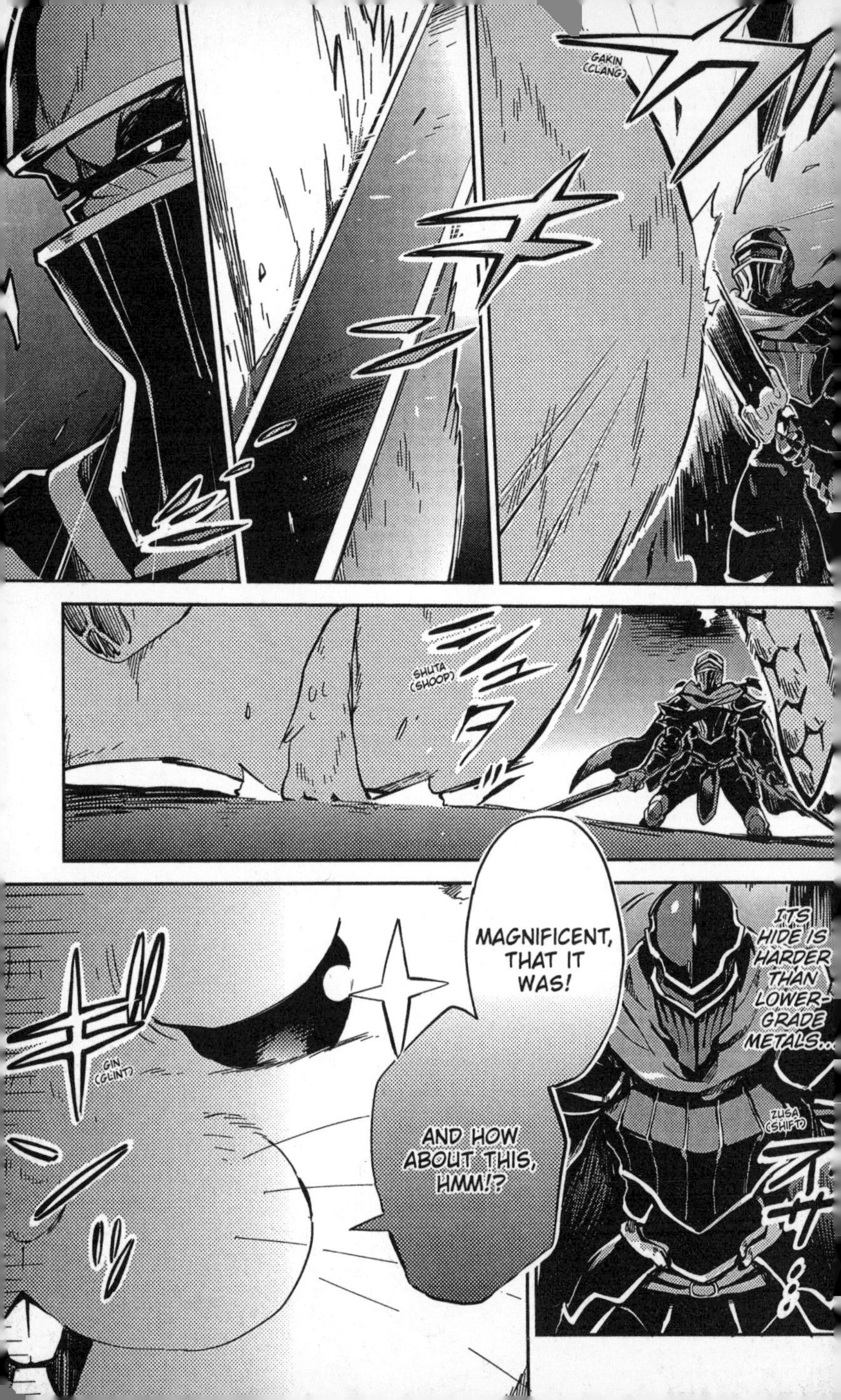
GAKIN (CLANG)
SHUTA (SHOOP)
ITS HIDE IS HARDER THAN LOWER-GRADE METALS...
MAGNIFICENT, THAT IT WAS!
ZUSA (SHIFT)
AND HOW ABOUT THIS, HMM!?
GIN (GLINT)

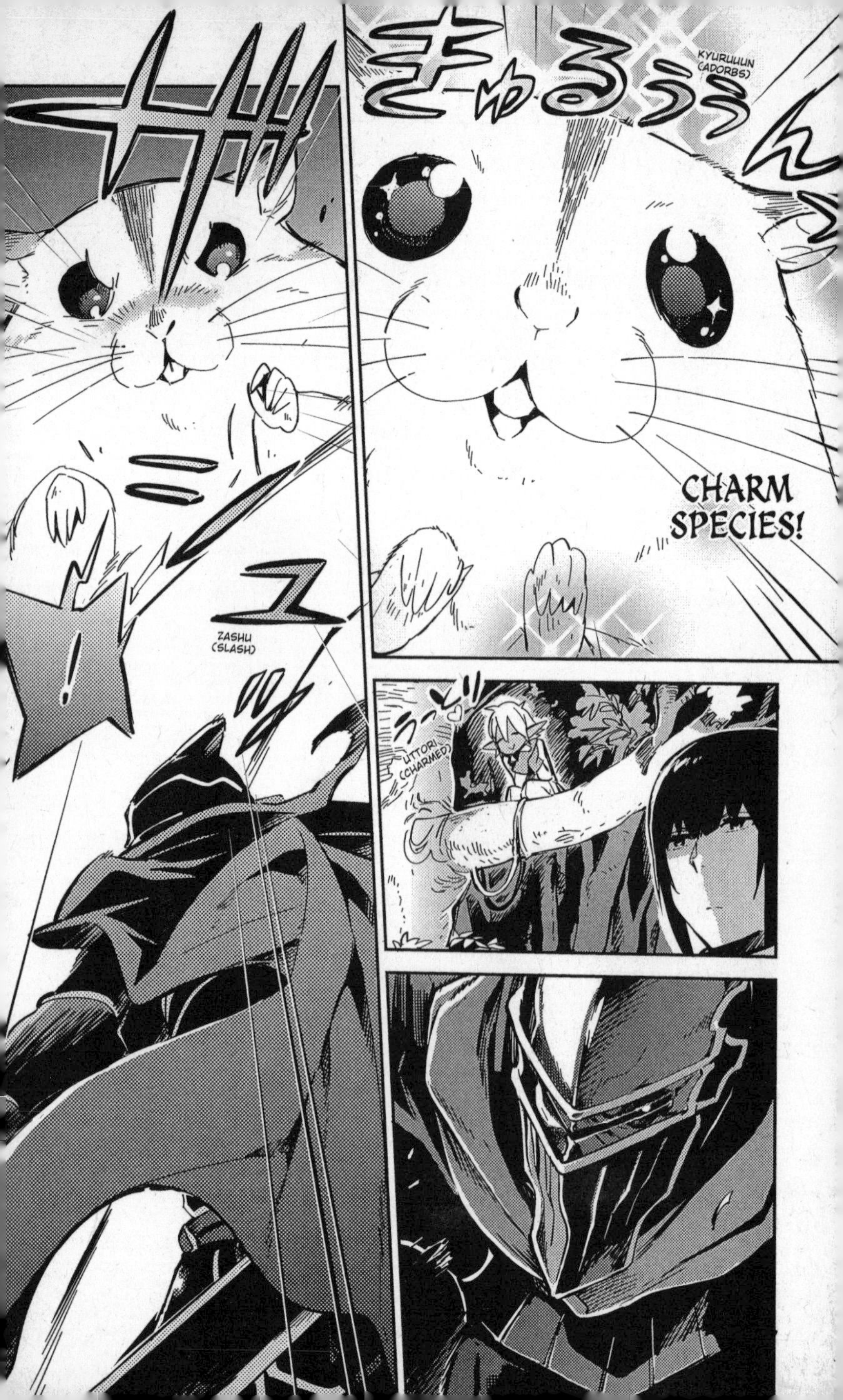
KYURUUUN (ADORBS)
CHARM SPECIES!
UTTORI (CHARMED)
ZASHU (SLASH)

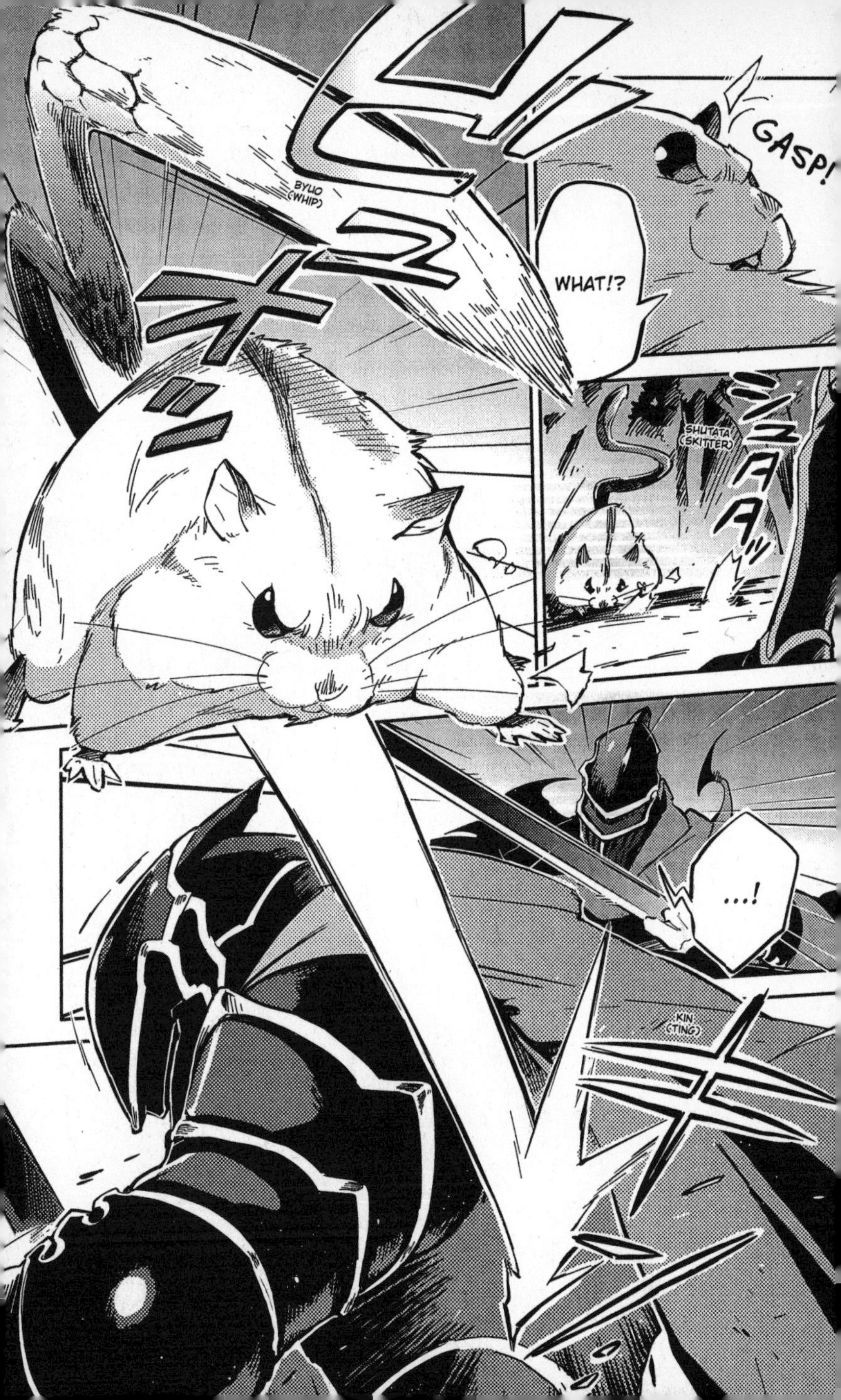
GASP!
WHAT!?
BYUO (WHIP)
SHUTATA (SKITTER)
...!
KIN (TING)

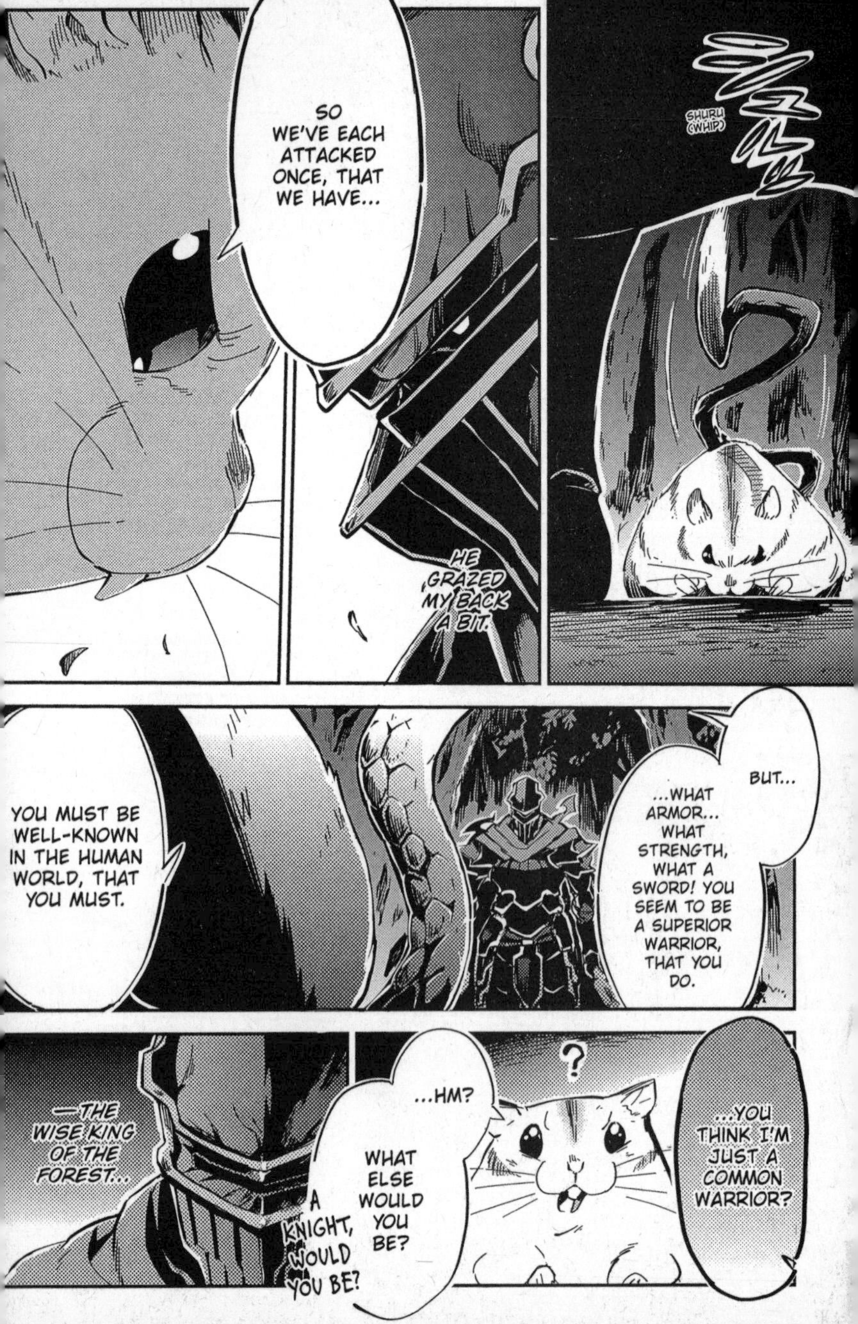
SHURU (WHIP)
SO WE'VE EACH ATTACKED ONCE, THAT WE HAVE...
HE GRAZED MY BACK A BIT.
BUT...
...WHAT ARMOR... WHAT STRENGTH, WHAT A SWORD! YOU SEEM TO BE A SUPERIOR WARRIOR, THAT YOU DO.
YOU MUST BE WELL-KNOWN IN THE HUMAN WORLD, THAT YOU MUST.
...YOU THINK I'M JUST A COMMON WARRIOR?
?
...HM?
WHAT ELSE WOULD YOU BE?
A KNIGHT, WOULD YOU BE?
—THE WISE KING OF THE FOREST...

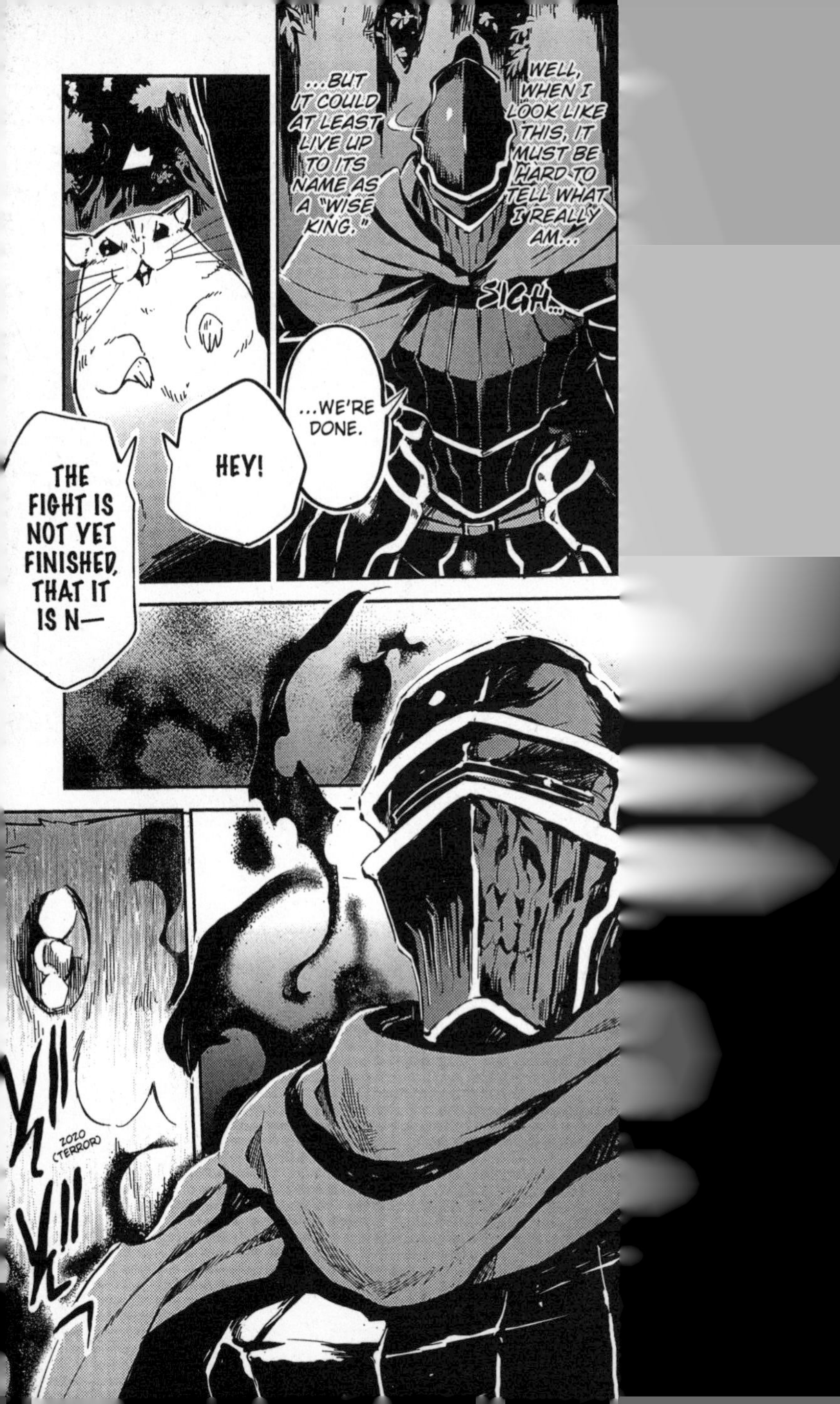

WELL, WHEN I LOOK LIKE THIS, IT MUST BE HARD TO TELL WHAT I REALLY AM...
...BUT IT COULD AT LEAST LIVE UP TO ITS NAME AS A "WISE KING."
SIGH...
...WE'RE DONE.
HEY!
THE FIGHT IS NOT YET FINISHED, THAT IT IS N—
ZOZO (TERROR)

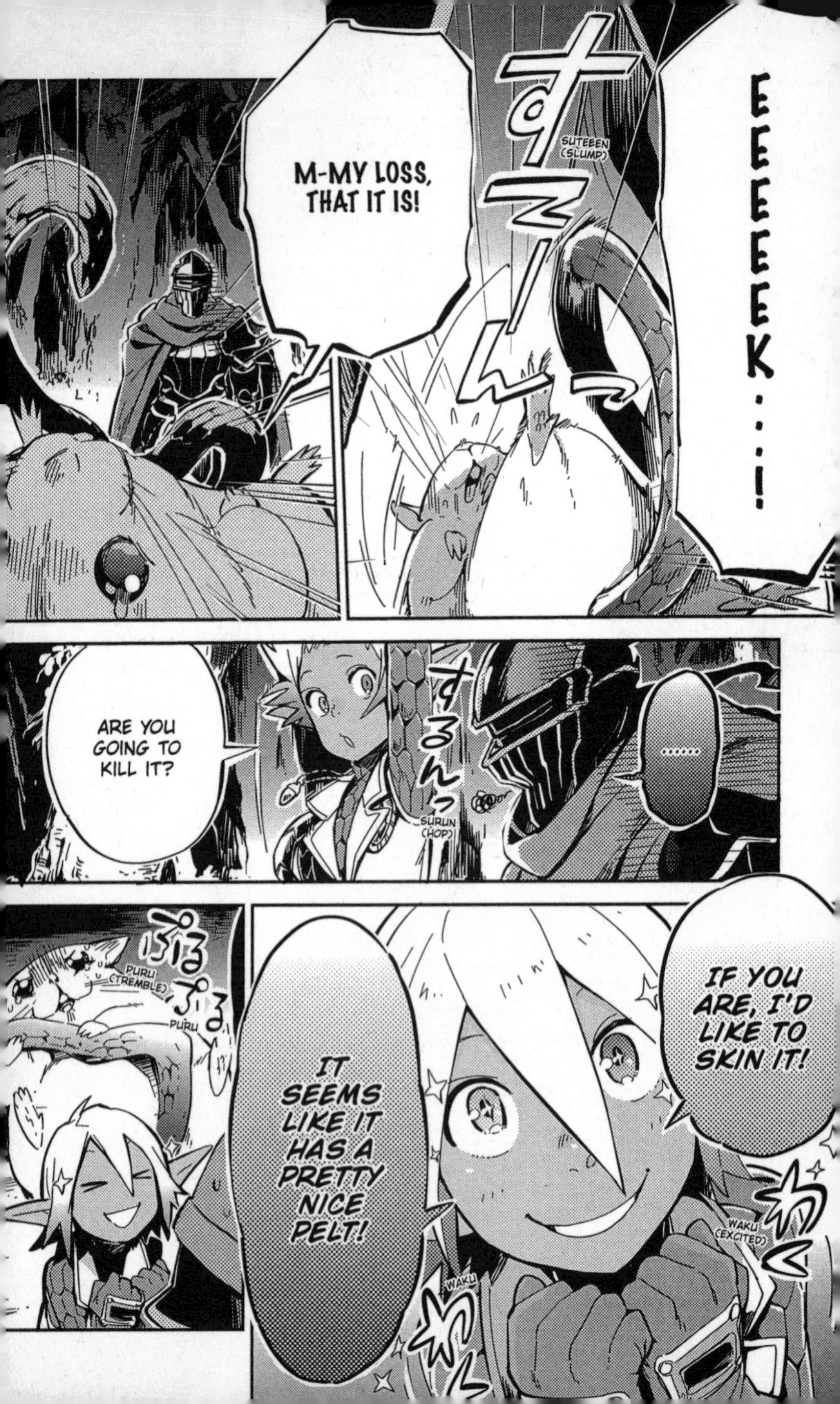

EEEEEEK...!
SUTEEEN (SLUMP)
M-MY LOSS, THAT IT IS!
......
SURUN (HOP)
ARE YOU GOING TO KILL IT?
IF YOU ARE, I'D LIKE TO SKIN IT!
WAKU (EXCITED)
WAKU
IT SEEMS LIKE IT HAS A PRETTY NICE PELT!
PURU (TREMBLE)
PURU

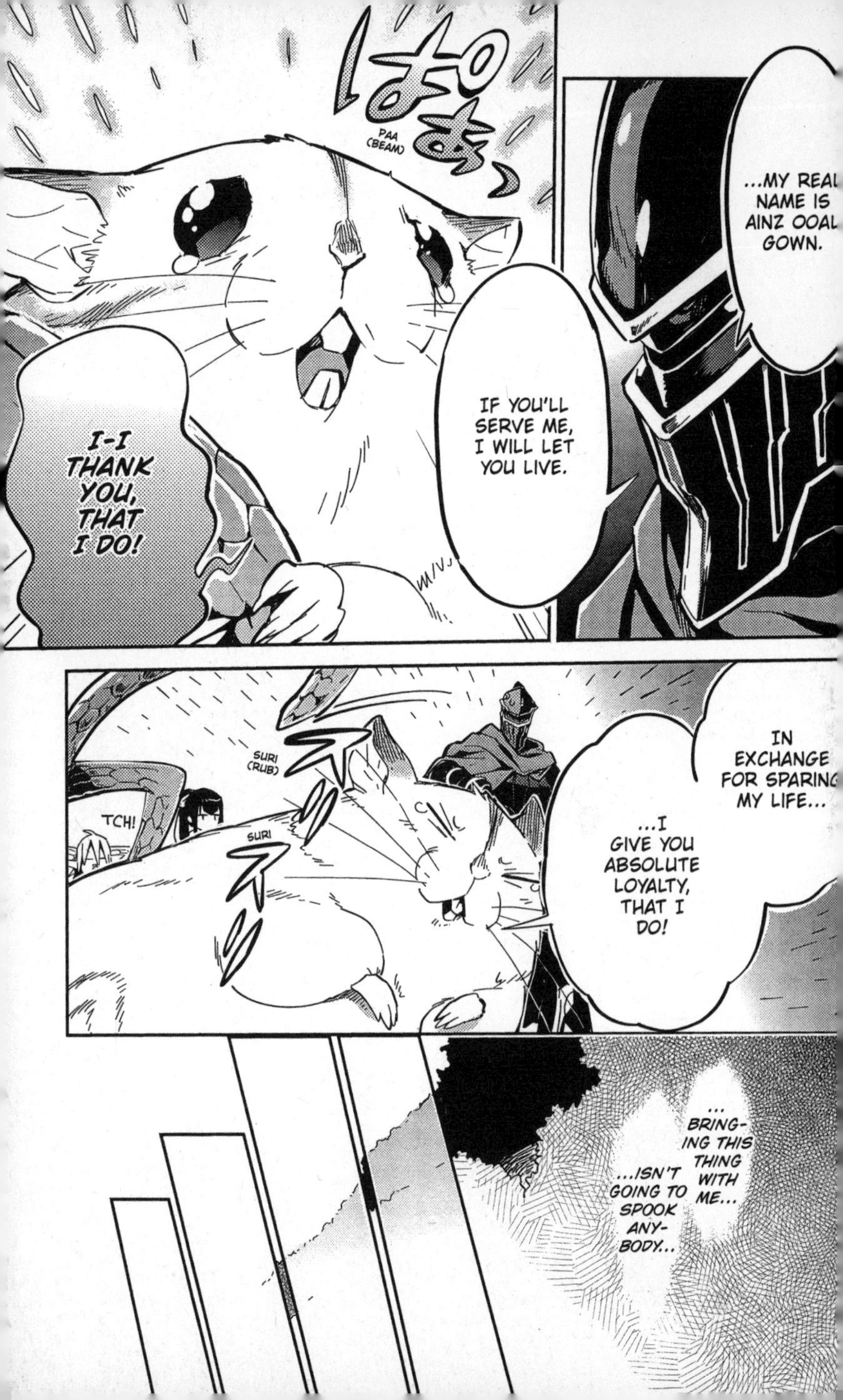
...MY REAL NAME IS AINZ OOAL GOWN.
IF YOU'LL SERVE ME, I WILL LET YOU LIVE.
ぱぁっ
PAA (BEAM)
I-I THANK YOU, THAT I DO!
IN EXCHANGE FOR SPARING MY LIFE...
...I GIVE YOU ABSOLUTE LOYALTY, THAT I DO!
SURI (RUB)
SURI
TCH!
...BRINGING THIS THING WITH ME...
...ISN'T GOING TO SPOOK ANYBODY...

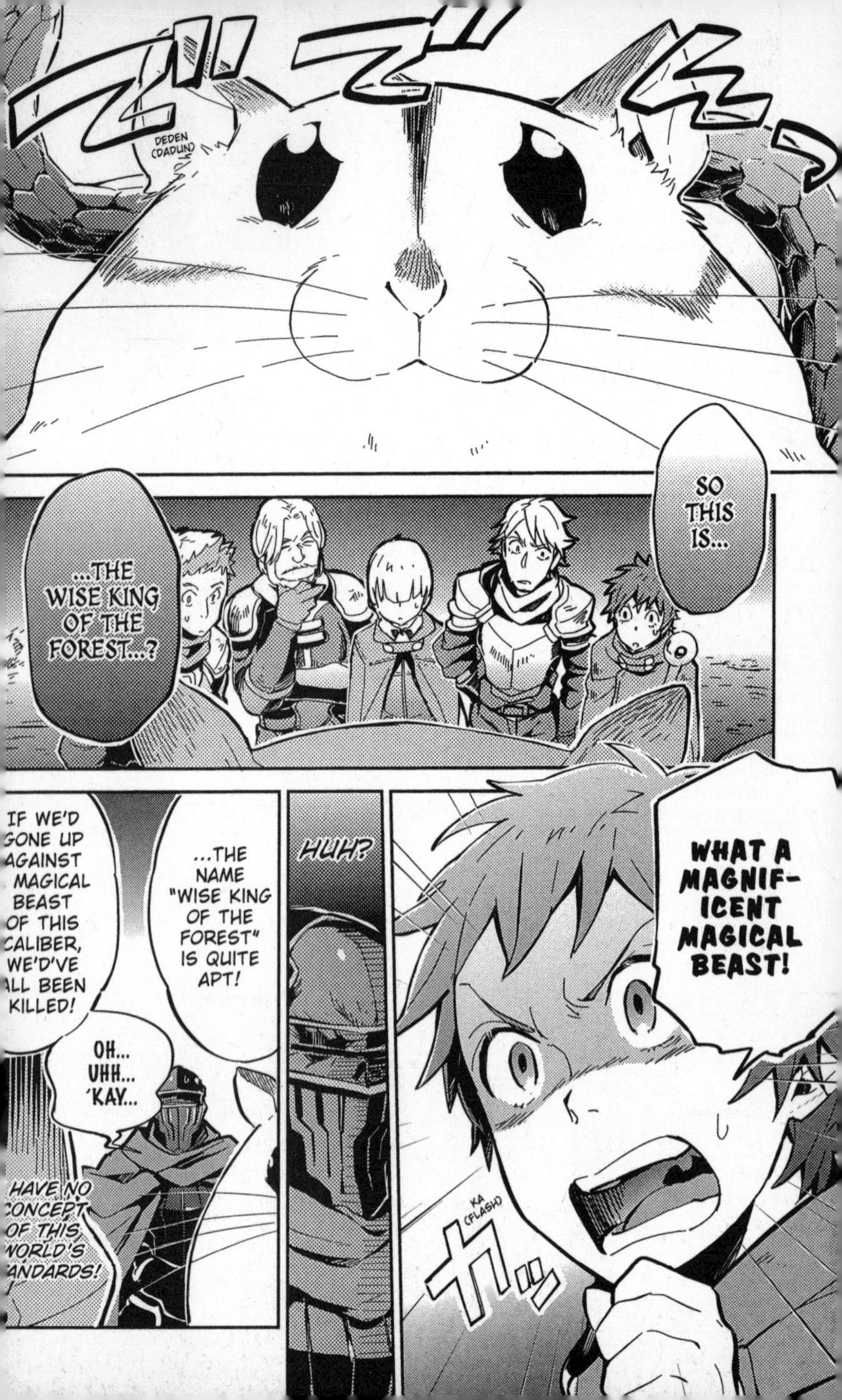
DEDEN (DADUN)
SO THIS IS...
...THE WISE KING OF THE FOREST...?
WHAT A MAGNIF- ICENT MAGICAL BEAST!
KA (FLASH)
HUH?
...THE NAME "WISE KING OF THE FOREST" IS QUITE APT!
IF WE'D GONE UP AGAINST MAGICAL BEAST OF THIS CALIBER, WE'D'VE LL BEEN KILLED!
OH... UHH... 'KAY...
HAVE NO CONCEPT OF THIS WORLD'S ANDARDS!

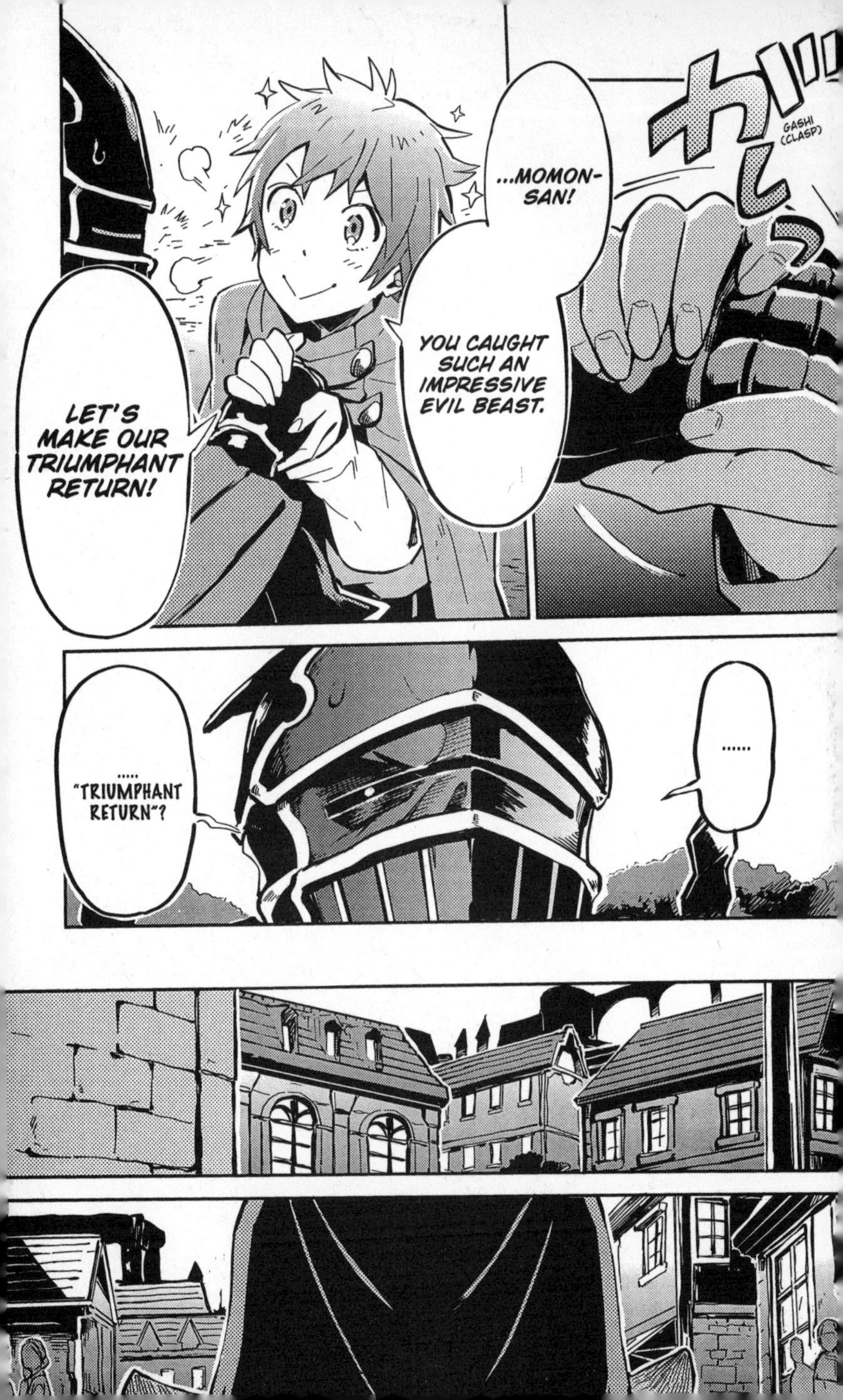
GASHI (CLASP)
...MOMON-SAN!
YOU CAUGHT SUCH AN IMPRESSIVE EVIL BEAST.
LET'S MAKE OUR TRIUMPHANT RETURN!
......
..... "TRIUMPHANT RETURN"?

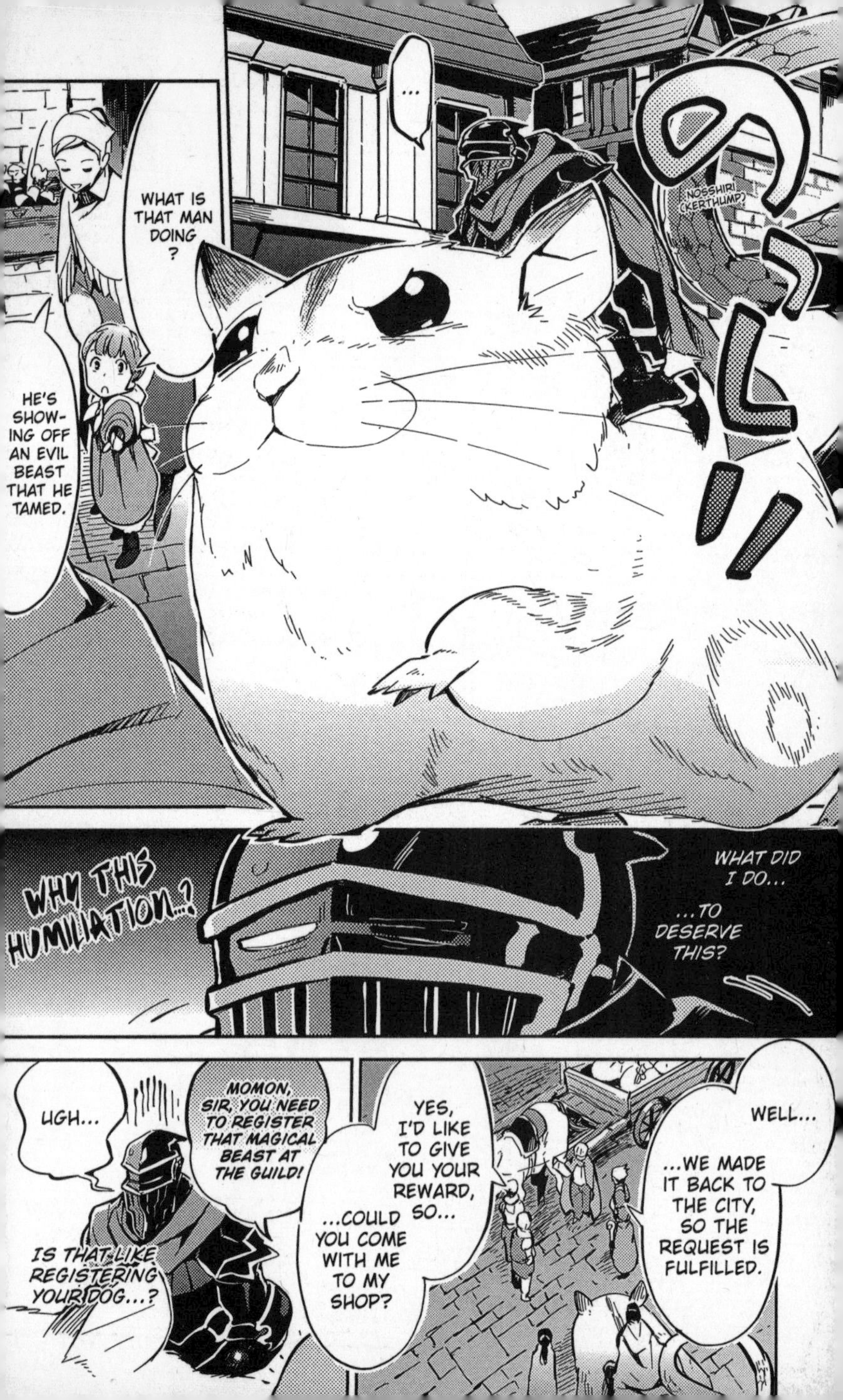
NOSSHIRI (KERTHUMP)
...
WHAT IS THAT MAN DOING?
HE'S SHOWING OFF AN EVIL BEAST THAT HE TAMED.
WHAT DID I DO...
...TO DESERVE THIS?
WHY THIS HUMILIATION...?
WELL...
...WE MADE IT BACK TO THE CITY, SO THE REQUEST IS FULFILLED.
YES, I'D LIKE TO GIVE YOU YOUR REWARD, SO...
...COULD YOU COME WITH ME TO MY SHOP?
MOMON, SIR, YOU NEED TO REGISTER THAT MAGICAL BEAST AT THE GUILD!
UGH...
IS THAT LIKE REGISTERING YOUR DOG...?

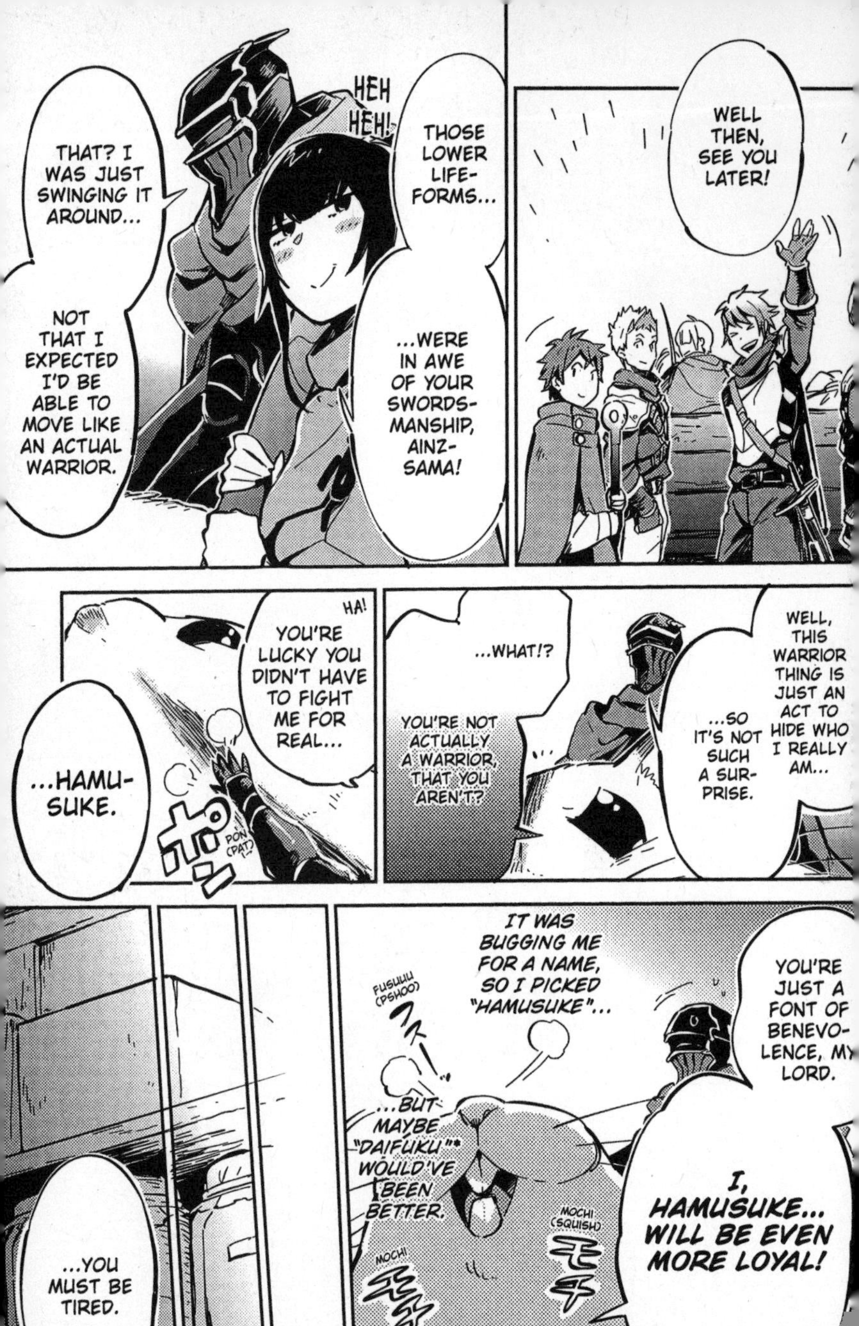
WELL THEN, SEE YOU LATER!
HEH HEH!
THOSE LOWER LIFE-FORMS...
...WERE IN AWE OF YOUR SWORDS-MANSHIP, AINZ-SAMA!
THAT? I WAS JUST SWINGING IT AROUND...
NOT THAT I EXPECTED I'D BE ABLE TO MOVE LIKE AN ACTUAL WARRIOR.
WELL, THIS WARRIOR THING IS JUST AN ACT TO HIDE WHO I REALLY AM...
...SO IT'S NOT SUCH A SUR-PRISE.
...WHAT!?
YOU'RE NOT ACTUALLY A WARRIOR, THAT YOU AREN'T?
HA!
YOU'RE LUCKY YOU DIDN'T HAVE TO FIGHT ME FOR REAL...
PON (PAT)
...HAMU-SUKE.
YOU'RE JUST A FONT OF BENEVO-LENCE, MY LORD.
I, HAMUSUKE... WILL BE EVEN MORE LOYAL!
IT WAS BUGGING ME FOR A NAME, SO I PICKED "HAMUSUKE"...
FUSUUU (PSHOO)
...BUT MAYBE "DAIFUKU"* WOULD'VE BEEN BETTER.
MOCHI (SQUISH)
MOCHI
...YOU MUST BE TIRED.

*DAIFUKU: A KIND OF MOCHI (RICE CAKE) WITH SWEET FILLING THAT IS ROUND AND FLUFFY.

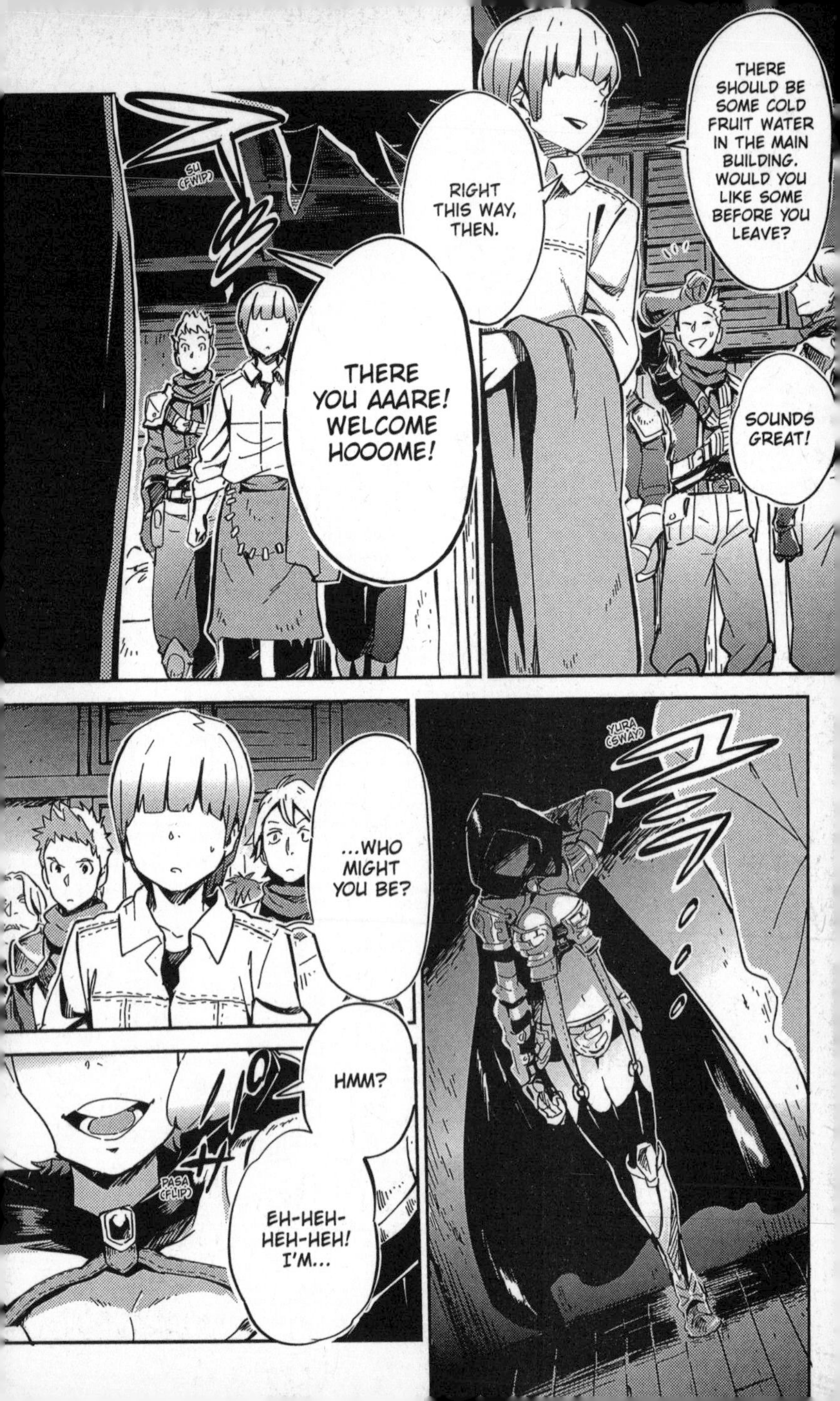
THERE SHOULD BE SOME COLD FRUIT WATER IN THE MAIN BUILDING. WOULD YOU LIKE SOME BEFORE YOU LEAVE?
RIGHT THIS WAY, THEN.
SOUNDS GREAT!
SU (FWIP)
THERE YOU AAARE! WELCOME HOOOME!
YURA (SWAY)
...WHO MIGHT YOU BE?
HMM?
PASA (FLIP)
EH-HEH-HEH-HEH! I'M...

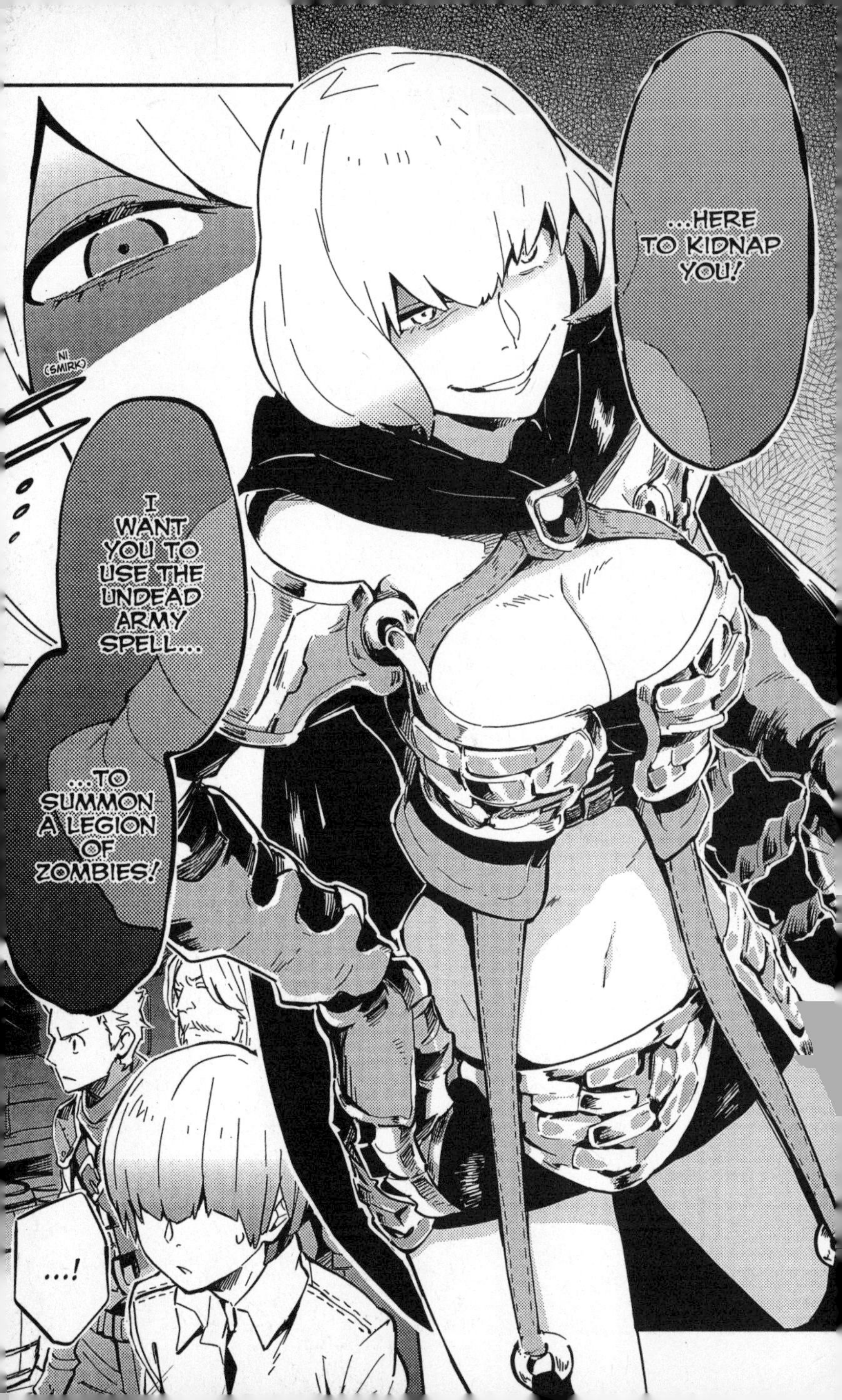
...HERE TO KIDNAP YOU!
NI (SMIRK)
I WANT YOU TO USE THE UNDEAD ARMY SPELL...
...TO SUMMON A LEGION OF ZOMBIES!
...!

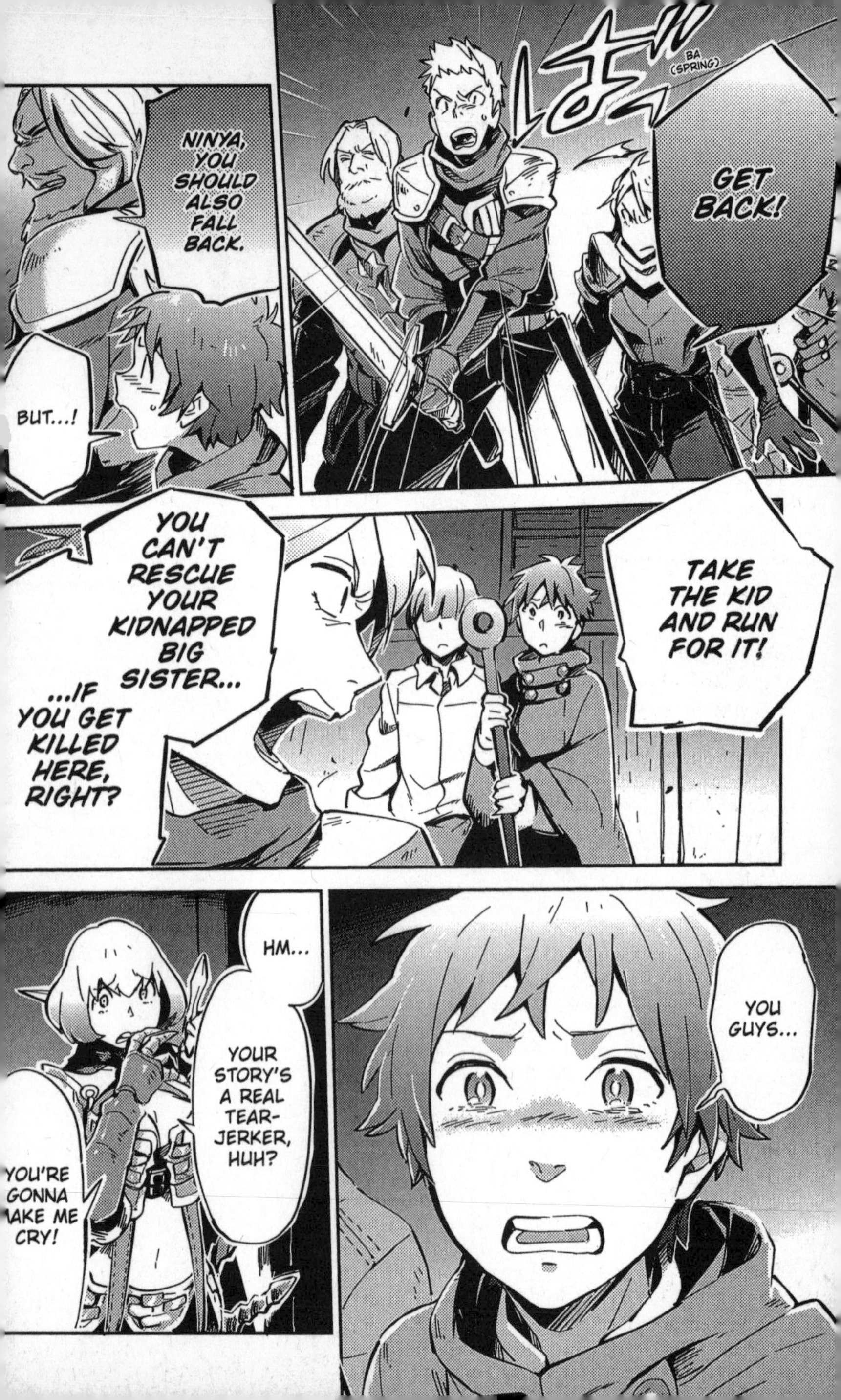
BA (SPRING)
GET BACK!
NINYA, YOU SHOULD ALSO FALL BACK.
BUT...!
TAKE THE KID AND RUN FOR IT!
YOU CAN'T RESCUE YOUR KIDNAPPED BIG SISTER...
...IF YOU GET KILLED HERE, RIGHT?
YOU GUYS...
HM...
YOUR STORY'S A REAL TEAR-JERKER, HUH?
YOU'RE GONNA AKE ME CRY!

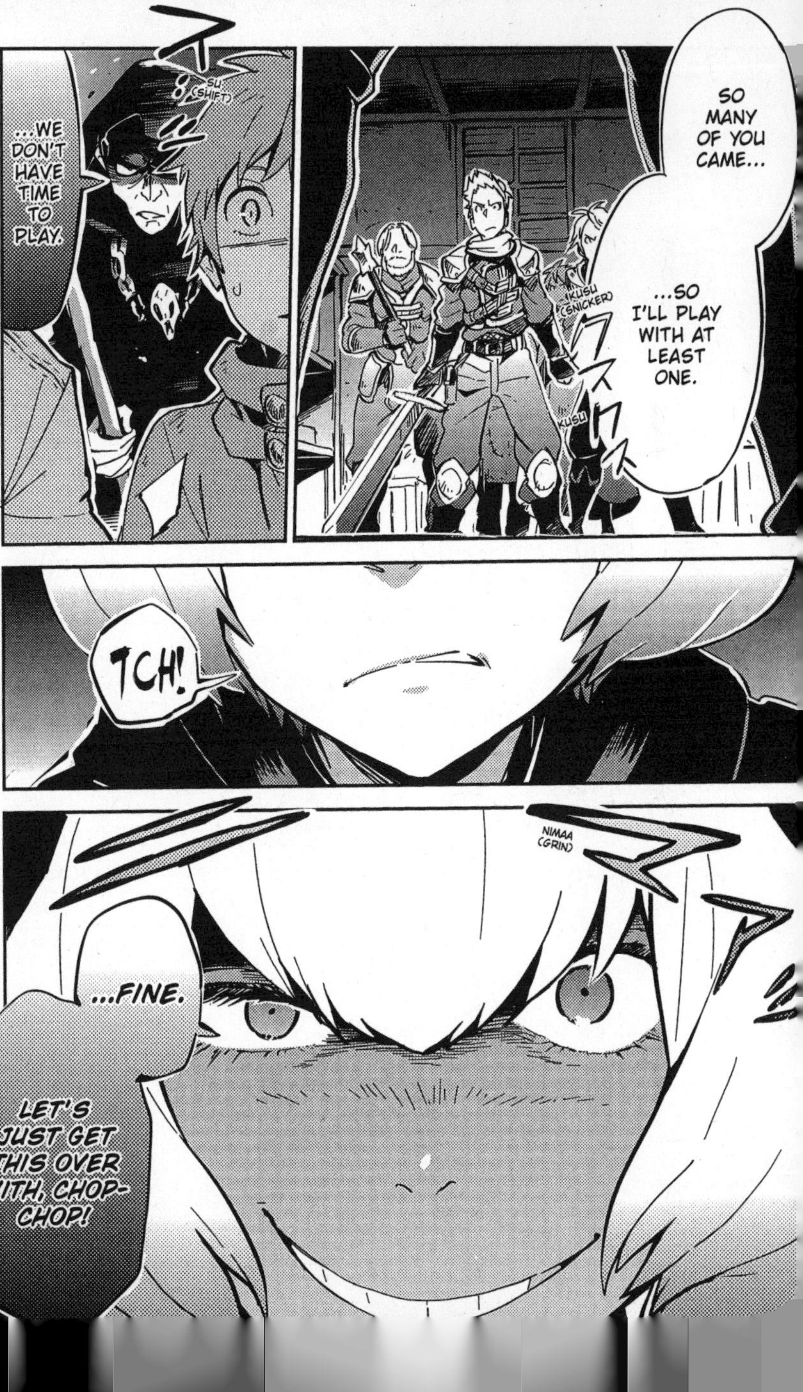
SO MANY OF YOU CAME...
...SO I'LL PLAY WITH AT LEAST ONE.
KUSU (SNICKER)
KUSU
SU (SHIFT)
...WE DON'T HAVE TIME TO PLAY.
TCH!
NIMAA (GRIN)
...FINE.
LET'S JUST GET THIS OVER WITH, CHOP-CHOP!

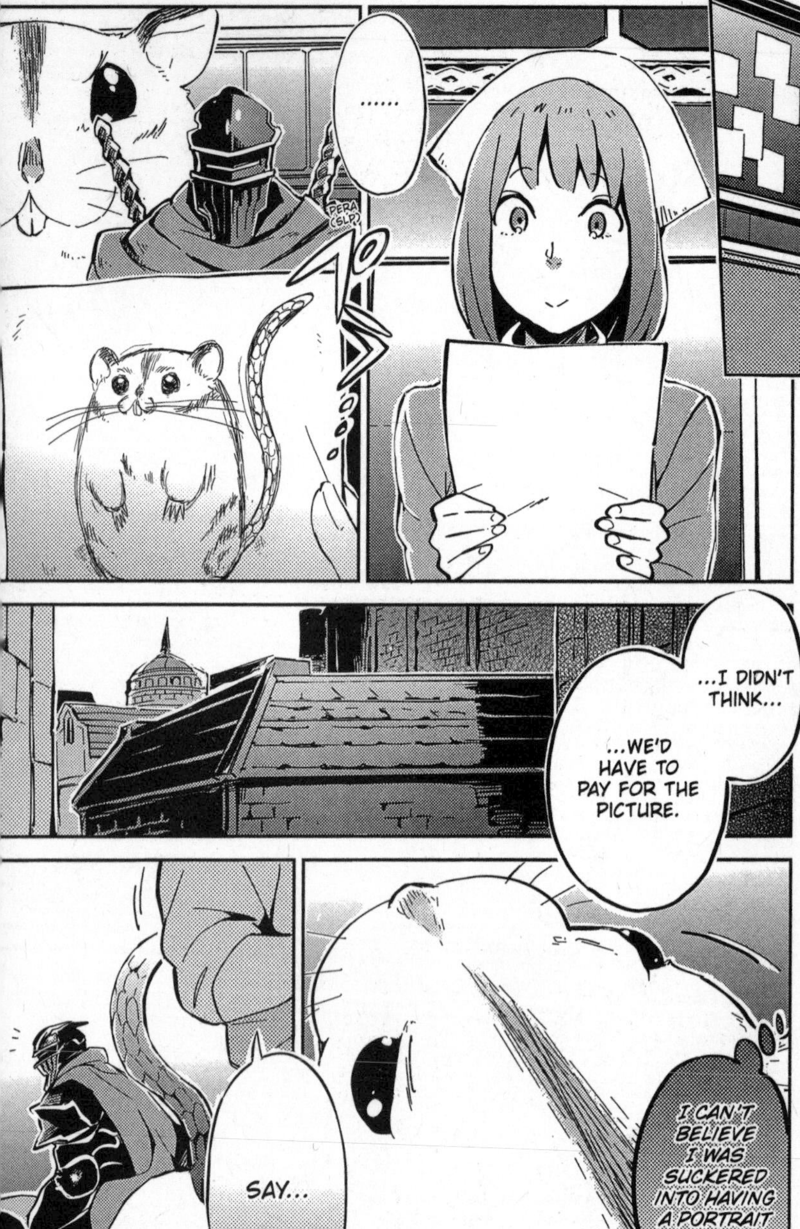
......
PERA (SLP)
...I DIDN'T THINK...
...WE'D HAVE TO PAY FOR THE PICTURE.
I CAN'T BELIEVE I WAS SUCKERED INTO HAVING A PORTRAIT DRAWN...
SAY...

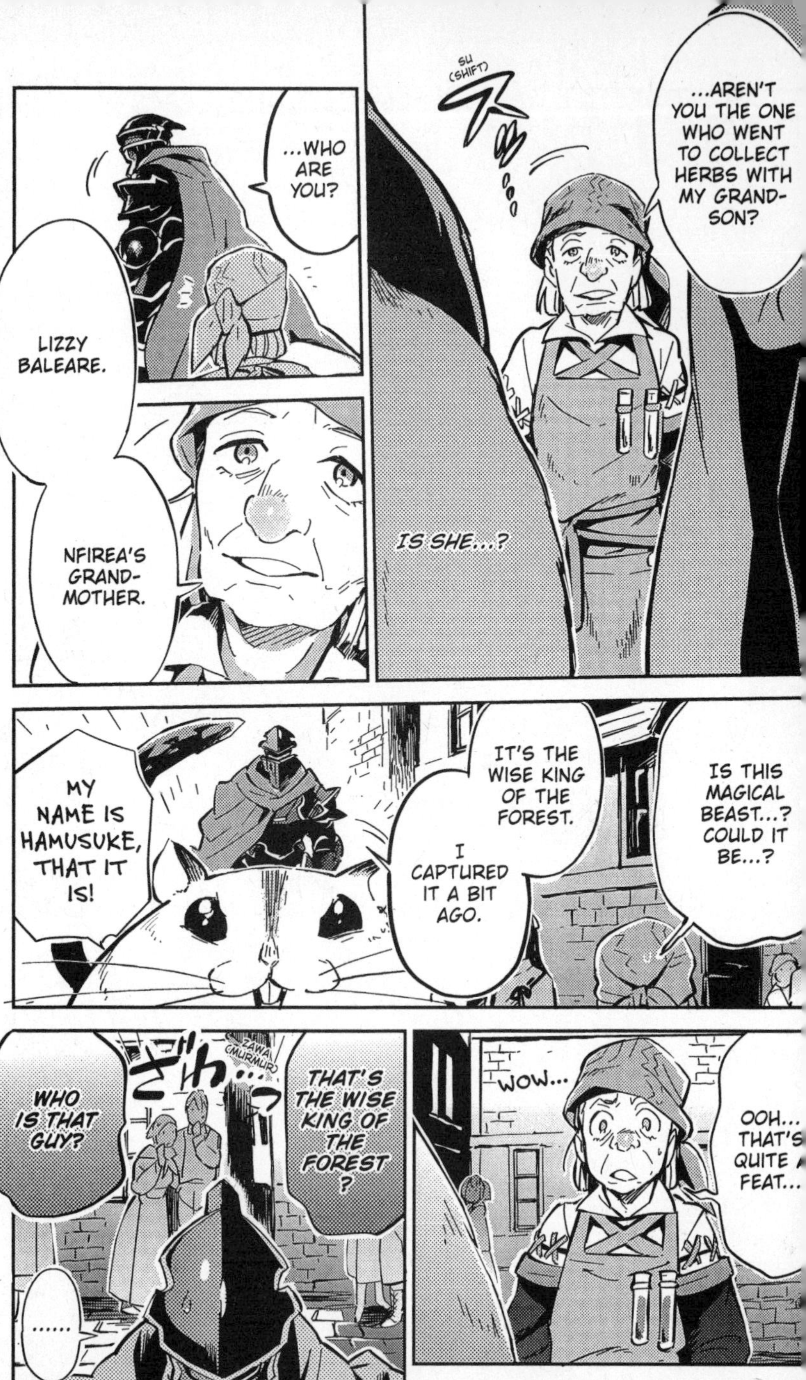
SU (SHIFT)
...AREN'T YOU THE ONE WHO WENT TO COLLECT HERBS WITH MY GRANDSON?
IS SHE...?
...WHO ARE YOU?
LIZZY BALEARE.
NFIREA'S GRANDMOTHER.
IS THIS MAGICAL BEAST...? COULD IT BE...?
IT'S THE WISE KING OF THE FOREST.
I CAPTURED IT A BIT AGO.
MY NAME IS HAMUSUKE, THAT IT IS!
OOH... THAT'S QUITE A FEAT...
WOW...
ZAWA (MURMUR)
THAT'S THE WISE KING OF THE FOREST?
WHO IS THAT GUY?
......

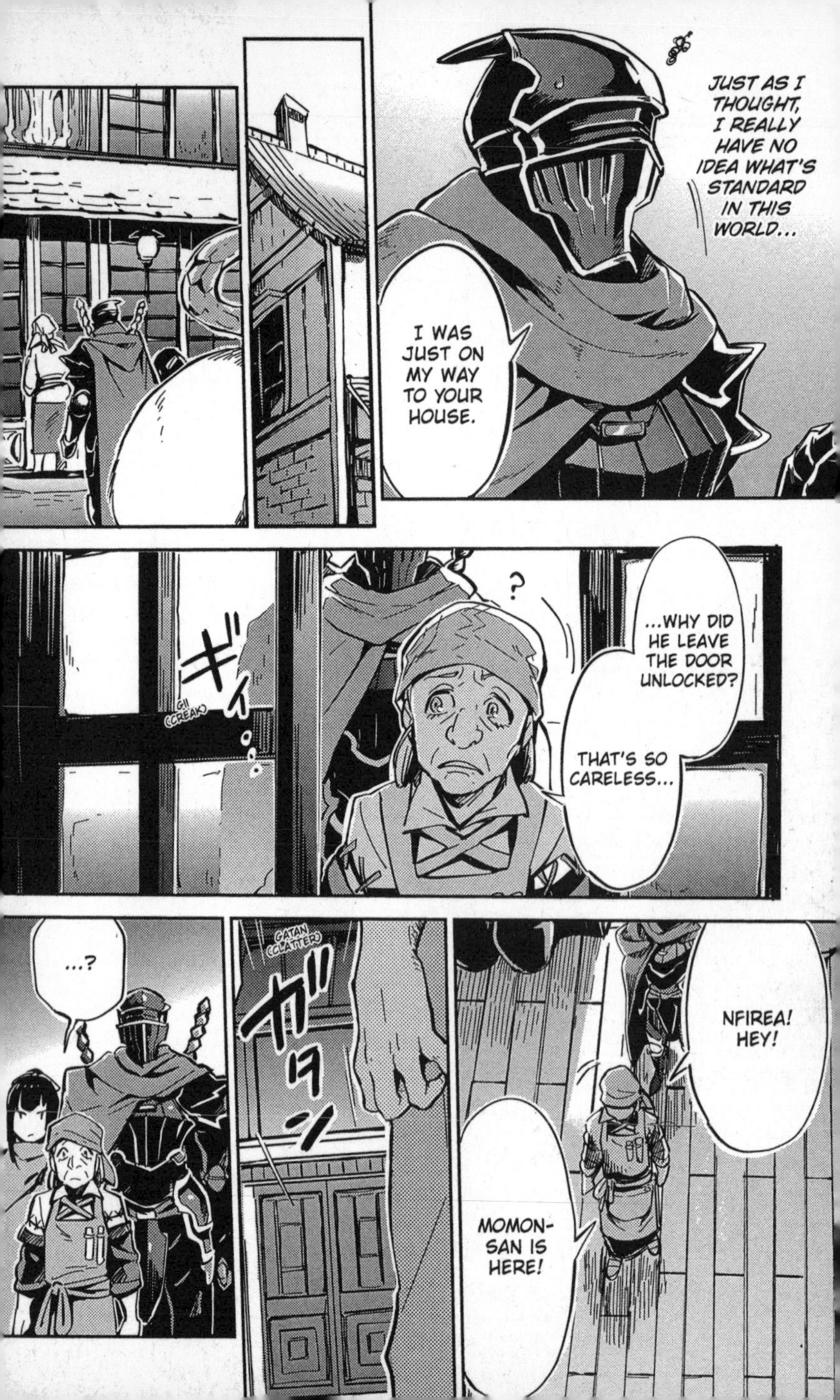
JUST AS I THOUGHT, I REALLY HAVE NO IDEA WHAT'S STANDARD IN THIS WORLD...
I WAS JUST ON MY WAY TO YOUR HOUSE.
?
...WHY DID HE LEAVE THE DOOR UNLOCKED?
THAT'S SO CARELESS...
ギィ…
GII (CREAK)
NFIREA! HEY!
MOMON-SAN IS HERE!
GATAN (CLATTER)
ガタッ
...?

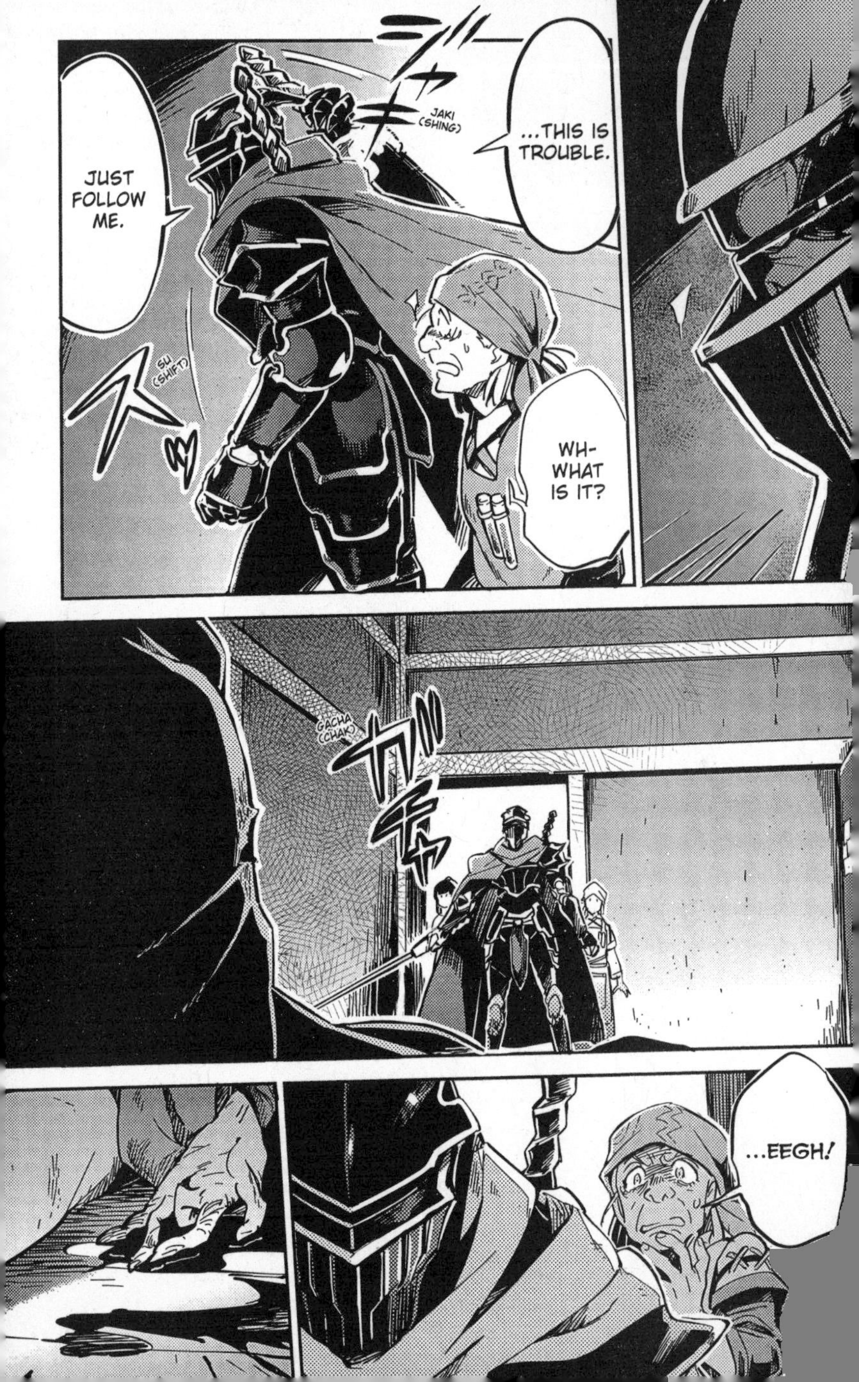
...THIS IS TROUBLE.
JAKI (SHING)
JUST FOLLOW ME.
WH- WHAT IS IT?
SU (SHIFT)
GACHA (CHAK)
...EEGH!

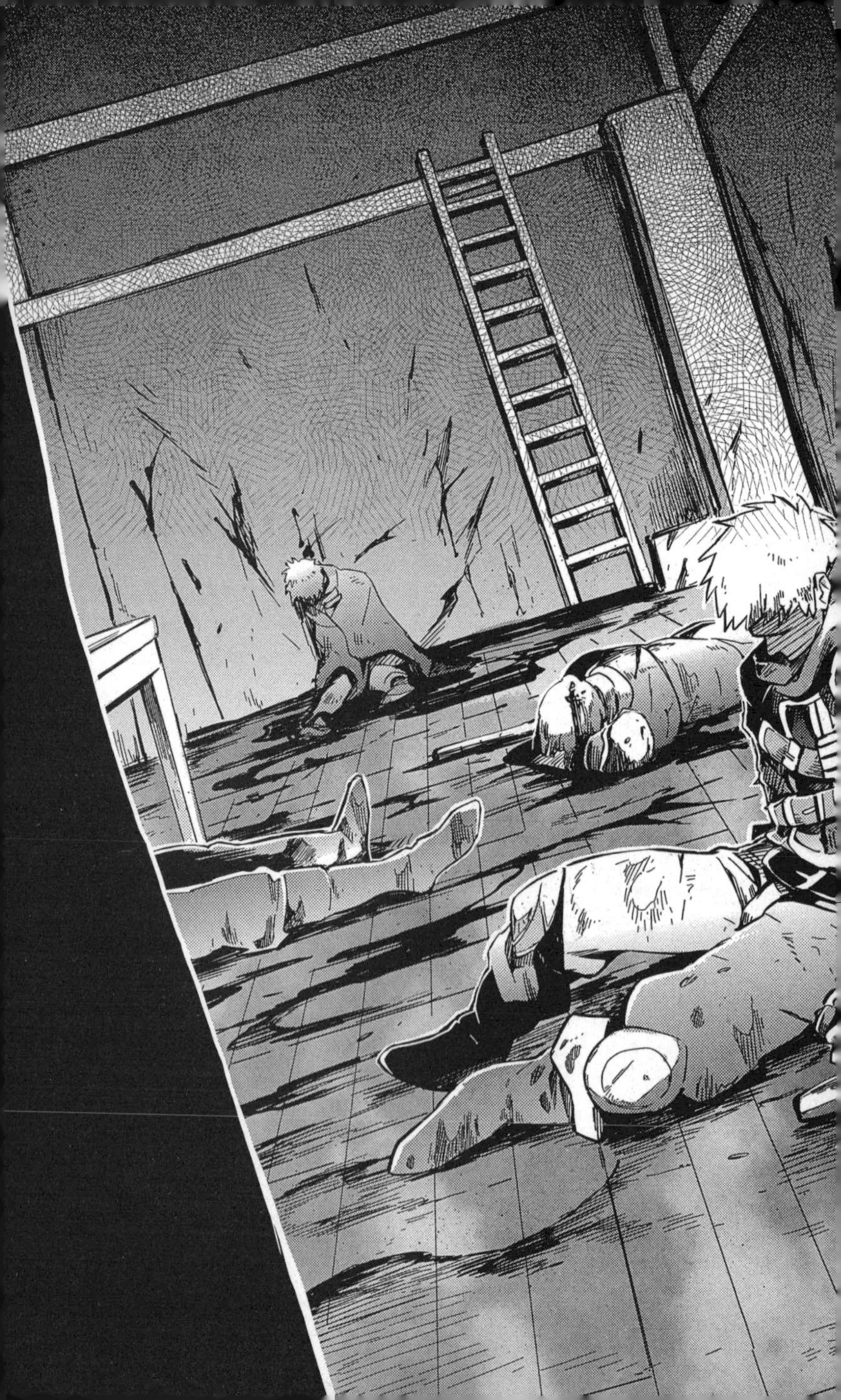

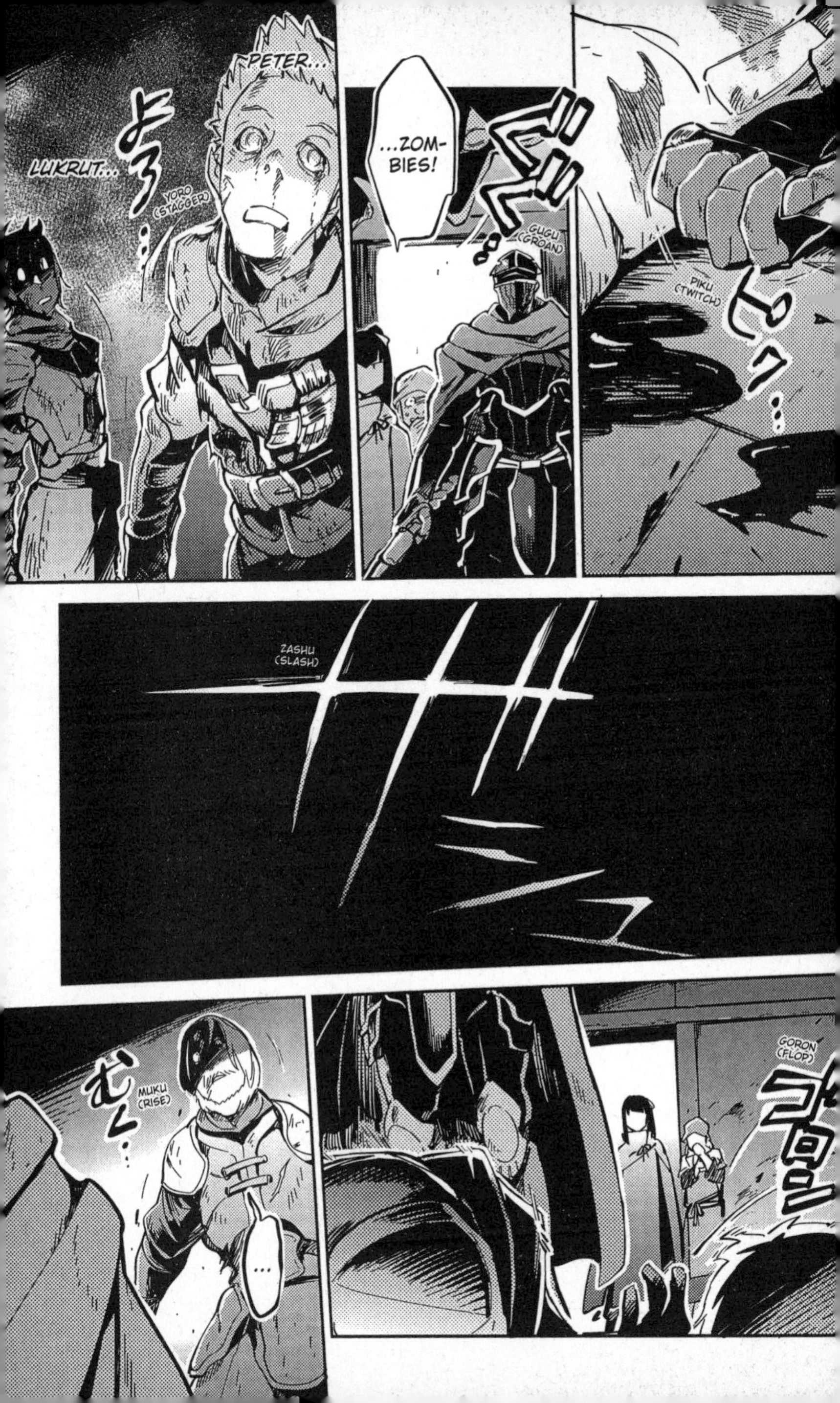
PIKU (TWITCH)
...ZOM-BIES!
GUGU (GROAN)
PETER...
LUKRUT...
YORO (STAGGER)
ZASHU (SLASH)
GORON (FLOP)
MUKU (RISE)
...

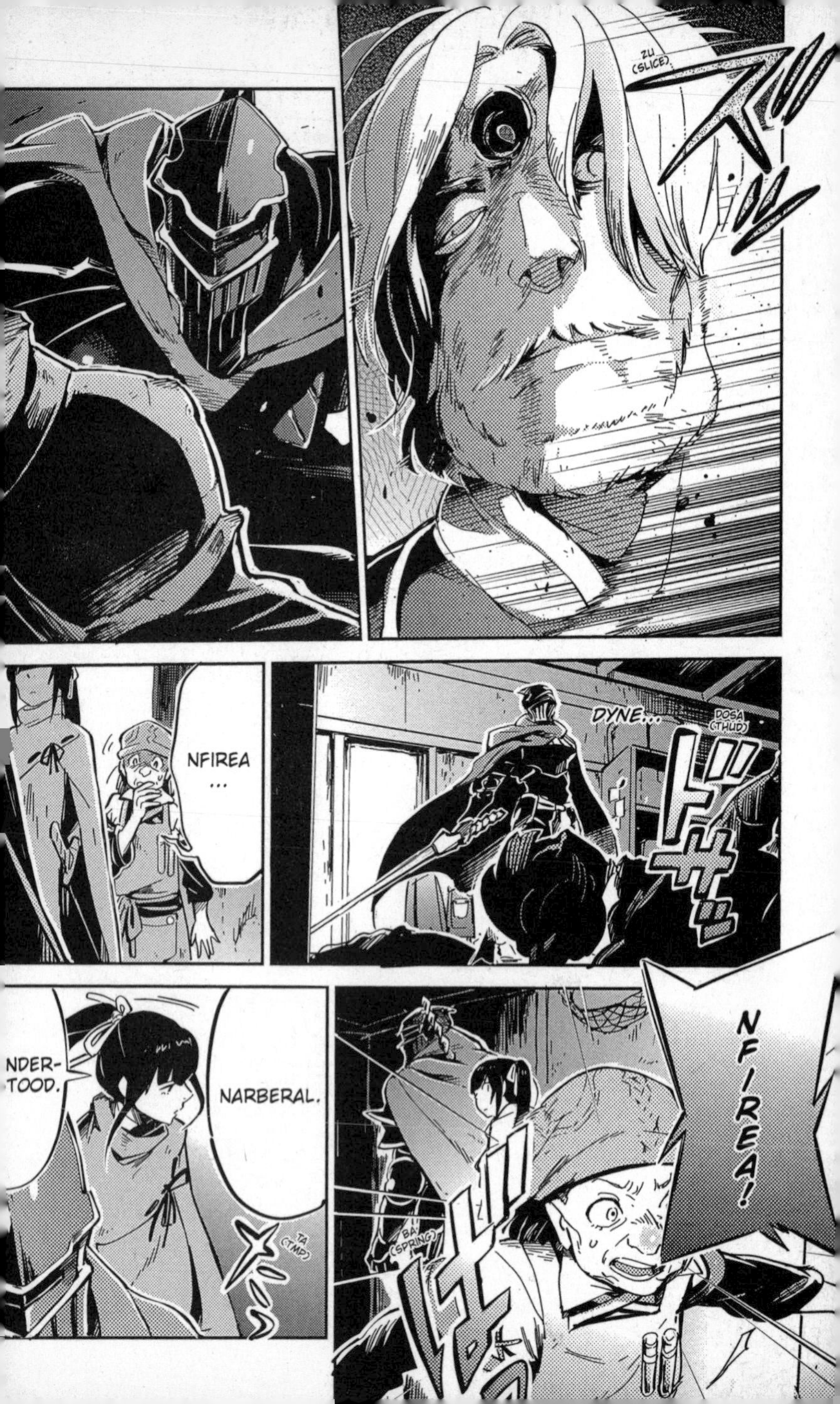
ZU (SLICE)
DYNE...
DOSA (THUD)
NFIREA ...
NFIREA!
BA (SPRING)
NARBERAL.
NDER-TOOD.
TA (TMP)

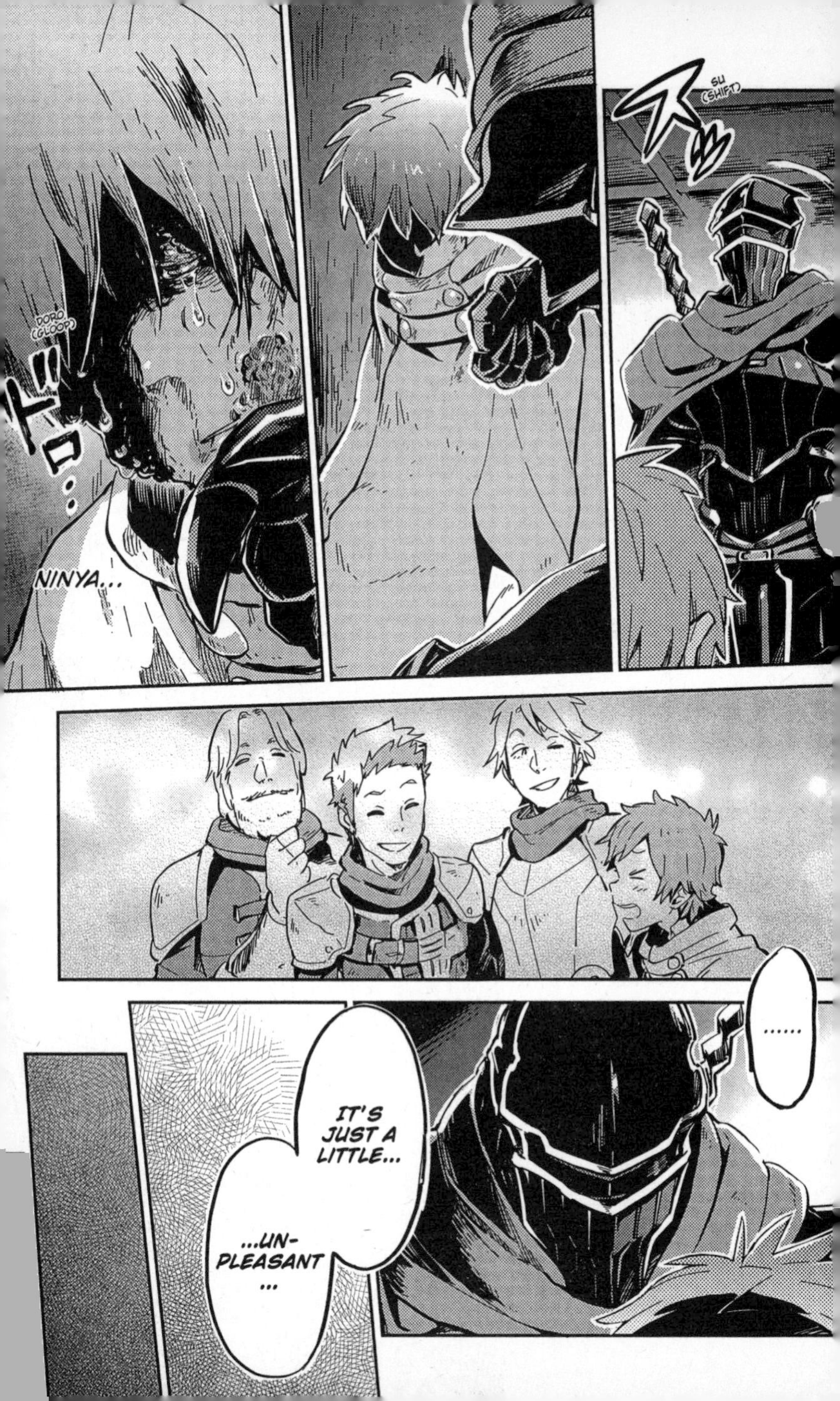
スッ
SU (SHIFT)
ドロ‥
DORO (GLOOP)
NINYA...
......
IT'S JUST A LITTLE...
...UN-PLEASANT...

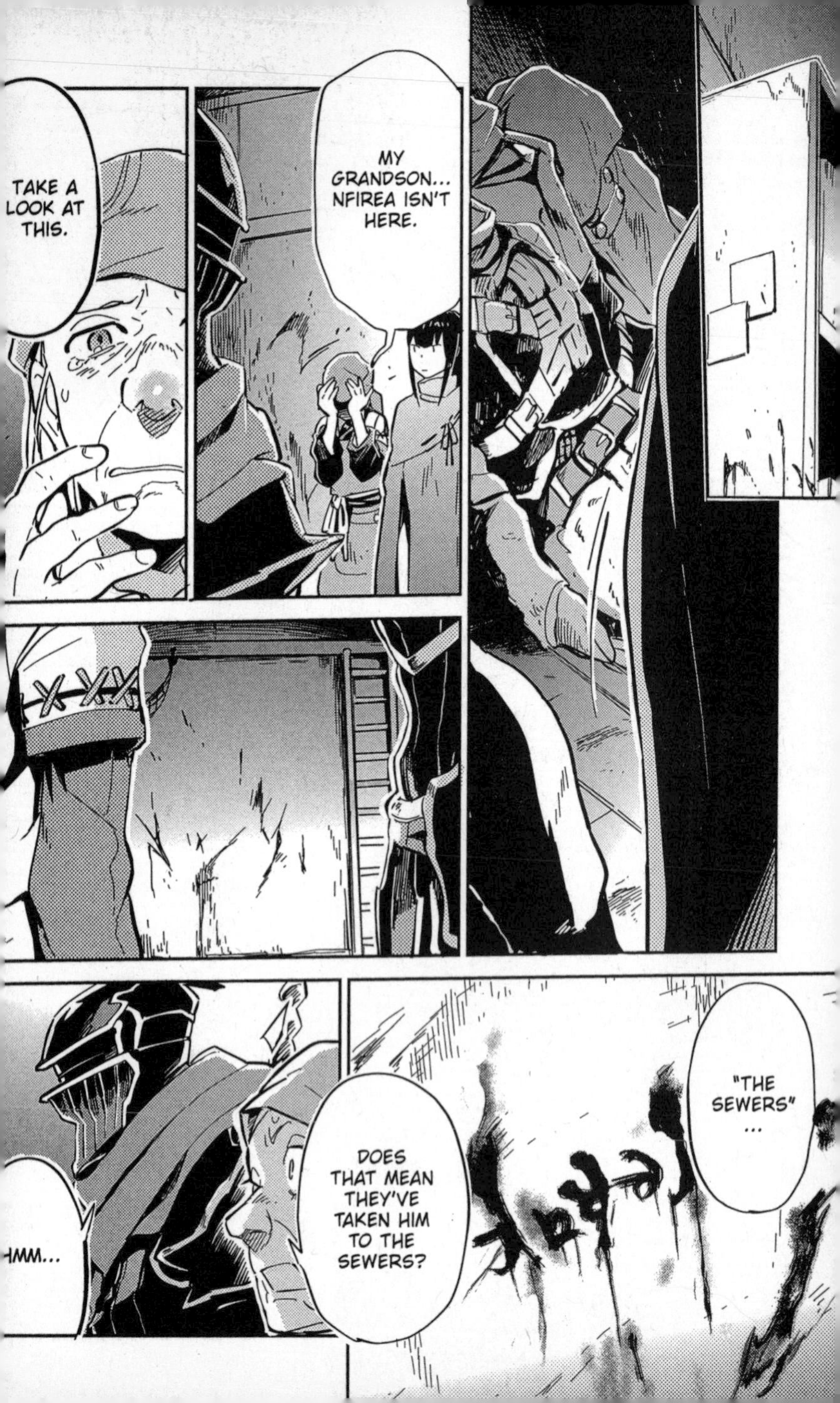
MY GRANDSON... NFIREA ISN'T HERE.
TAKE A LOOK AT THIS.
"THE SEWERS" ...
DOES THAT MEAN THEY'VE TAKEN HIM TO THE SEWERS?
HMM...

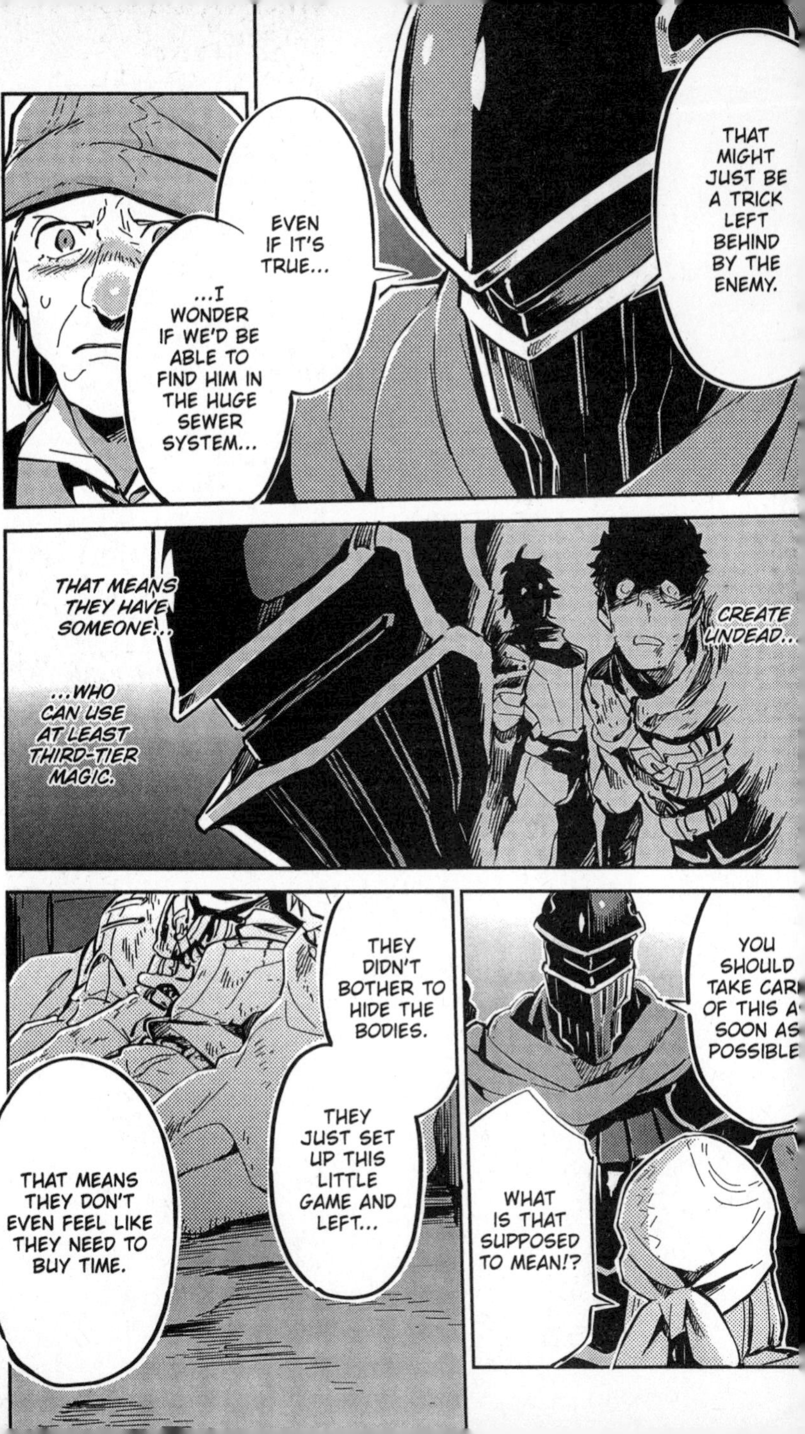
THAT MIGHT JUST BE A TRICK LEFT BEHIND BY THE ENEMY.
EVEN IF IT'S TRUE...
...I WONDER IF WE'D BE ABLE TO FIND HIM IN THE HUGE SEWER SYSTEM...
CREATE UNDEAD...
THAT MEANS THEY HAVE SOMEONE...
...WHO CAN USE AT LEAST THIRD-TIER MAGIC.
YOU SHOULD TAKE CAR OF THIS A SOON AS POSSIBLE
WHAT IS THAT SUPPOSED TO MEAN!?
THEY DIDN'T BOTHER TO HIDE THE BODIES.
THEY JUST SET UP THIS LITTLE GAME AND LEFT...
THAT MEANS THEY DON'T EVEN FEEL LIKE THEY NEED TO BUY TIME.

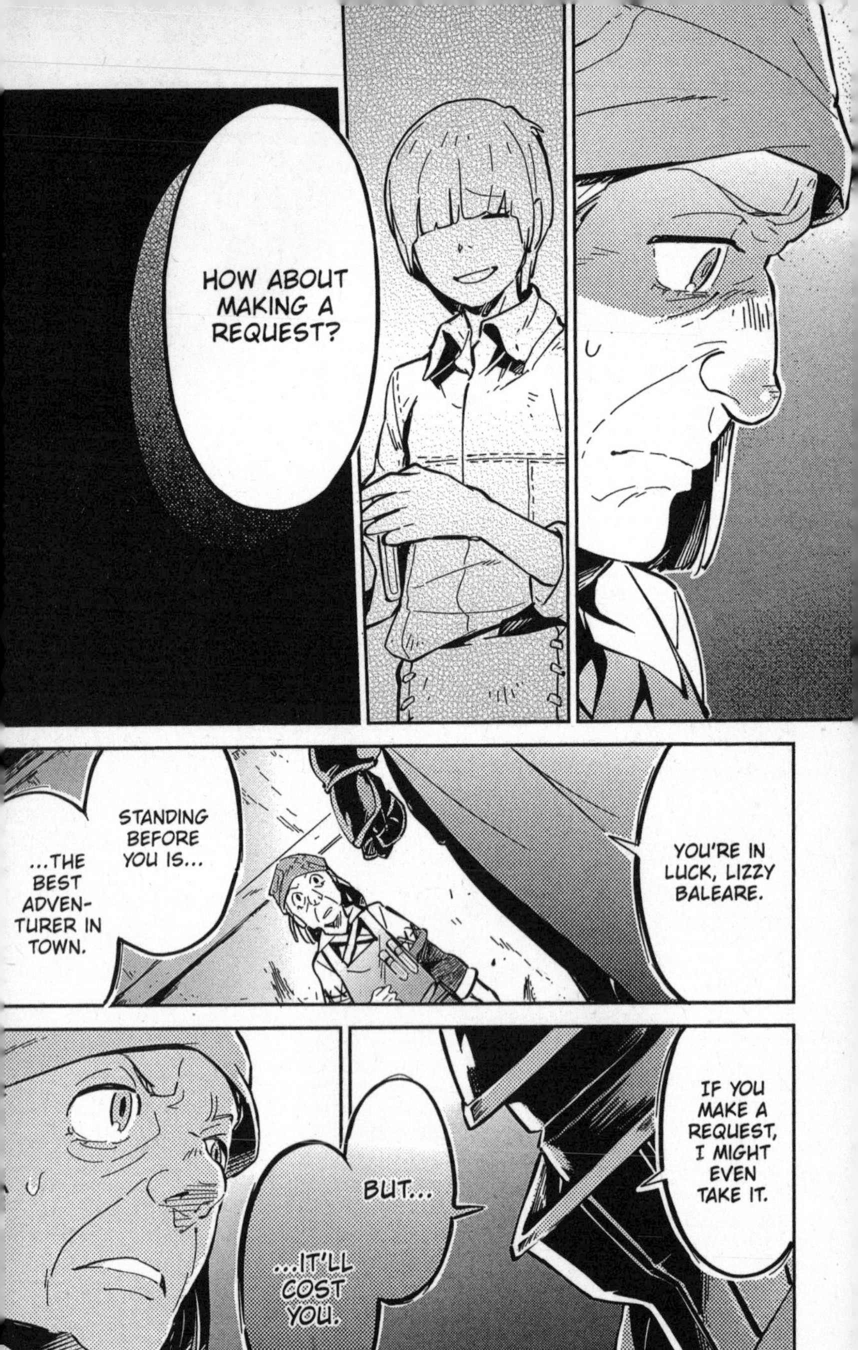
HOW ABOUT MAKING A REQUEST?
YOU'RE IN LUCK, LIZZY BALEARE.
STANDING BEFORE YOU IS...
...THE BEST ADVEN-TURER IN TOWN.
IF YOU MAKE A REQUEST, I MIGHT EVEN TAKE IT.
BUT...
...IT'LL COST YOU.

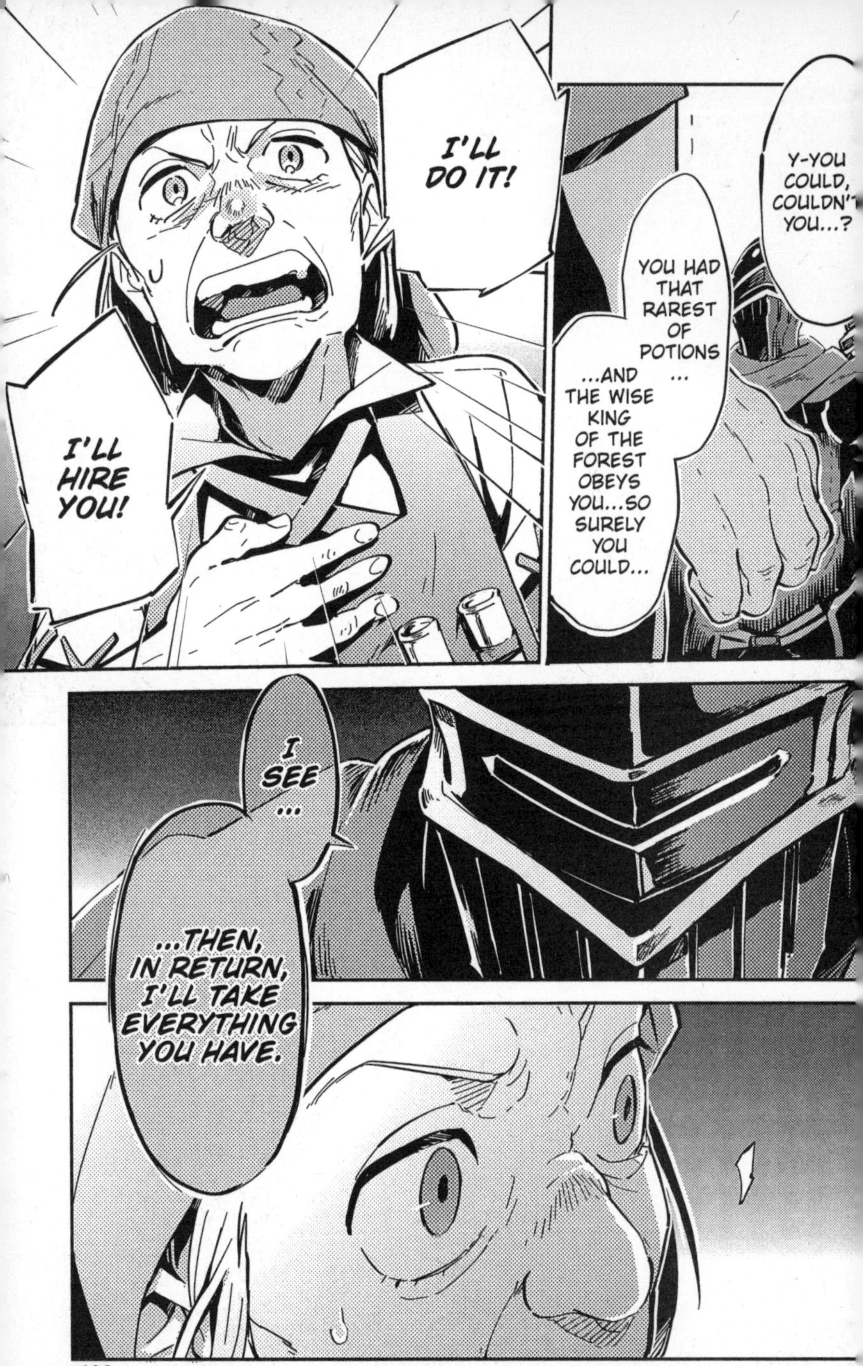
Y-YOU COULD, COULDN'T YOU...?
YOU HAD THAT RAREST OF POTIONS...
...AND THE WISE KING OF THE FOREST OBEYS YOU...SO SURELY YOU COULD...
I'LL DO IT!
I'LL HIRE YOU!
I SEE...
...THEN, IN RETURN, I'LL TAKE EVERYTHING YOU HAVE.

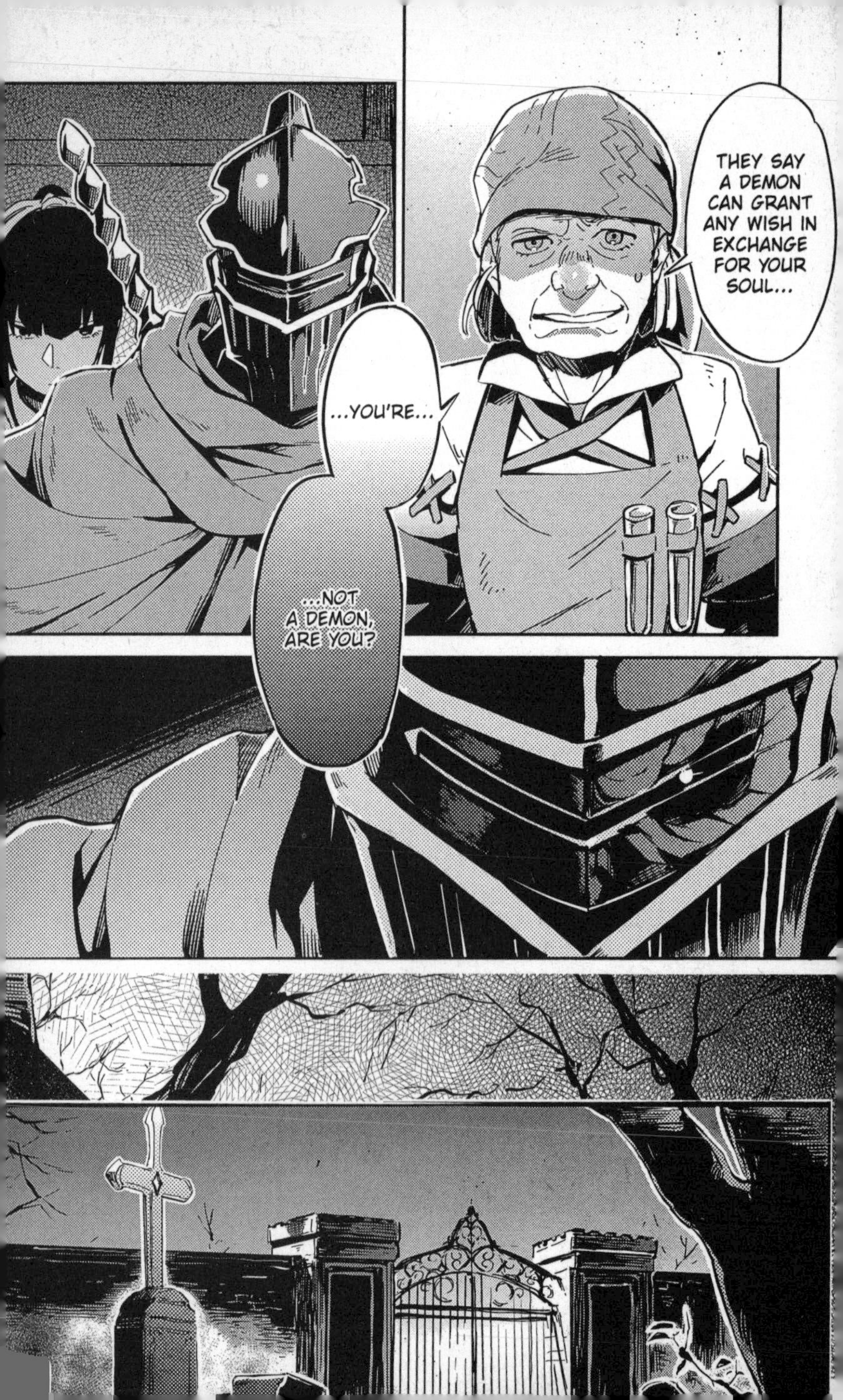
THEY SAY A DEMON CAN GRANT ANY WISH IN EXCHANGE FOR YOUR SOUL...
...YOU'RE...
...NOT A DEMON, ARE YOU?

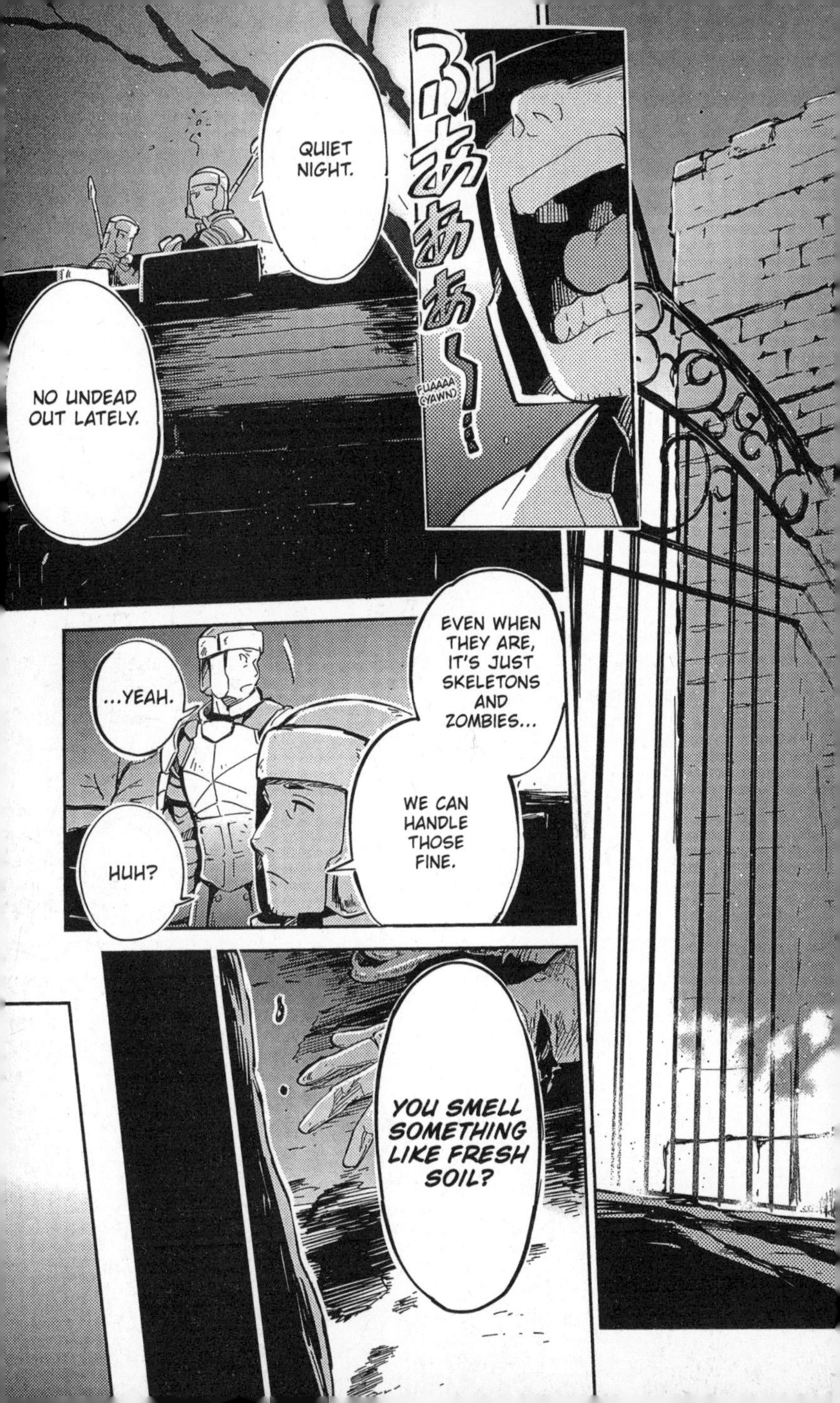
ふあああ～！！
FUAAAA (YAWN)
QUIET NIGHT.
NO UNDEAD OUT LATELY.
EVEN WHEN THEY ARE, IT'S JUST SKELETONS AND ZOMBIES...
WE CAN HANDLE THOSE FINE.
...YEAH.
HUH?
YOU SMELL SOMETHING LIKE FRESH SOIL?

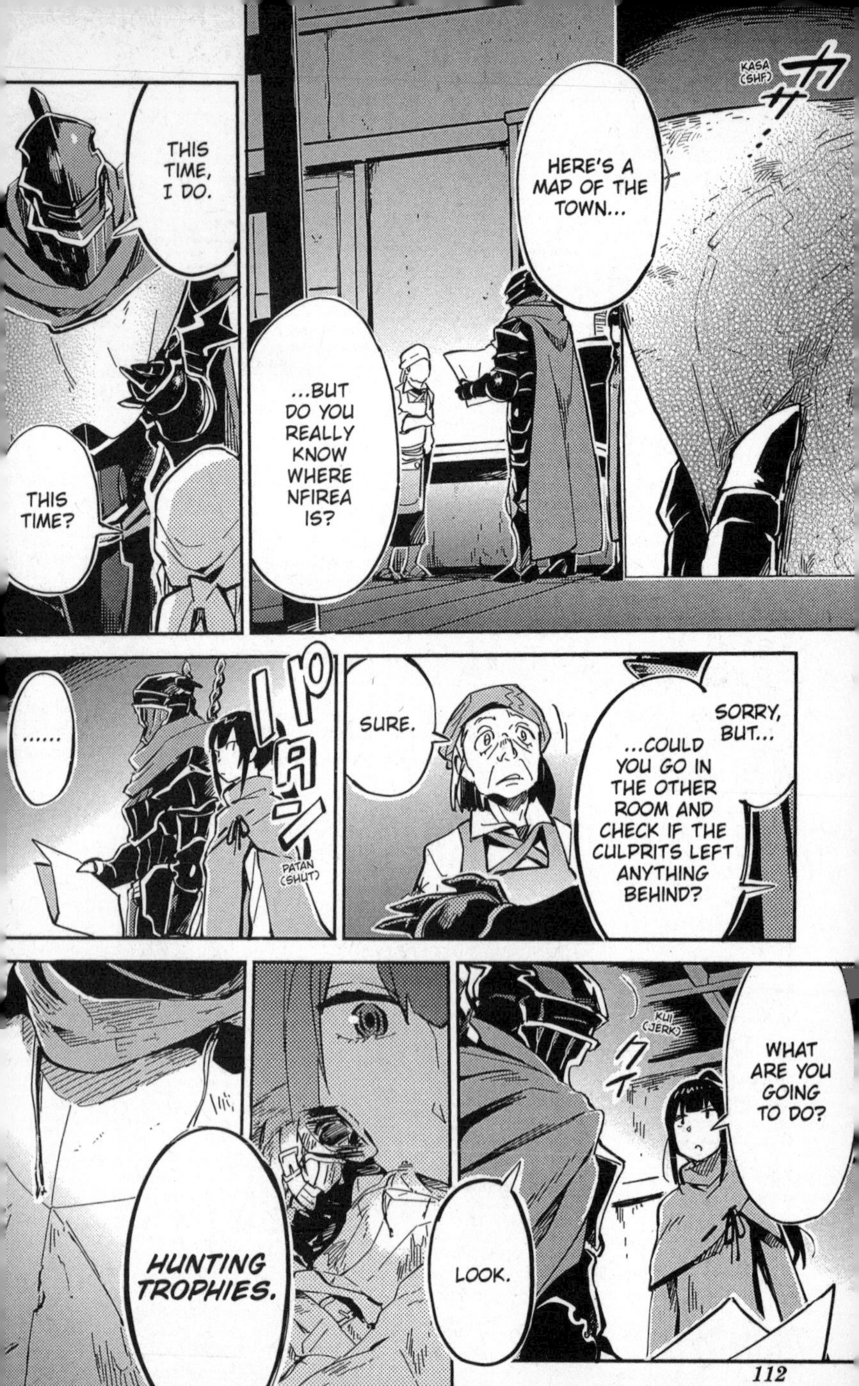
KASA (SHF)
HERE'S A MAP OF THE TOWN...
...BUT DO YOU REALLY KNOW WHERE NFIREA IS?
THIS TIME, I DO.
THIS TIME?
SORRY, BUT...
...COULD YOU GO IN THE OTHER ROOM AND CHECK IF THE CULPRITS LEFT ANYTHING BEHIND?
SURE.
PATAN (SHUT)
......
WHAT ARE YOU GOING TO DO?
KUI (JERK)
LOOK.
HUNTING TROPHIES.

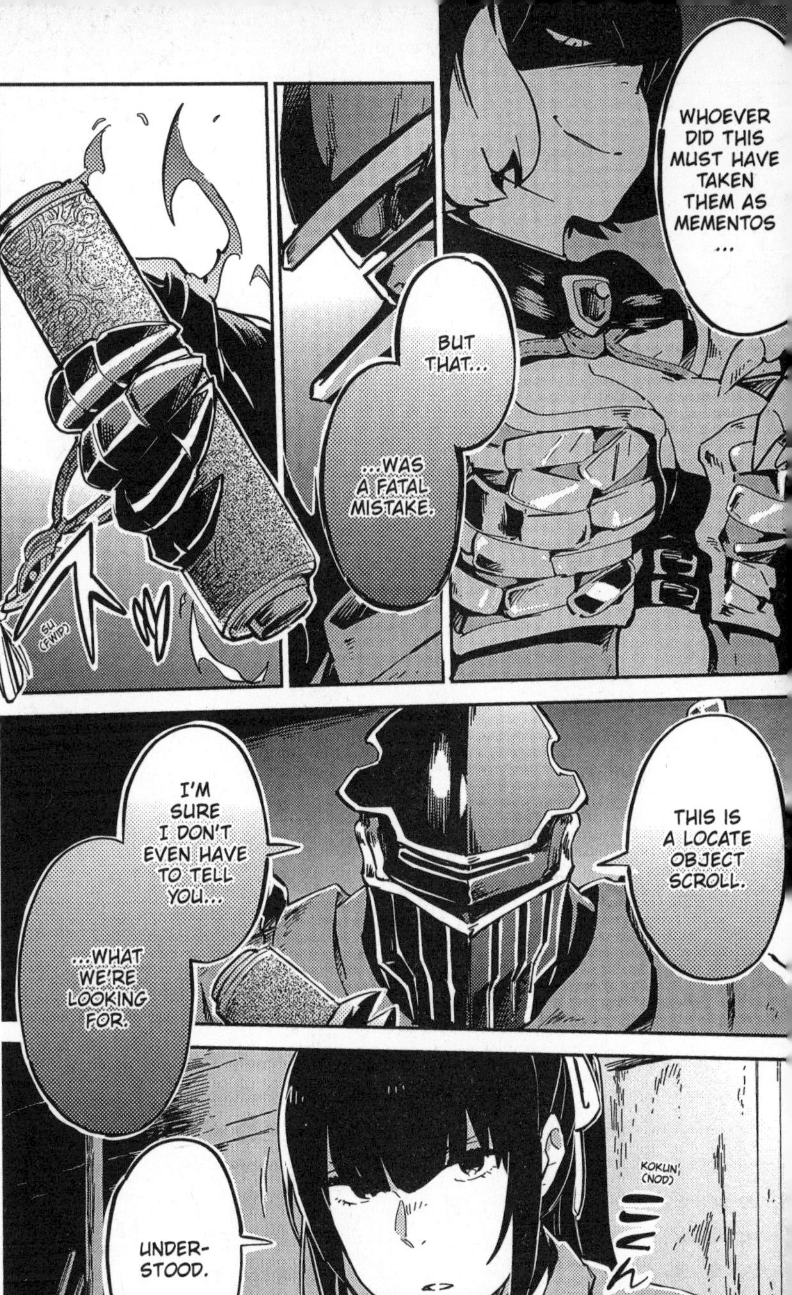
WHOEVER DID THIS MUST HAVE TAKEN THEM AS MEMENTOS ...
BUT THAT...
...WAS A FATAL MISTAKE.
SU (FWIP)
THIS IS A LOCATE OBJECT SCROLL.
I'M SURE I DON'T EVEN HAVE TO TELL YOU...
...WHAT WE'RE LOOKING FOR.
KOKUN (NOD)
UNDER-STOOD.

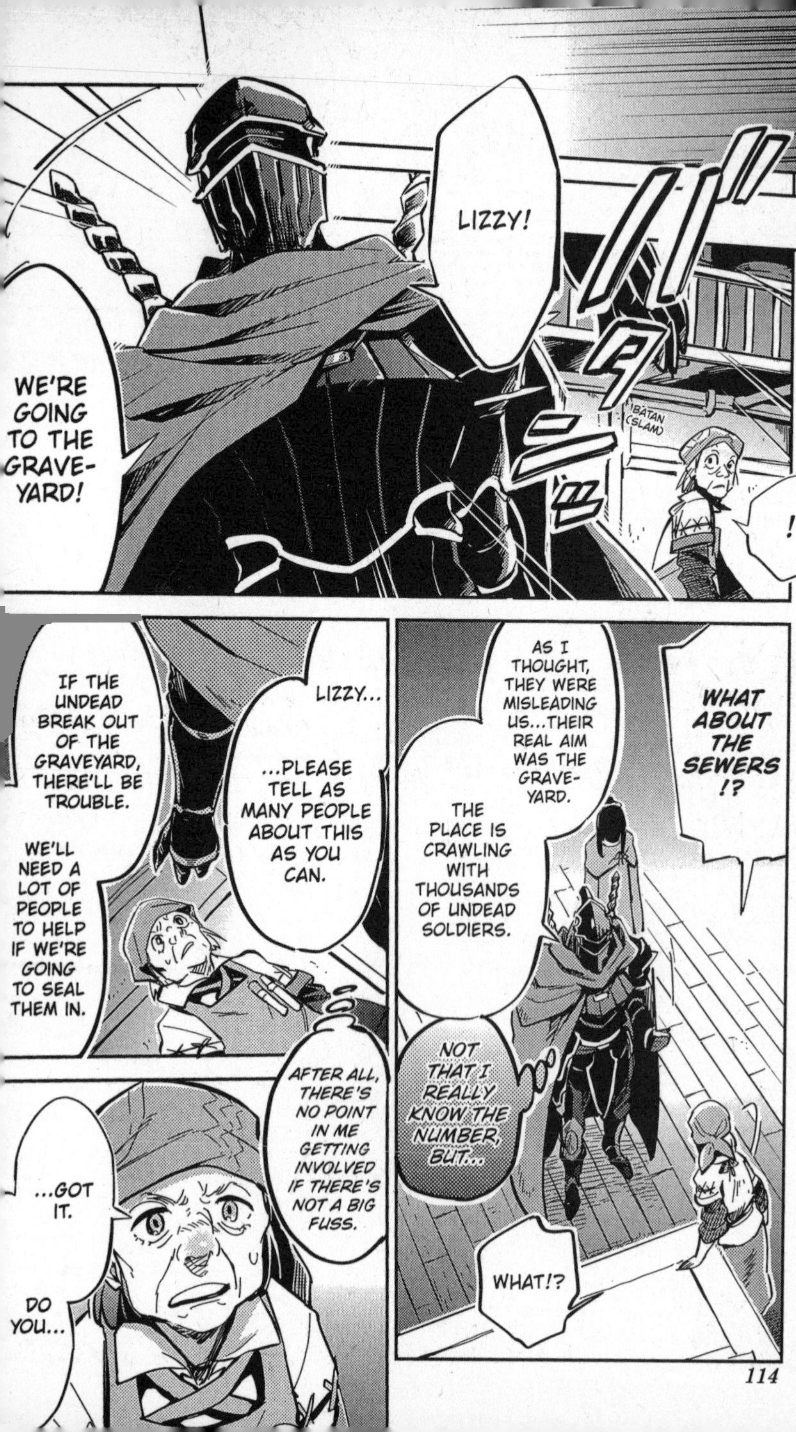

LIZZY!
BATAN (SLAM)
!
WE'RE GOING TO THE GRAVEYARD!
WHAT ABOUT THE SEWERS!?
AS I THOUGHT, THEY WERE MISLEADING US...THEIR REAL AIM WAS THE GRAVEYARD.
THE PLACE IS CRAWLING WITH THOUSANDS OF UNDEAD SOLDIERS.
NOT THAT I REALLY KNOW THE NUMBER, BUT...
WHAT!?
LIZZY...
...PLEASE TELL AS MANY PEOPLE ABOUT THIS AS YOU CAN.
IF THE UNDEAD BREAK OUT OF THE GRAVEYARD, THERE'LL BE TROUBLE.
WE'LL NEED A LOT OF PEOPLE TO HELP IF WE'RE GOING TO SEAL THEM IN.
AFTER ALL, THERE'S NO POINT IN ME GETTING INVOLVED IF THERE'S NOT A BIG FUSS.
...GOT IT.
DO YOU...

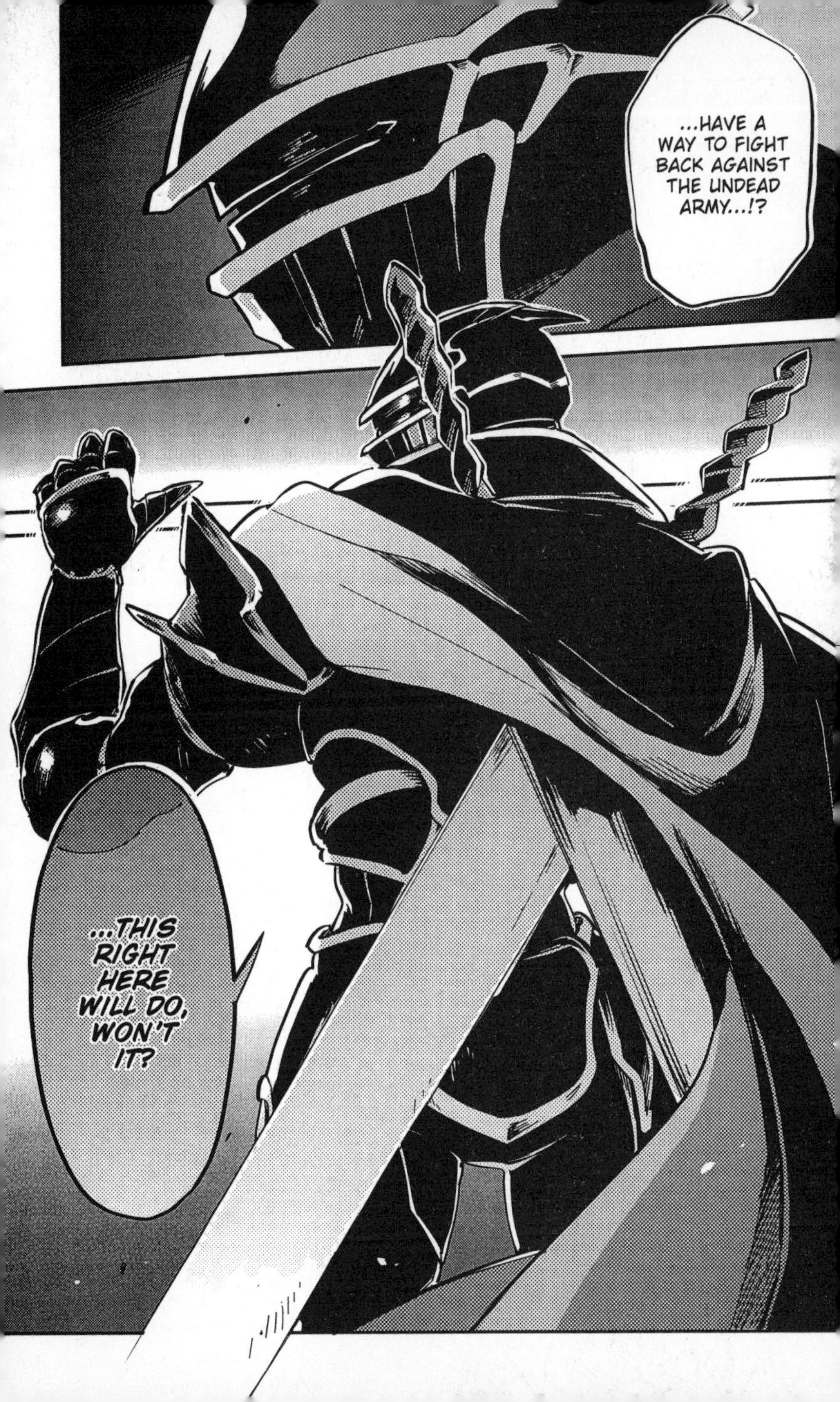
...HAVE A WAY TO FIGHT BACK AGAINST THE UNDEAD ARMY...!?
...THIS RIGHT HERE WILL DO, WON'T IT?

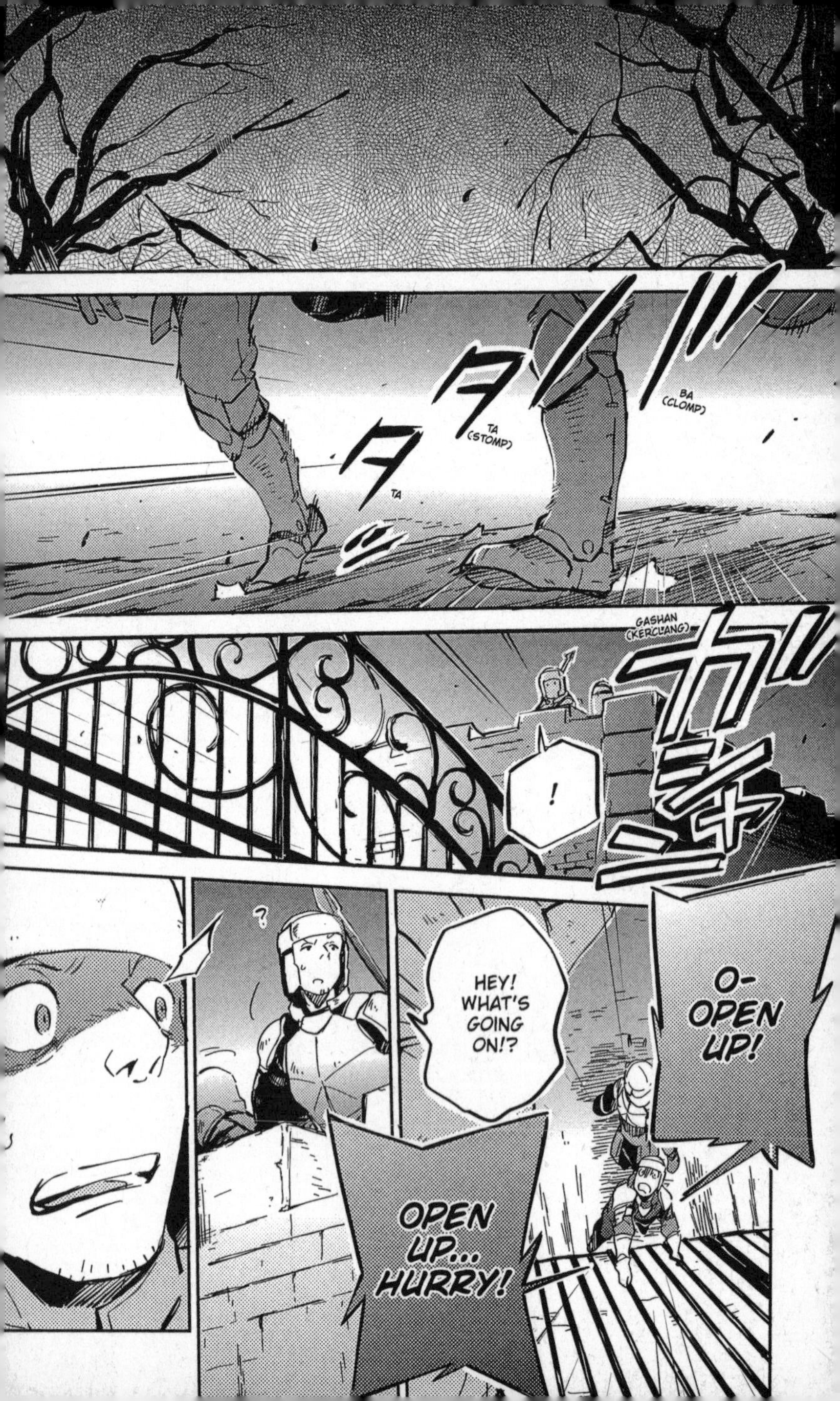
BA (CLOMP)
TA (STOMP)
TA
GASHAN (KERCLANG)
!
O-OPEN UP!
HEY! WHAT'S GOING ON!?
OPEN UP... HURRY!
?

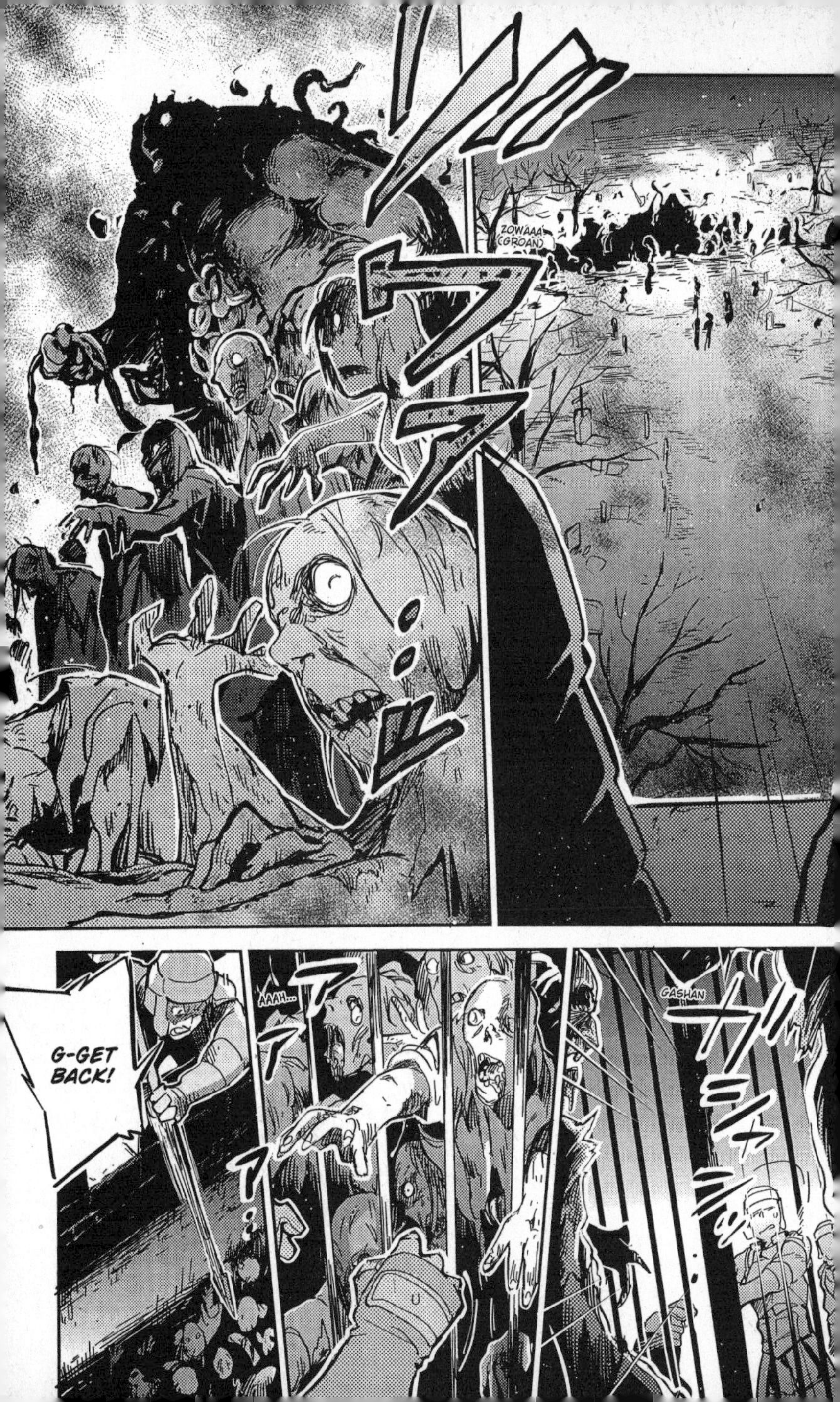
ZOWAAA (GROAN)
GASHAN
AAAH...
G-GET BACK!

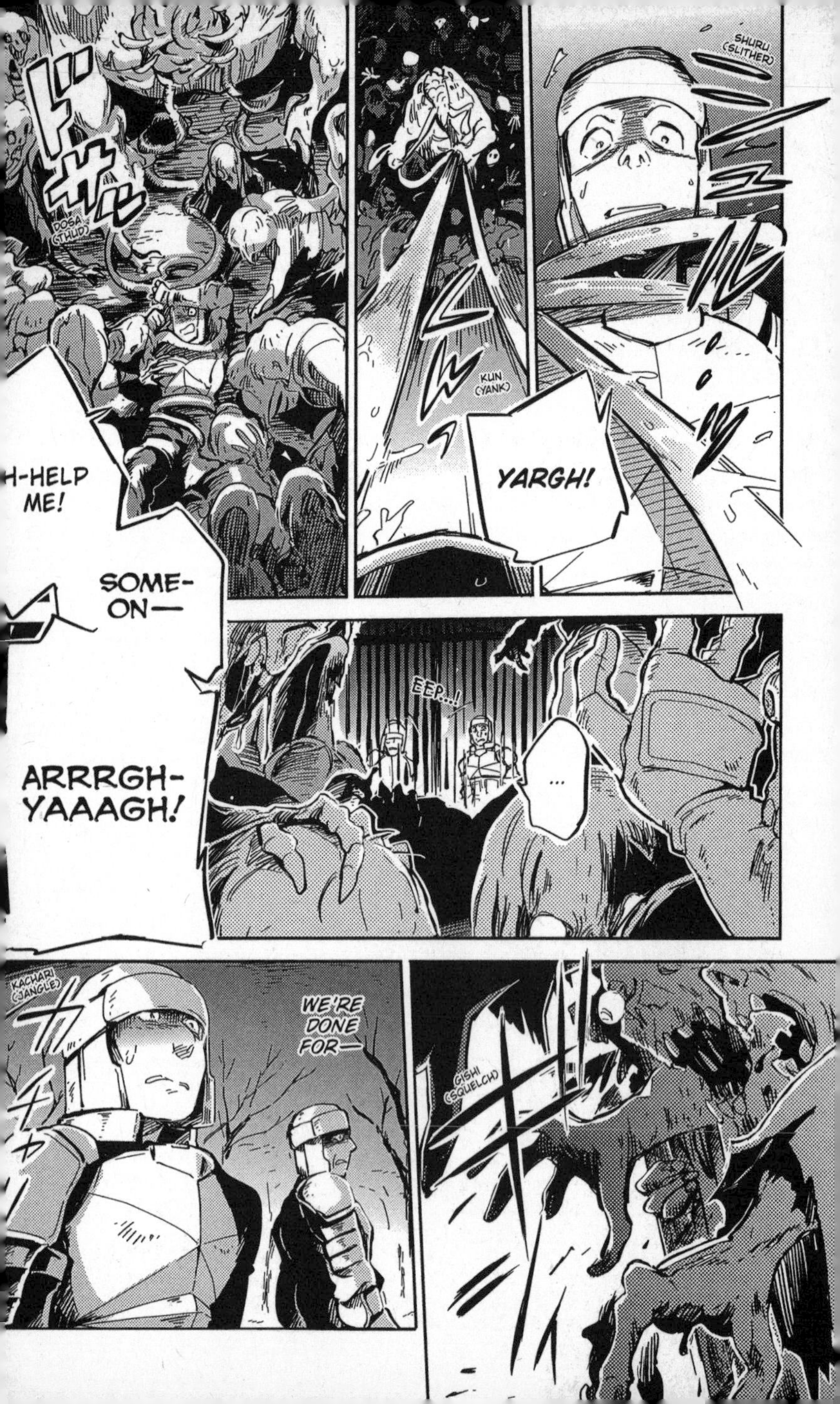
SHURU (SLITHER)
YARGH!
KUN (YANK)
DOSA (THUD)
H-HELP ME!
SOME-ON—
ARRRGH-YAAAGH!
EEP...!
...
GISHI (SQUELCH)
KACHARI (JANGLE)
WE'RE DONE FOR—

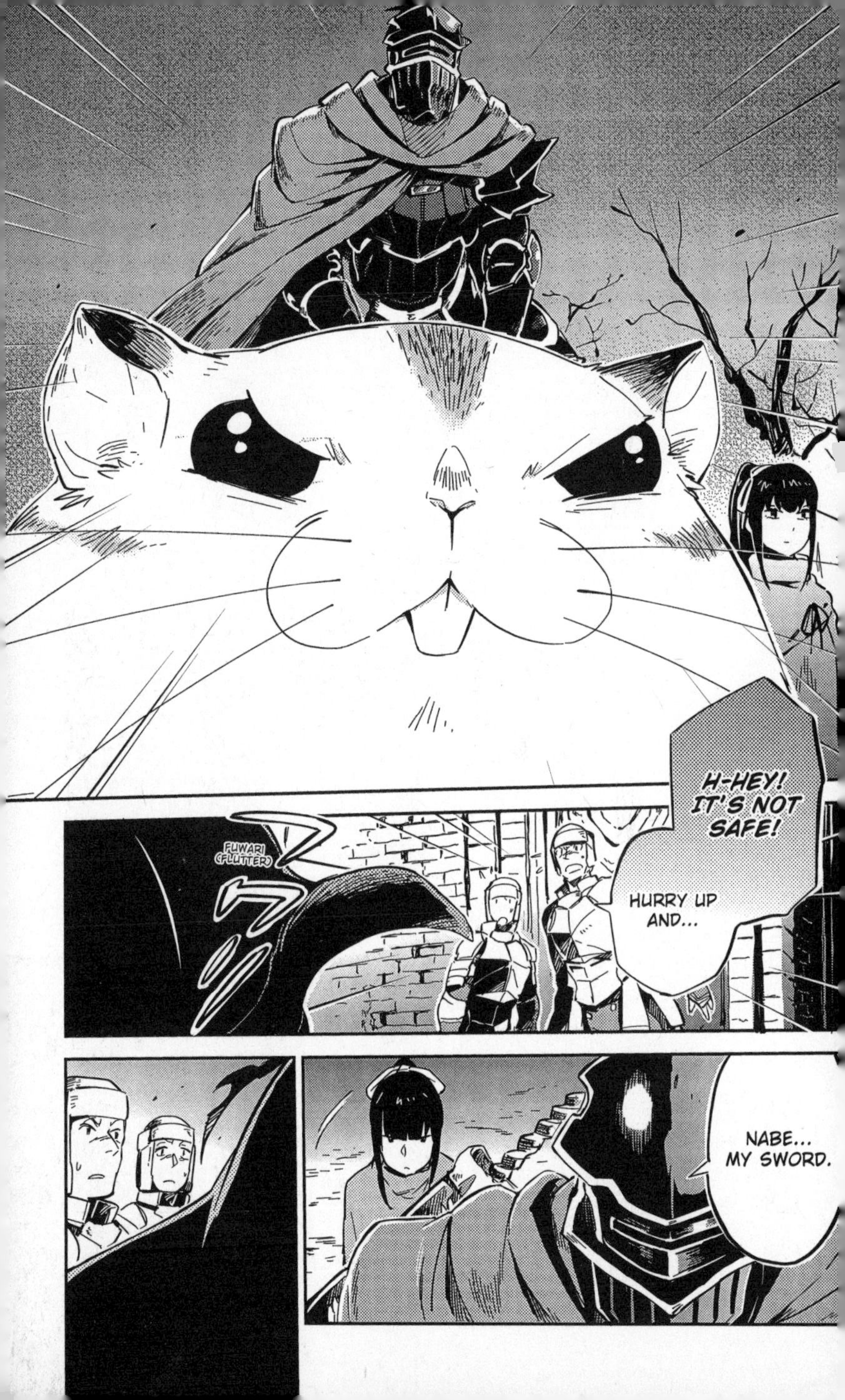
H-HEY! IT'S NOT SAFE!
HURRY UP AND...
FUWARI (FLUTTER)
NABE... MY SWORD.

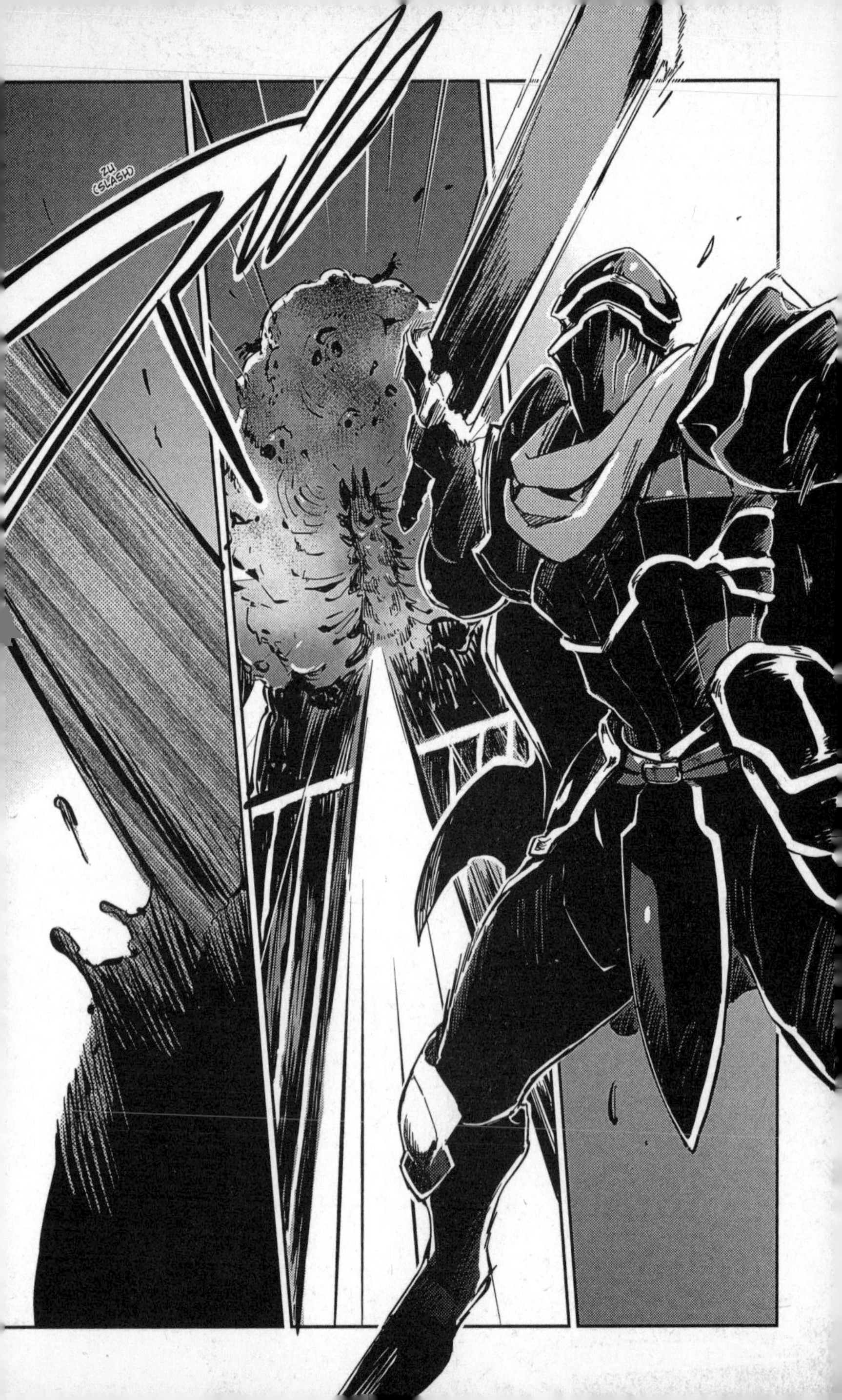
ZU
(SLASH)

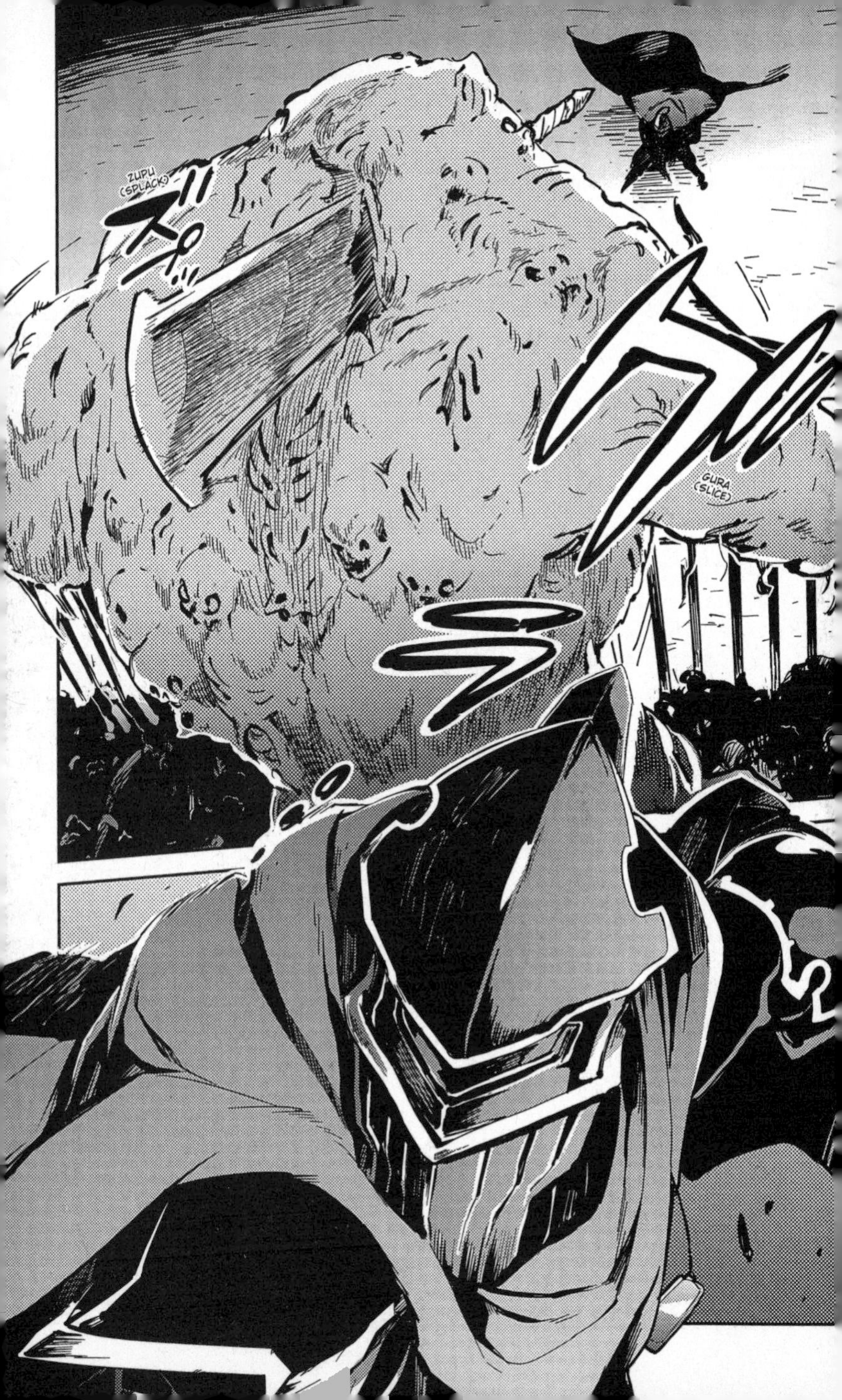
ZUPU (SPLACK)
GURA (SLICE)

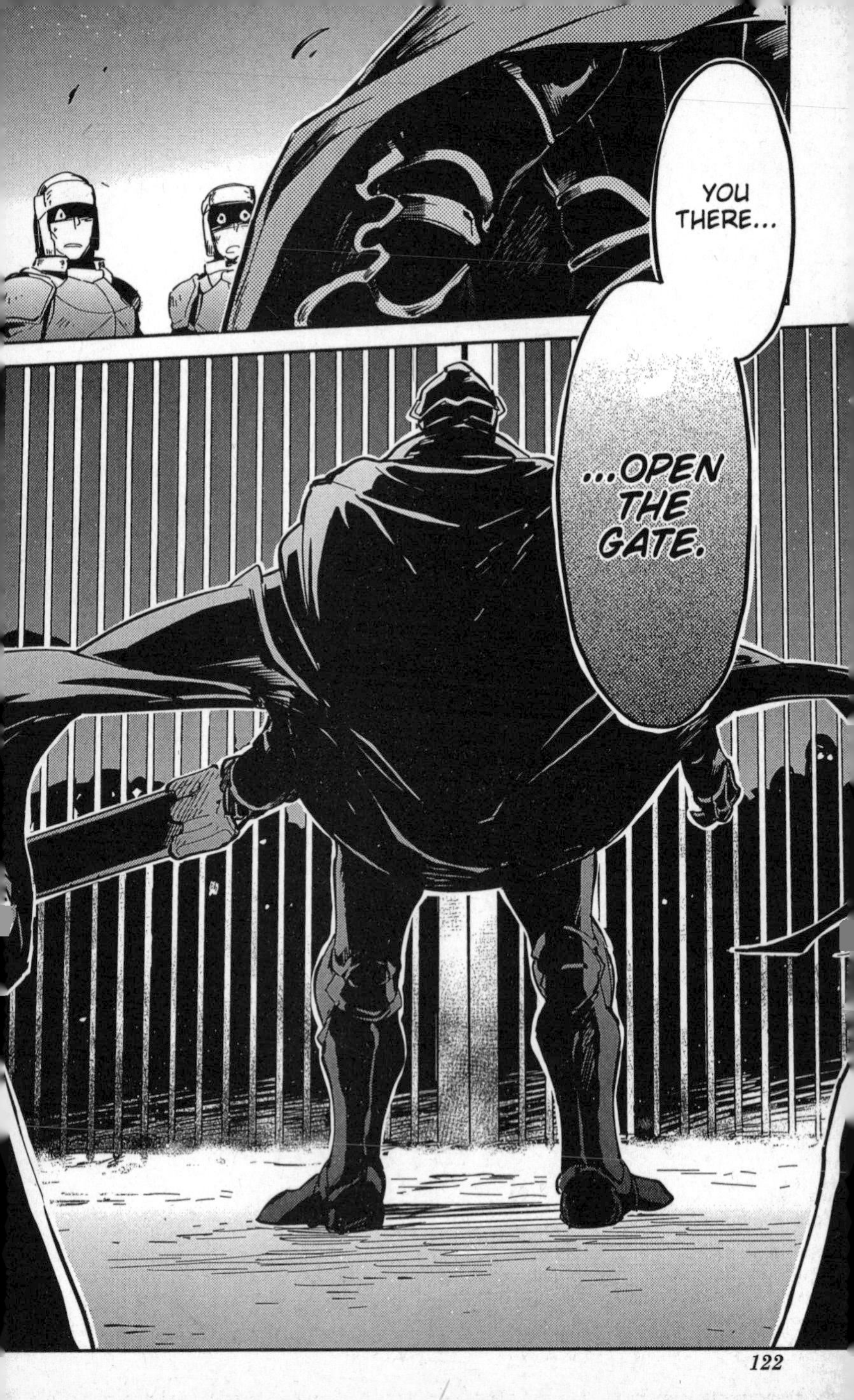
YOU THERE...
...OPEN THE GATE.

Interpretive notes of the OVERLORD
Chapter 7

Abilities That People Are Born With—*Talents*

Talents are powers that exist in this world but did not exist in *Yggdrasil*. Approximately one in every two hundred people is born with one of these abilities. There are many types of talents, from things like predicting the next day's weather with 70% accuracy to being able to speed up the harvest times of grass family grains by a couple of days or using the magic of the dragons who once ruled this world.

These types of abilities are fixed at birth—it's not possible to select or change powers later in life. That means that sometimes talents don't match the natures of the holders. For example, if someone is born with the talent to boost the destructive power of spells but doesn't have the inclination, ability, or physical strength necessary to become a caster, then they can't make good use of their talent.

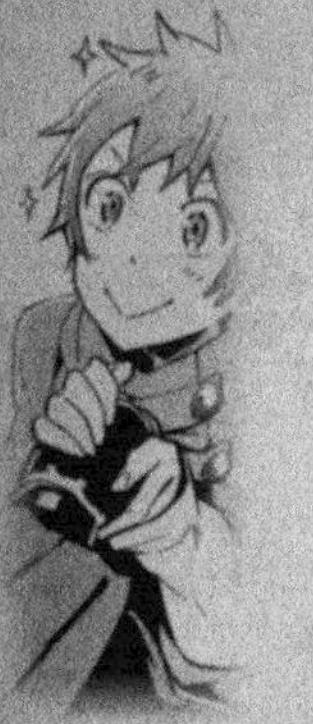

Examples of Talents

○ Ninya......Magic Aptitude

Ninya had a high aptitude for magic thanks to his talent. Spells that would normally take eight years to master, he did in four.

Famous as a genius magic caster, Ninya's nickname was "The Spell Master," but being called that embarrassed him. This is a tangent, but Ninya was an example of someone whose latent abilities matched his talent very well. If he could have grown up, he might have achieved hero-level powers and rivaled the great magic casters of the Baharuth Empire.

○ Nfirea Baleare......Use Any Magic Item

Some magic items have racial limitations on who can use them, or sometimes the limitation is unique to the item type—for example, to use a scroll, one has to have mastered the magic tree it comes from, or it won't work. However, thanks to his talent, Nfirea can use any magic item. He could even use items that require royal blood or the Staff of Ainz Ooal Gown, which normally only the guild master can use.

○ Nigun Grid Lewin......Strengthen Summoned Monsters

Nigun, captain of the Sunlit Scripture, summoned monsters that were ever so slightly more powerful than normal summons. For that reason, he had a lot of confidence in his monsters—until he met Ainz.

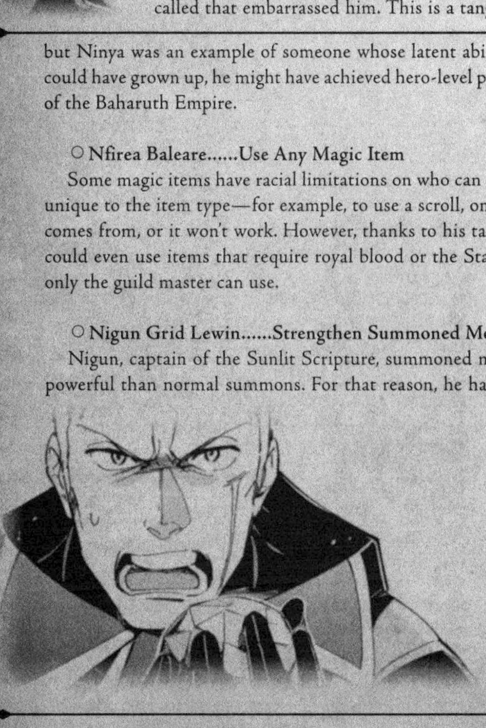

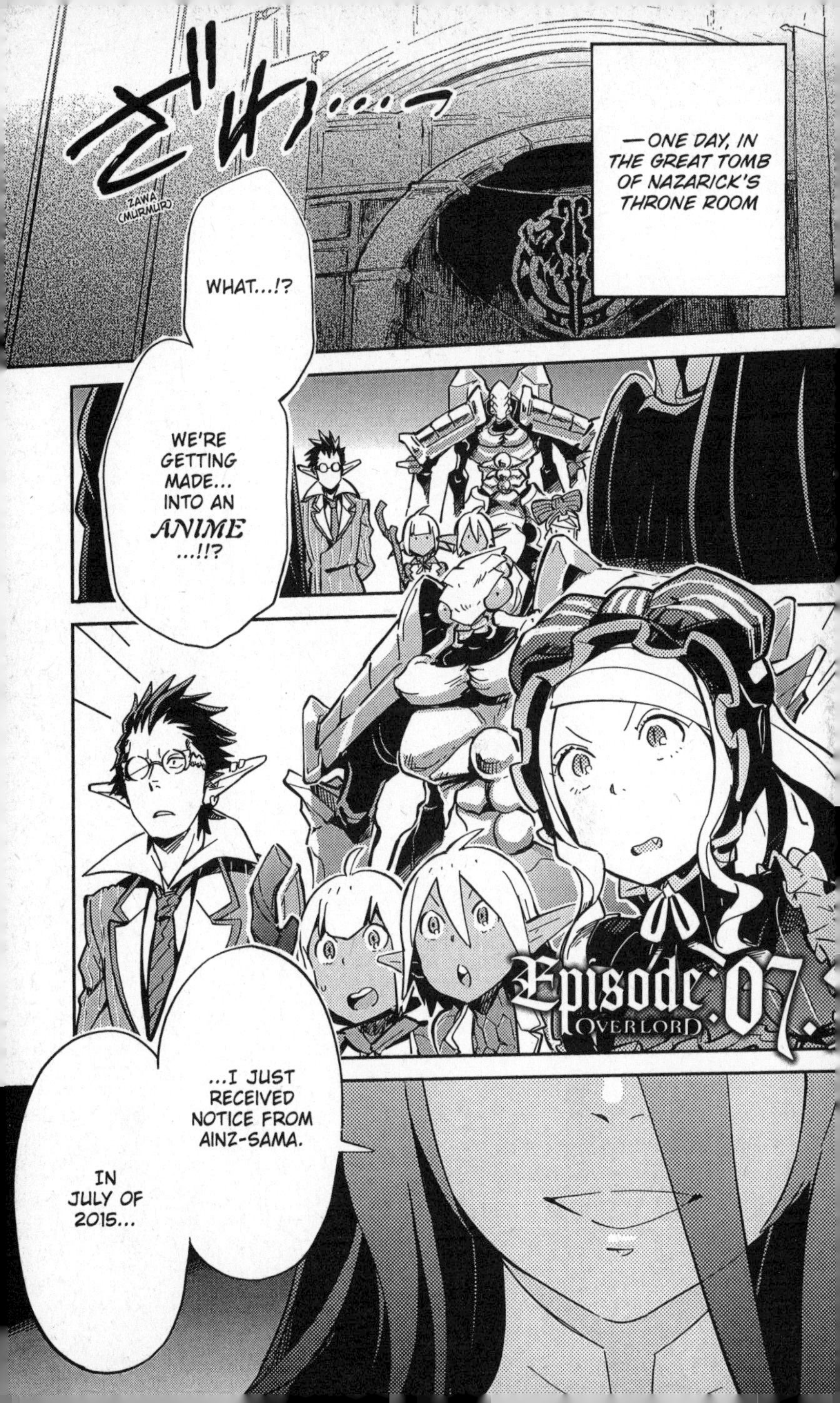
—ONE DAY, IN THE GREAT TOMB OF NAZARICK'S THRONE ROOM
ざわっ…っ
ZAWA (MURMUR)
WHAT...!?
WE'RE GETTING MADE... INTO AN ANIME ...!!?
Episode 07
OVERLORD
...I JUST RECEIVED NOTICE FROM AINZ-SAMA.
IN JULY OF 2015...

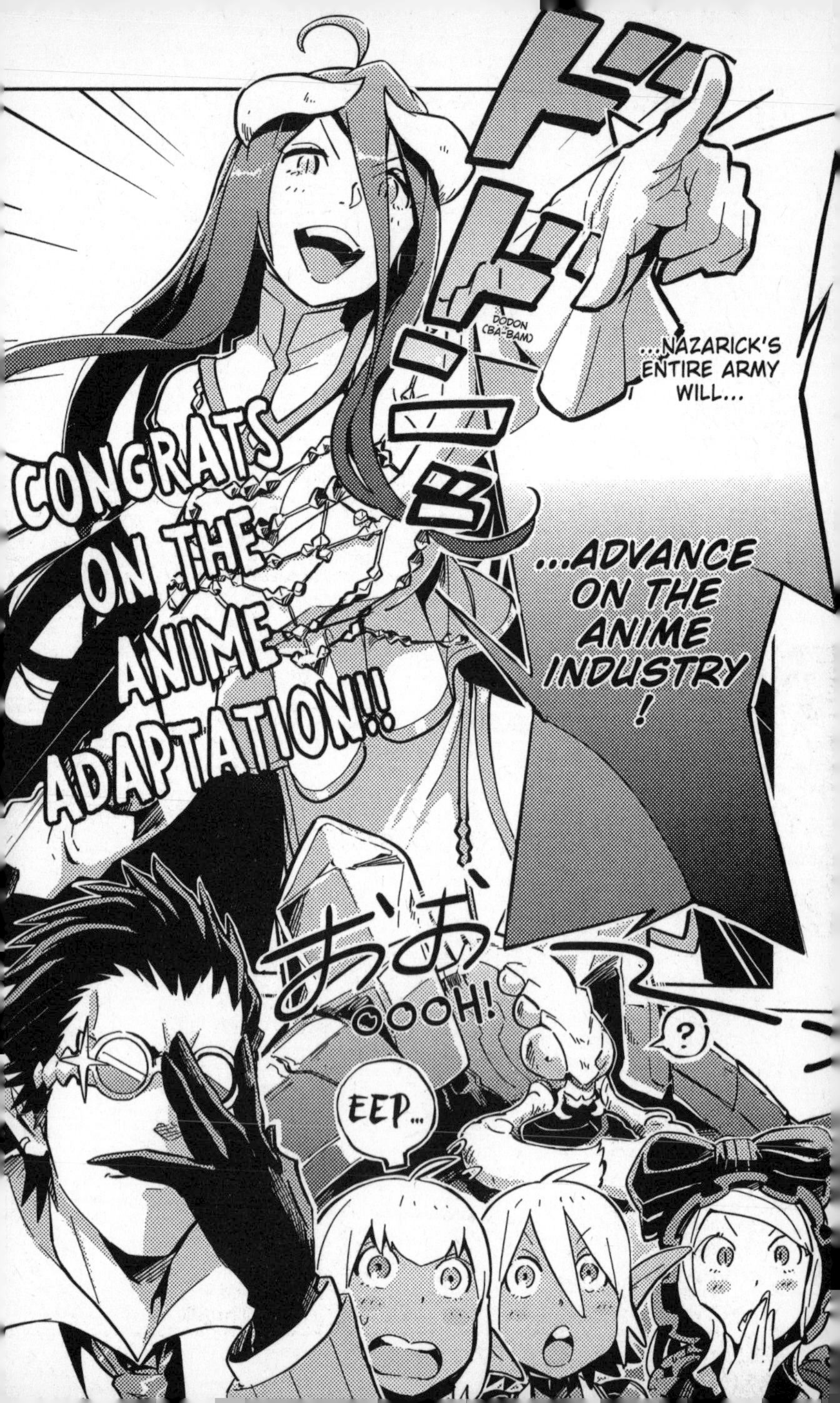
DODON (BA-BAM)
...NAZARICK'S ENTIRE ARMY WILL...
...ADVANCE ON THE ANIME INDUSTRY!
CONGRATS ON THE ANIME ADAPTATION!!
OOOH!
?
EEP...

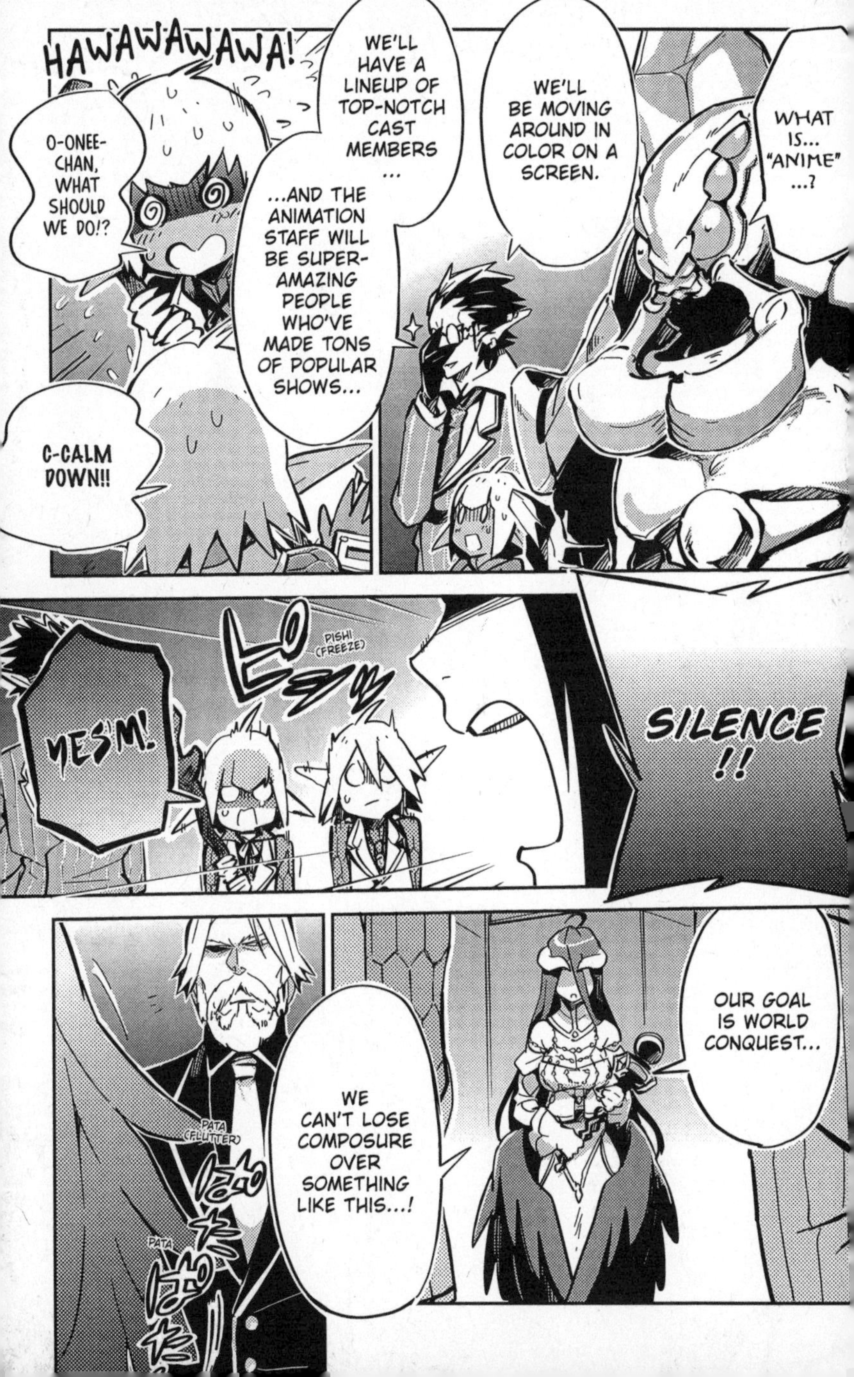
WHAT IS... "ANIME" ...?
WE'LL BE MOVING AROUND IN COLOR ON A SCREEN.
WE'LL HAVE A LINEUP OF TOP-NOTCH CAST MEMBERS ...
...AND THE ANIMATION STAFF WILL BE SUPER-AMAZING PEOPLE WHO'VE MADE TONS OF POPULAR SHOWS...
HAWAWAWAWA!
O-ONEE-CHAN, WHAT SHOULD WE DO!?
C-CALM DOWN!!
SILENCE!!
PISHI (FREEZE)
YESM!
OUR GOAL IS WORLD CONQUEST...
WE CAN'T LOSE COMPOSURE OVER SOMETHING LIKE THIS...!
PATA (FLUTTER)
PATA

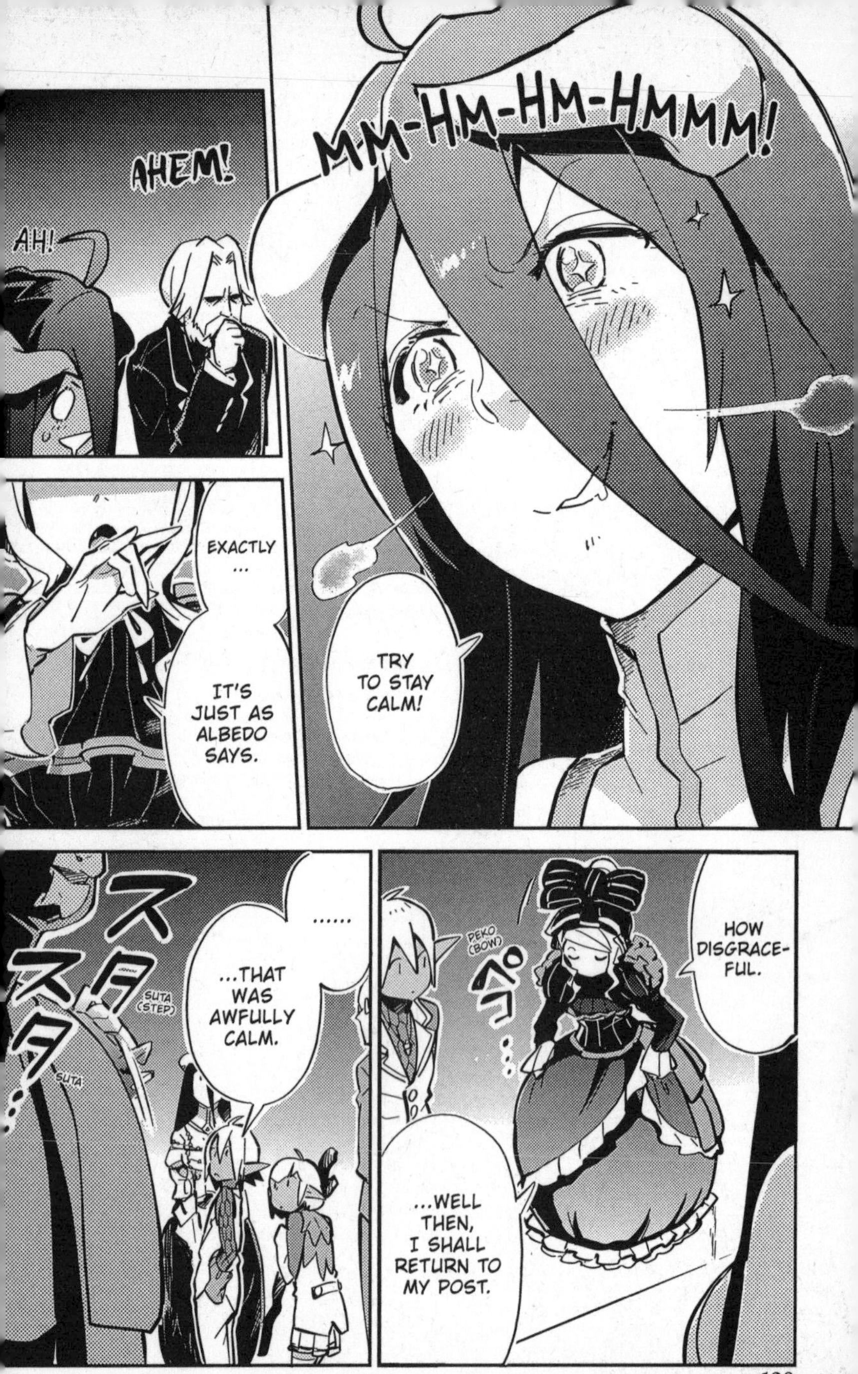
MM-HM-HM-HMMM!
TRY TO STAY CALM!
AHEM!
AH!
EXACTLY ...
IT'S JUST AS ALBEDO SAYS.
HOW DISGRACE-FUL.
PEKO (BOW)
ペコ…
...WELL THEN, I SHALL RETURN TO MY POST.
......
...THAT WAS AWFULLY CALM.
スタスタ…
SUTA (STEP)
SUTA

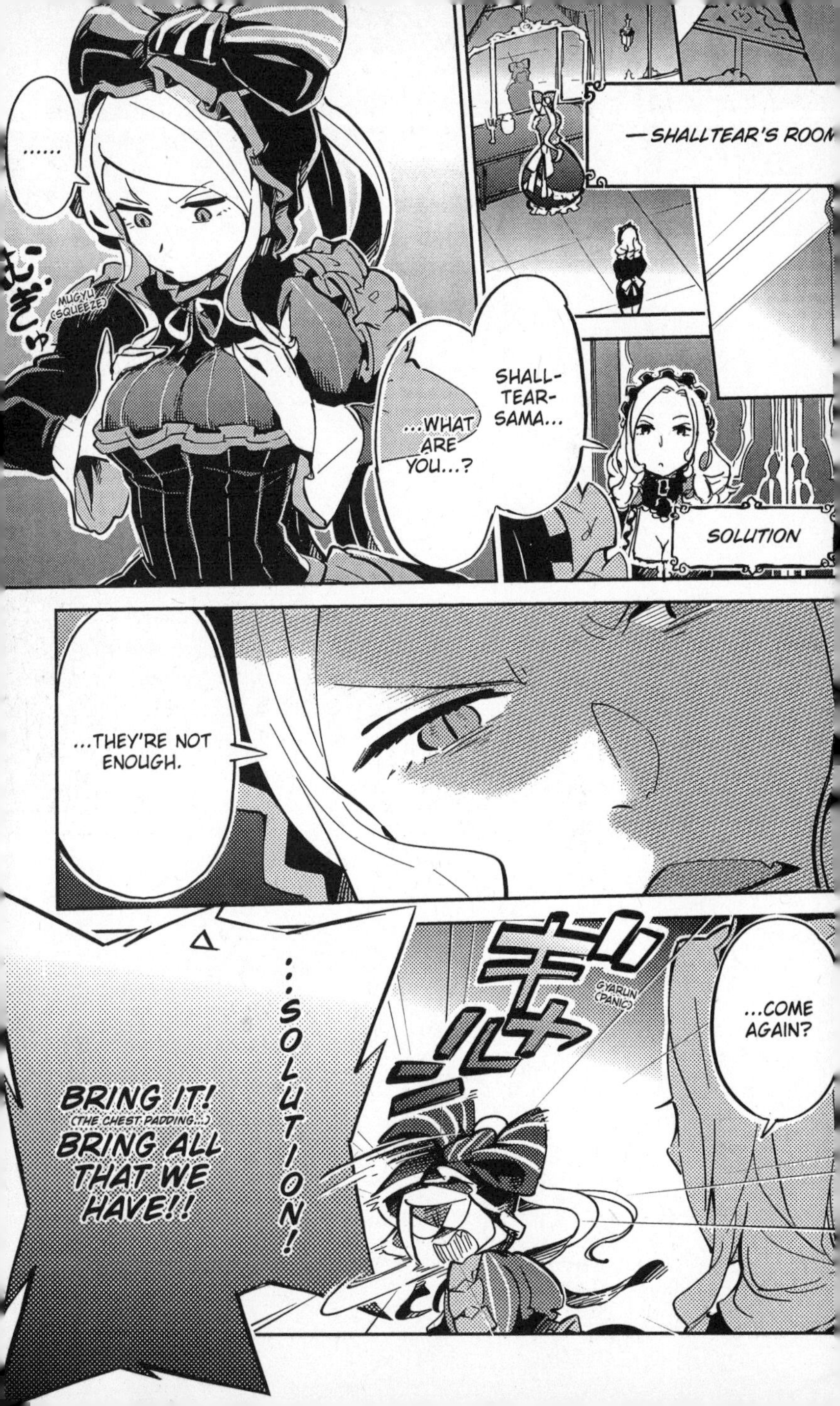
—SHALLTEAR'S ROOM
SHALL-TEAR-SAMA... ...WHAT ARE YOU...?
SOLUTION
......
MUGYU (SQUEEZE)
...THEY'RE NOT ENOUGH.
...COME AGAIN?
GYARUN (PANIC)
...SOLUTION!
BRING IT! (THE CHEST PADDING...) BRING ALL THAT WE HAVE!!

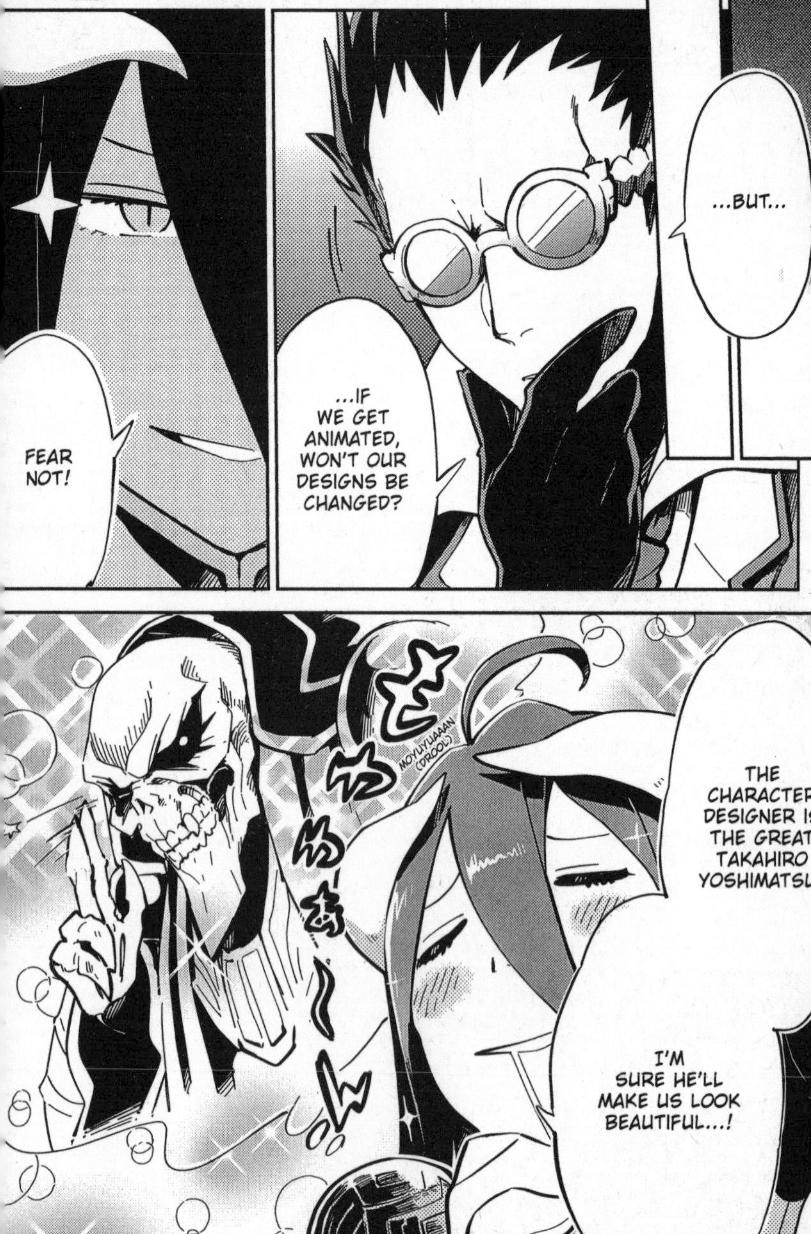
...BUT...
...IF WE GET ANIMATED, WON'T OUR DESIGNS BE CHANGED?
FEAR NOT!
THE CHARACTER DESIGNER IS THE GREAT TAKAHIRO YOSHIMATSU!
I'M SURE HE'LL MAKE US LOOK BEAUTIFUL...!
MOYUYUAAAN (DROOL)

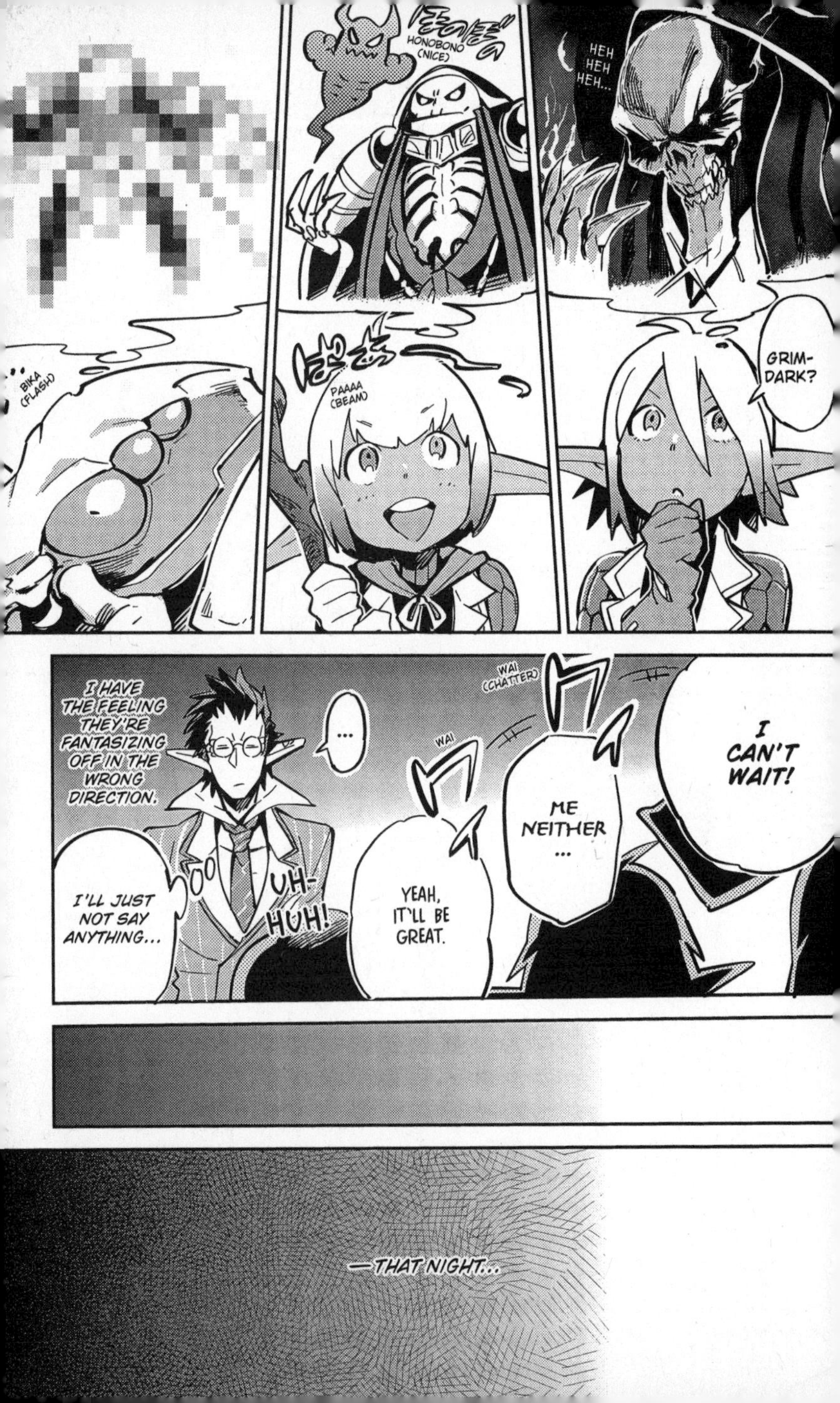
HEH HEH HEH...
HONOBONO (NICE)
GRIM-DARK?
PAAAA (BEAM)
BIKA (FLASH)
I CAN'T WAIT!
ME NEITHER ...
WAI (CHATTER)
WAI
YEAH, IT'LL BE GREAT.
UH-HUH!
...
I HAVE THE FEELING THEY'RE FANTASIZING OFF IN THE WRONG DIRECTION.
I'LL JUST NOT SAY ANYTHING...
—THAT NIGHT...

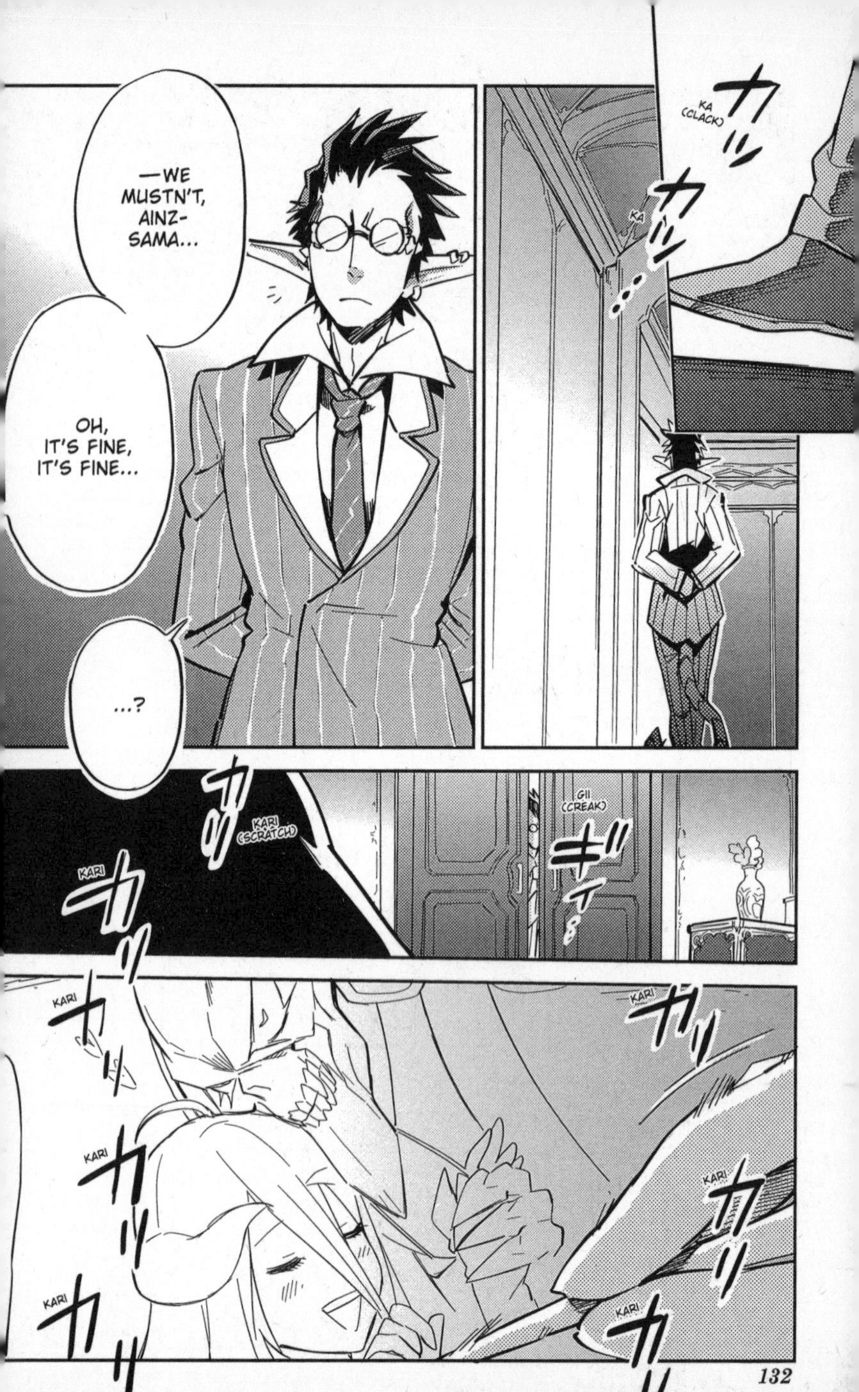
KA (CLACK)
KA
—WE MUSTN'T, AINZ-SAMA...
OH, IT'S FINE, IT'S FINE...
...?
GII (CREAK)
KARI (SCRATCH)
KARI
KARI
KARI
KARI
KARI
KARI
KARI

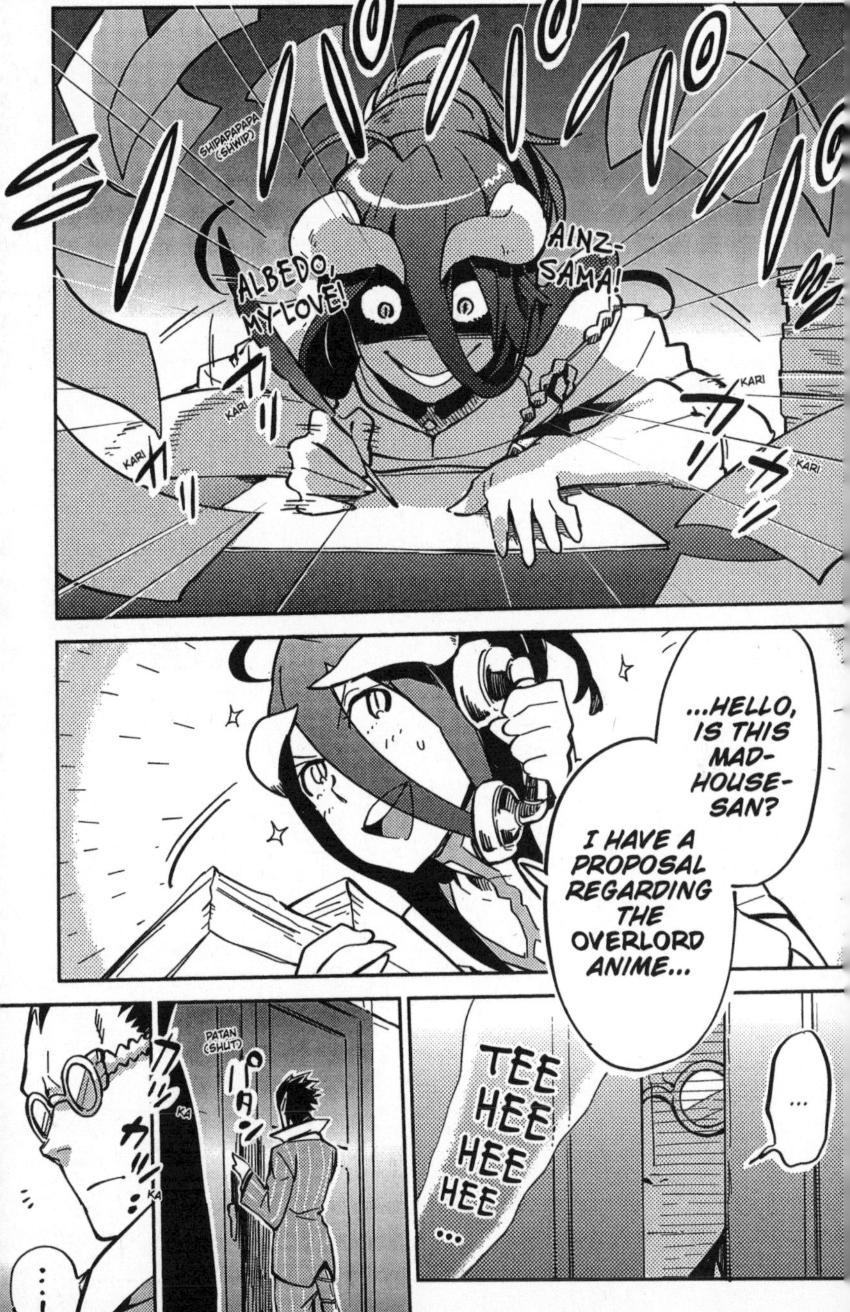

AINZ-SAMA!
ALBEDO, MY LOVE!
SHIPAPAPAPA (SHWIP)
KARI
KARI
KARI
KARI
...HELLO, IS THIS MAD-HOUSE-SAN?
I HAVE A PROPOSAL REGARDING THE OVERLORD ANIME...
...
TEE HEE HEE HEE...
PATAN (SHUT)
KA
KA
...!

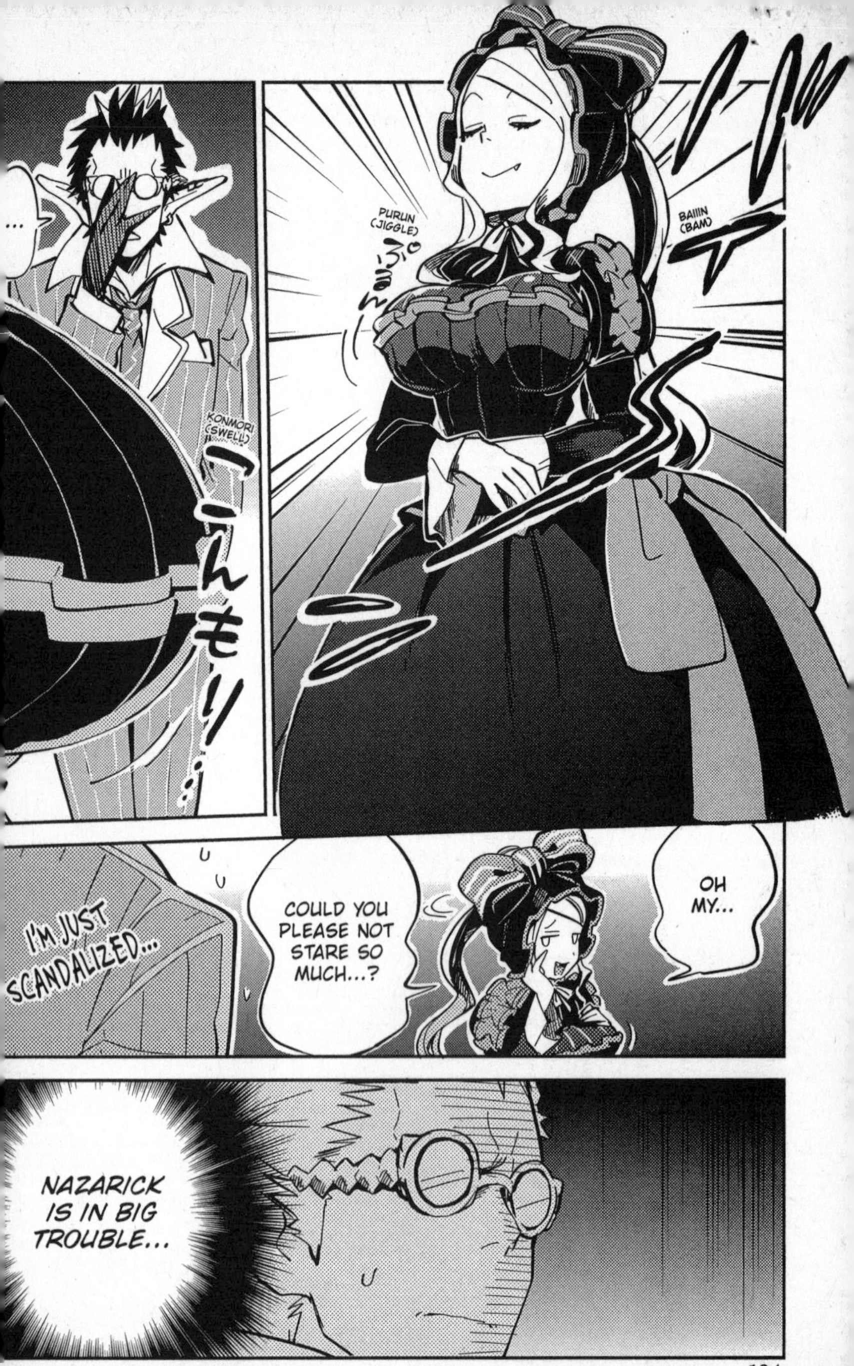
BAIIIN (BAM)
PURUN (JIGGLE)
ぷるん
...
KONMORI (SWELL)
こんもり…!!
OH MY...
COULD YOU PLEASE NOT STARE SO MUCH...?
I'M JUST SCANDALIZED...
NAZARICK IS IN BIG TROUBLE...

Six major gods descended to this world six hundred years ago. They rule light (or life), darkness (or death), fire, wind, water, and earth. They created the foundations of the Slane Theocracy. The items they left behind are known as sacred relics and are kept under lock and key.

Ainz suspects these Six Gods were players transported to this world like himself. Though six hundred years have passed, grotesques have no notion of life span, and some classes have extra life expectancy, so it's even possible that the Six Gods could still be alive.

The Six Gods

The Six Gods and the Slane Theocracy

The Slane Theocracy is a religious nation that believes in the Six Gods. The other countries in the area, such as the Re-Estize Kingdom and the Baharuth Empire, believe in the Four Gods. There is, of course, a reason for this, which will be discussed later.

The Slane Theocracy's national policy is that the human race must prevail and prosper over all other races. Unlike the world in which Ainz once lived, in this one, humans are considered one of the inferior races. The reason they live in open fields where there is nowhere to hide is because they aren't strong enough to survive in the mountains or forests. There are also countries made up of subhumans and grotesques which prey on humans.

The reason a superior race hasn't taken over the world is that, when the Eight Kings of Avarice tried to rule it five hundred years ago, the ensuing struggle resulted in diminished power across all races. Additionally, the Eight Kings of Avarice treated humans rather well, in a way—subhumans and grotesques were even hunted.

In order to protect humans from the threat of other races, the Slane Theocracy binds people together with faith.

If the Six Gods are still behind the Slane Theocracy, and if they really are players, it's possible that the country is using their power to create warriors comparable to level-100 players. For this reason, Ainz is keeping his eye on them.

OVERLORD ❷

Art: Hugin Miyama
Original Story: Kugane Maruyama
Character Design: so-bin
Scenario: Satoshi Oshio

Translation: Emily Balistrieri • Lettering: Brndn Blakeslee

This book is a work of fiction. Names, characters, places, and incidents are the product of the author's imagination or are used fictitiously. Any resemblance to actual events, locales, or persons, living or dead, is coincidental.

OVERLORD Volume 2
© Hugin MIYAMA 2015
© Satoshi OSHIO 2015
© 2012 Kugane Maruyama
First published in Japan in 2015 by KADOKAWA CORPORATION, Tokyo
English Translation rights arranged with KADOKAWA CORPORATION, Tokyo
through Tuttle Mori Agency, Inc.

English translation © 2016 by Yen Press, LLC

Yen Press, LLC supports the right to free expression and the value of copyright. The purpose of copyright is to encourage writers and artists to produce the creative works that enrich our culture.

The scanning, uploading, and distribution of this book without permission is a theft of the author's intellectual property. If you would like permission to use material from the book (other than for review purposes), please contact the publisher. Thank you for your support of the author's rights.

Yen Press
1290 Avenue of the Americas
New York, NY 10104

Visit us at yenpress.com
facebook.com/yenpress
twitter.com/yenpress
yenpress.tumblr.com

First Yen Press Edition: September 2016

Yen Press is an imprint of Yen Press, LLC.
The Yen Press name and logo are trademarks of Yen Press, LLC.

The publisher is not responsible for websites (or their content) that are not owned by the publisher.

Library of Congress Control Number: 2016932688

ISBNs: 978-0-316-39766-7 (paperback)
          978-0-316-39767-4 (ebook)
          978-0-316-39768-1 (app)

10 9 8 7 6 5 4 3 2 1

BVG

Printed in the United States of America

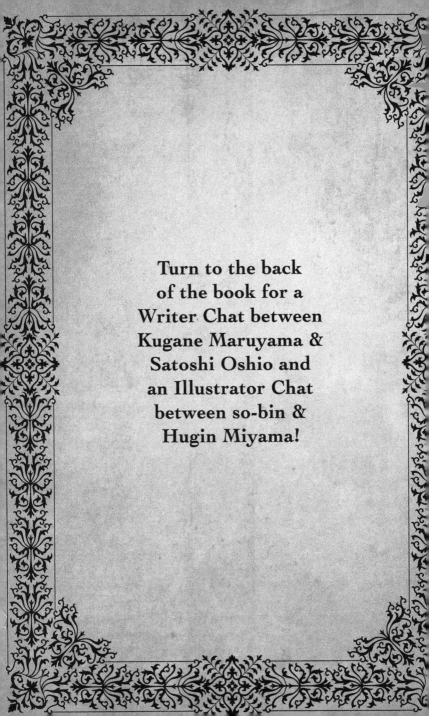

Turn to the back
of the book for a
Writer Chat between
Kugane Maruyama &
Satoshi Oshio and
an Illustrator Chat
between so-bin &
Hugin Miyama!

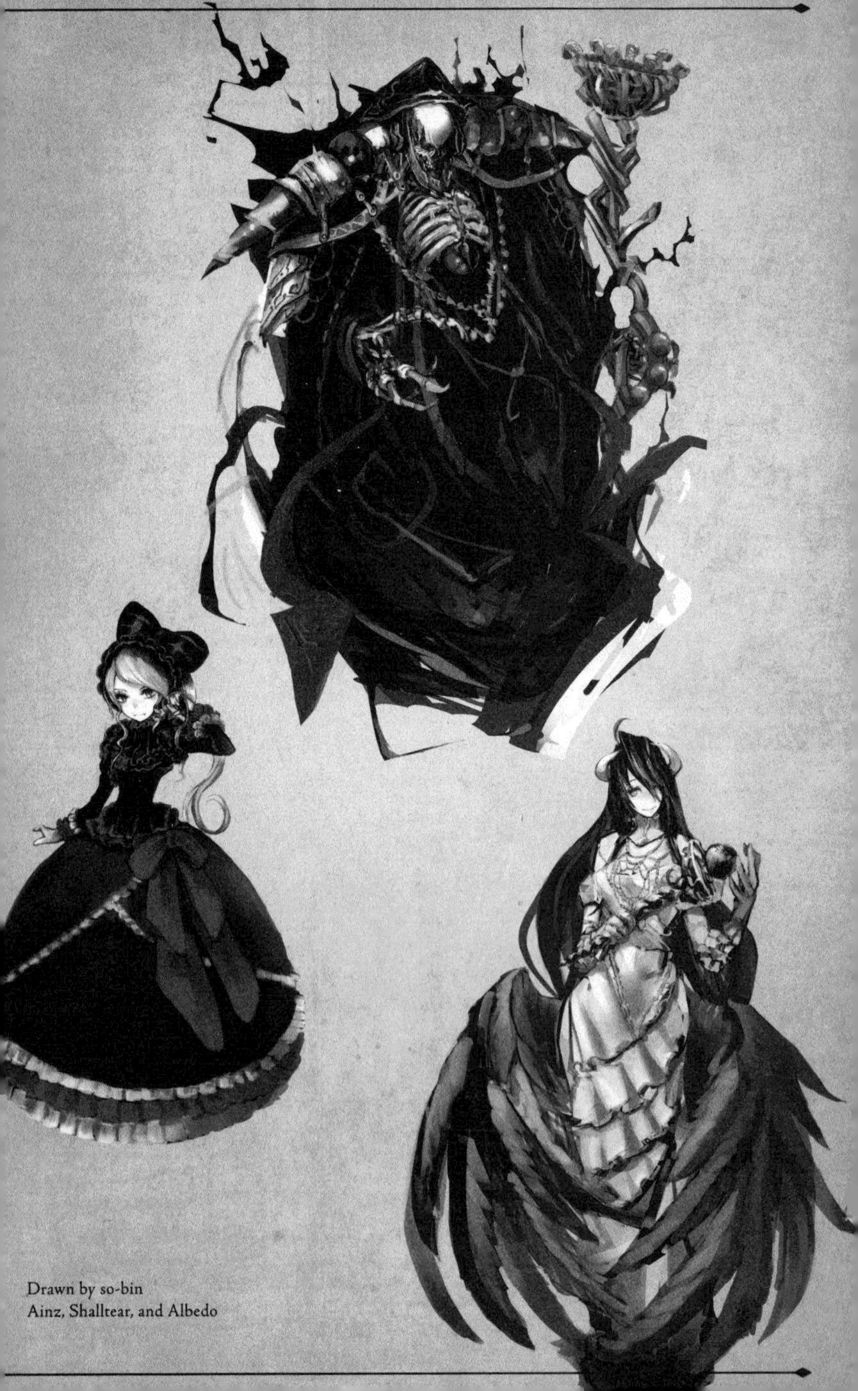

Drawn by so-bin
Ainz, Shalltear, and Albedo

The Anime and Manga Versions from the Character Designer's Point of View

Miyama: I'm really looking forward to seeing the *Overlord* characters move around in the anime. Is there anything in particular you're excited for?

so-bin: There are so many people involved in making an anime. For starters, there are the directors and the animation staff, then there are the people doing designs for characters and creatures, the people who make the backgrounds, the people who make the music—all kinds of people are giving their all for this project. So I'm looking forward, in a general way, to seeing what happens when all of those people come together. I think a lot of it will come down to how the scenes are directed. This is a hardcore story that will be difficult to adapt, but I'd be so happy if it turns out to be the kind of series you want to watch over and over again.

Miyama: And please let me know—is there is anything you're hoping for from the manga...?

so-bin: Even though I have the idea of the *Overlord* world in my head, there are still so many things I haven't quite been able to visualize. So when I read the first chapter of the manga, my first thought was, "Thank you for giving all of this shape at last!" I think you have a part heavily featuring Nabe coming up and some dynamic scenes—I'm excited for Hamusuke, too!

His Encounter with *Overlord* and Behind-the-Scenes on His Design Process

Miyama: What do you think of *Overlord*'s plot?

so-bin: When I first got offered the job, I wasn't sure if I should take it or not. I was like, "It's a story where some bones do some stuff or something? What is that about?" But then, I tried reading the web version and got pretty into the scenes where Shalltear talks a lot. I got hooked and ended up reading the whole thing. It was so interesting that I'd sit at work reading instead of doing my job—I was surprised. I'd be reading on the train and find myself going "heh-heh!" [laughs] Then, once I thought it was interesting, I was like, "So now you're gonna draw this...?" It has horror elements, but it's also funny and has some slice-of-life parts, yet there's a darker underbelly, so the world is steeped in this perfect mixture. Also, I think it's quite a feat that the web and book versions are different. By the time you get to Volume 6, it's insane. And he did a whole volume of lizardmen! That was amazing!

Miyama: Each of *Overlord*'s characters have their charms, but is there anything specific you pay attention to or get particular about while designing them?

so-bin: Maruyama-san's text helps me out a lot. All I do is read what's there and draw exactly what pops into my head...

Miyama: Are there any characters that were particularly hard or fun or that you are particularly fond of? I'd really like to hear some production secrets.

so-bin: When I look at them now, I can't help but think, "That looks crummy," or, "Couldn't you have done a little better?" about some things, but I'm attached to all of them, so I like them all. There's this one character called the "Duke of Terror." Maybe it's because I once drew him with tears streaming down my face? But I'm glad he got popular.

Miyama: Please teach me your tricks for how to make Lord Ainz look cool!

so-bin: You need fighting spirit. But I'm not sure if I'm even managing to draw him cool.

Miyama: What's your favorite illustration you've done for *Overlord* so far?

so-bin: The cover for Volume 4 is the only one I can see even now and think, "Wow, nice job."

The cover illustration for Volume 4 that so-bin mentioned as his favorite

Miyama: What kind of exchanges do you have with the author?

so-bin: He sometimes treats me to a meal. And every time he gets pissed, he tells me to work till I vomit blood. Thanks to that, I'm getting a lot done. I'm truly grateful.

Illustrator Chat

Overlord character designer so-bin
gives rapid answers to *Overlord*
manga artist Hugin Miyama's
many questions!

Interviewee: Illustrator of the novel version of *Overlord*

so-bin

Interviewer: Artist of the manga version of *Overlord*

Hugin Miyama

— OVERLORD —

Getting Closer to the Secrets of the Ever-Disciplined so-bin

Miyama: What got you started drawing illustrations?

so-bin: I graduated high school and became a regular desk jockey, but I really wanted to be a graphic designer—and I was under the mistaken impression that graphic designers had to be able to draw. I guess that's how I started. I didn't have even the slightest idea illustration itself would end up being my job.

Miyama: Do you have artists you like or artists who have influenced you?

so-bin: There are a lot, both Japanese and from other countries. And not only illustrators, but people in the credits on anime, games, or movies, and some people I know personally. Once I started drawing, I began to take more interest in all kinds of art, so I'm constantly being stimulated by new things.

Miyama: You upload a lot of sketches and things to your website, including some that are quite studious. Do you practice drawing every day? And how long would you say you spend drawing per day?

so-bin: I learned a few years ago that, sadly, if you don't draw every day, your art doesn't improve. So while I don't worry too much about how much time I spend, I do practice every day...because I'm always bummed out about how much I suck. I don't have the basics down, so I feel like I still need to look at all kinds of different things and practice a lot. If I weren't doing *Overlord*, I don't think I'd be a pro illustrator, so I want to show how grateful I am by improving as much as I can.

1 **Shōsetsuka ni Narō:** A site where users can browse and post stories for free. There are over 300,000 works uploaded. The web version of *Overlord* is still being updated there.

2 **"Reimei":** *Kagetsu Tōya* is a fandisk for the Type-Moon visual novel *Tsukihime*. Three player-created scenarios were selected for inclusion, and Maruyama's *"Reimei"* was among them.

3 **D&D replay novels:** A genre that is not fiction but a record of tabletop RPG (e.g. Dungeons & Dragons) sessions.

4 **F-ta the editor:** A female editor who creates hits mainly by turning web novels into published books. She is known for being very passionate about the content, and there are many delightful anecdotes about her. She is loved by authors and readers alike. Other projects of hers include *Maoyu* and *Ninja Slayer*.

5 **Clementine:** One of the leaders of the heretical religious group Zurrernorn (to the left in this picture). A cruel female warrior who has absolute confidence in her stabbing weapon combat skills.

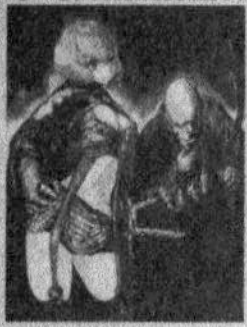

6 ***Log Horizon* tabletop RPG replay:** A replay series where Mamare Touno, the author of the *Log Horizon* novels, is the game master. Kugane Maruyama and three other authors participate. There are currently four volumes out.

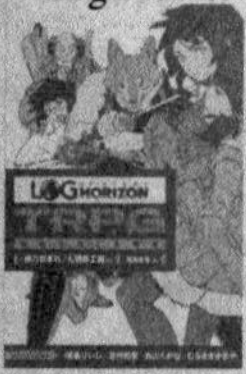

7 **Cocytus:** Guardian of Nazarick's fifth level. A warrior with an insect-like appearance and a conscientious personality.

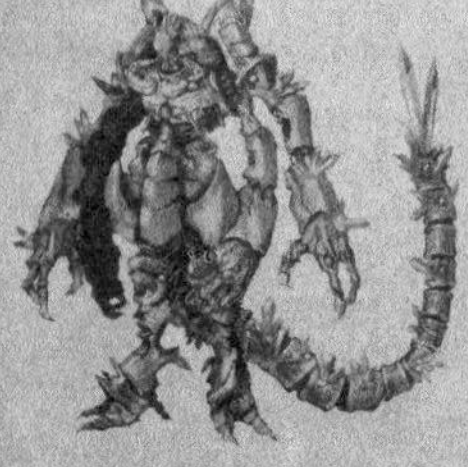

8 **Enterbrain:** A Kadokawa-brand company in Japan that publishes the *Overlord* novels. In addition to light novels, they also often have publications focused on video games.

Oshio: And finally, a message for *Comptiq* magazine readers, please.

Maruyama: Mine is one of the more offbeat titles in *Comptiq* and *Compace*, etc., but if you enjoy it, that makes me happy.

Oshio: So then, where do you find these weirdos? Do you observe people around you?

Maruyama: Nobody's that weird. [laughs]

Oshio: So it's your imagination?

Maruyama: Yeah, it's imagination. Pretty much all the characters in *Overlord* are strange, especially the women—the more beautiful they are on the outside, the more warped they are on the inside. Not that I set out to make it that way...

Oshio: So I'm going to ask you straight up: Do you already know how the *Overlord* novels will end?

Maruyama: Of course. I have the main plot points from beginning to end all done in my head. If you don't have that, you can't foreshadow.

Oshio: Aha. How many volumes do you think it will take to get there?

Maruyama: The next one coming out is Volume 9, so I think it'll probably be about nine more? Ainz's story will still continue, but *Overlord*, at least, will end there.

Oshio: The pace now is about a book every four months?

Maruyama: Yes. But up until now, I've only been editing and adding to what was already published online. After Volume 9, I don't have that stock, so the pace will probably change.

The *Overlord* World Expands into Anime and Manga

Oshio: How did you feel when you heard *Overlord* was getting an anime?

Maruyama: I thought, "Enterbrain[8] is awesome!" [laughs] I'd talked with my editor at some point, like, "It'd be cool if it got turned into an anime..." But before I knew it, things got rolling, and it was decided. It's a strange book, so I'm looking forward to seeing how the anime ends up. I think animating the spells and whatnot will be particularly tricky.

Oshio: How much will you be involved in the anime production?

Maruyama: I attend the script meetings every week.

Oshio: What kinds of stuff do you say in them?

Maruyama: I mostly answer questions the director has about *Overlord* lore. I told him a lot of things. For example, I told him some of the stuff that will be revealed in the final volume. Now and then, he'd ask me a pointed question, and I'd be like, "Ask my past-self from three years ago," and almost had to escape. Oh, and about the voice actors—the drama CDs that came with the deluxe editions of the books were perfect, so I didn't have any complaints.

Oshio: What do you think are the main differences between the *Overlord* novels and the anime and manga?

Maruyama: Definitely the way it's represented. In words, all I have to do is write "an army of 100,000," but for the manga or anime, they have to show that with pictures. It must be tough. Oh, and Albedo. I don't remember writing such a cute lady character. I was surprised how cute she was in the manga.

Oshio: Do you sometimes roll the dice, like in a tabletop RPG, and end up with a stronger character?

Maruyama: I don't create characters for my novels with dice. [laughs]

Oshio: By the way, do you have a favorite type of character in tabletop RPGs, one that you tend to use when you play?

Maruyama: I don't, actually. No matter what character I play, I'm a gag character announcing my presence like, "Hey, Kugane Maruyama is here!" If you read the *Log Horizon* tabletop RPG replay,[6] you'll kinda get what I mean...to throw in a plug. [laughs]

The Secret Origin of *Overlord* Characters

Oshio: So I'd like to ask if there were any scenes that you had a hard time writing. Or any that went really smoothly?

Maruyama: I always have a hard time. Really. Emotional scenes are especially hard.

Oshio: So, scenes where characters are sharing their emotions are difficult, huh?

Maruyama: Yeah, it's tough to write emotions that readers will find believable.

Oshio: But the protagonist, Ainz, is undead, so his emotions don't vary too much in the first place, right?

Maruyama: Well, he still has functioning emotions. Strong ones are just suppressed—it's not as if all his emotions are gone. Put another way, it's just that the big mood swings are contained.

Oshio: So, Ainz looks like a skeleton. What made you decide on those visuals?

Maruyama: I wanted to create the strongest protagonist. Normal people die if they get stabbed. And they get tired if they don't sleep, but while they're sleeping, they could be killed. They can be poisoned. So that's why he ended up as an undead who doesn't require food nor sleep.

Oshio: I see. So you were thinking about all this from the very beginning. If you had to pick a favorite character out of all of them, including Ainz, who would it be?

Maruyama: I love all my characters. But if I start to feel like I don't need someone to drive the story along anymore, I kill them off. [laughs]

Oshio: And who do you fanboy the most?

Maruyama: I like Cocytus.[7] [laughs]

Oshio: That's a good answer. [laughs] He's the least human-looking, but in some ways, he's the most human.

Maruyama: Yeah, he's a good guy.

Oshio: I don't think he ever says anything wrong.

Maruyama: He's doing the best he can, in a lot of ways.

Oshio: Do the characters ever reflect a part of yourself?

Maruyama: I don't think so. I'm not that weird. [laughs]

The Story's Theme and the Author's True Intentions

Oshio: So I'd like to look a little closer at your work's content here. Your first original novel, *Overlord*, has this MMORPG motif. Have you played quite a few of them yourself?

Maruyama: I've tried a few of the well-known ones, but I always felt like you could do more in a tabletop RPG. So actually, even when I tried them out, I usually quit right away.

Oshio: So you really like tabletop RPGs, huh? Okay, if you had to give the theme of *Overlord* in a nutshell, what would you say?

Maruyama: "The strongest taken to extremes," I suppose. Or "survival of the fittest," "Might makes right," that sort of thing. I guess it's a bit immature.

Oshio: "The strongest" as a genre does feel like it has been taken to extremes, but this goes even further.

Maruyama: Well, when I started writing *Overlord*, there was no standout story for the "strongest army" genre yet, or at least probably not. Then again, I can't say I've read every last one, web-published stories included, so maybe there was one, but...

Oshio: What's the difference between other "summoned to another world" series and *Overlord*?

Maruyama: The protagonist is evil, and not just "dark hero" evil, either. That said, I'm thinking that from the reader's perspective—from my point of view, I'm not writing him as evil. Like I mentioned before, the basic tenets in the *Overlord* world are "survival of the fittest" and "might makes right." In a world where the struggle for existence is so intense, being weak is bad.

Oshio: Ah, I see. Ainz rules through power; he's not trying to be liked. Other than that, is there anything that you try to do when you write or that you pay specific attention to?

Maruyama: To never go halfway. I'm aiming for "the strongest" taken to extremes! My editor, F-ta, says this, too, but she says it more nicely to me—like, "You don't have to hold back!" [laughs]

Oshio: I was really on the edge of my seat during the Lizard Village arc.

Maruyama: Yeah, that was brutal.

Oshio: I think you took it right to the edge. It was certainly original; it was structured in a way I've never seen done before.

Maruyama: I know there won't be a lot of people who'll be on board with me, but I'm going there for those who are, yep.

Oshio: Anything else?

Maruyama: Umm, I kill female characters, too? They just never seem to die in light novels.

Oshio: You definitely don't discriminate based on gender. Women getting killed is the flip side of the fact that there are some women stronger than men in this series. It makes for a very gender-free world. Did it turn out that way subconciously?

Maruyama: Yeah, I guess it did.

Oshio: Especially Clementine[5] in Volume 2. She seemed really strong.

Maruyama: What a horrible death she died.

Oshio: I see. After that, there were ten years during which you didn't write anything, and then you wrote *Overlord*. What led to that?

Maruyama: The type of book I like didn't exist, so I figured I would write it. Also, I couldn't get my tabletop RPG group together, so we couldn't play...

Oshio: Do you read a lot of books?

Maruyama: More web novels than books.

Oshio: So the stories you read are usually from *Narō* or another site like that...

Maruyama: Or sometimes fanfic, etc. I've always liked fanfic, so I've been reading those kinds of stories for a long time.

Oshio: What kinds of original fiction do you like?

Maruyama: I guess ones like *Overlord*, where the protagonist is super strong and could even be said to be the strongest.

Oshio: So you were reading various things but couldn't seem to get hooked, and that's why you started writing your own.

Maruyama: I think it's because I'd always feel dissatisfied, thinking, "If it were me, I would've done it this way instead." For example—if a protagonist who was just transported to another world appears before the king and acts arrogant, that just feels weird to me.

Oshio: The protagonist in *Overlord* is a regular salaryman on the inside, so he always has some worry on his mind while he's speaking. But so, you're saying that, if you had found your ideal story, you might not have written *Overlord*?

OVERLORD

Maruyama: Yeah, of course not. I think the dissatisfaction is what was driving me.

Oshio: Are there other things besides Type-Moon games and web novels that inspired you?

Maruyama: Tabletop RPGs. I've been playing D&D forever. I think I've probably been influenced by replay novels,[3] too.

Oshio: What tabletop RPG were you into the most?

Maruyama: Probably *Sword World*, which I played back in high school.

Oshio: Oh, I've read one of those rulebooks. Like, "Slimes ooze out between the crevices in a cavern's rock wall and melt adventurers until only their metal is left, so slimes can drop metal." It was really interesting. So you played the most in high school?

Maruyama: Yeah. I was in a club. We'd play from 3 PM to around 8 PM, so five hours a day, five days a week.

Oshio: Five hours! By the way, what club was that?

Maruyama: The literature club.

Oshio: Oh! I see. Sounds kind of like a light novel [laughs], doing various things under the guise of a lit. club. I so would have wanted to be in a club like that.

Maruyama: I'm still in touch with those guys. In fact, we still play D&D together.

Oshio: Was your experience playing tabletop RPGs useful for developing your imagination?

Maruyama: Probably, I guess.

Writer Chat

Overlord creator Kugane Maruyama
and author of the manga script Satoshi Oshio
meet for the first time!

Interviewee: *Overlord* author

Kugane Maruyama

Interviewer: Scriptwriter for the *Overlord* manga

Satoshi Oshio

People in the Know, Know! The Roots of Dual-Job Author Kugane Maruyama!

Oshio: Before I start with questions...it says in your profile that you're a salaryman, but you're really wearing a suit and everything—you're very put together! [laughs] I meet a lot of visual artists in my line of work, and they're always so weird that I don't quite know how to deal with them. I half-expected you to show up dressed like dark lord Ainz or something.

Maruyama: I've gone out drinking with some writers from *Shōsetsuka ni Narō*,[1] and they all have it pretty together.

Oshio: So around when was it that you started writing novels while still juggling a busy work life?

Maruyama: It was about five years ago, in May of 2010.

Oshio: I hear you participated in a Type-Moon project before that.

Maruyama: The mini-scenario I submitted for *Kagetsu Tōya*, "Reimei,"[2] got picked up, but that was fourteen years ago, and I hadn't written anything since then.

Oshio: So was doing that project for Type-Moon what got you started writing stories?

Maruyama: At the time, I just liked Type-Moon games. And they just so happened to be looking for stories to include in *Kagetsu Tōya*, so I thought, "Okay, I'll give it my best shot!"

Oshio: Did you do anything to train up, like read books about how to write?

Maruyama: I've sworn to myself that I'll never read one of those. And as for training, there isn't anything I've written that I would say was specifically for practice.

OVERLORD
Special

— Writer Chat —

Kugane Maruyama ✕ Satoshi Oshio

— Illustrator Chat —

so-bin ✕ Hugin Miyama